本书获得

2022 年度浙江省社科联社科普及课题立项资助

（项目编号：22KPD10YB）

及浙江科技学院外国语学院高峰学科经费资助

浙江省社科联社科普及课题成果

走进亚运 体验杭州

（中英双语）

Enjoy Asian Games Explore Hosting City
(*Bilingual in Chinese and English*)

◎叶依群 潘 飞 石教旺／编著

浙江工商大学出版社 | 杭州
ZHEJIANG GONGSHANG UNIVERSITY PRESS

图书在版编目(CIP)数据

走进亚运 体验杭州．汉、英／叶依群，潘飞，石
教旺编著．—— 杭州：浙江工商大学出版社，2023.5
ISBN 978-7-5178-5469-2

Ⅰ．①走… Ⅱ．①叶… ②潘… ③石… Ⅲ．①杭州－
概况－汉、英 Ⅳ．①K925.51

中国国家版本馆CIP数据核字(2023)第072530号

走进亚运 体验杭州（中英双语）
ZOUJIN YAYUN TIYAN HANGZHOU (ZHONG-YING SHUANGYU)
叶依群 潘 飞 石教旺 编著

责任编辑	王 英
责任校对	何小玲
封面设计	望宸文化
责任印制	包建辉
出版发行	浙江工商大学出版社
	（杭州市教工路198号 邮政编码310012）
	（E-mail：zjgsupress@163.com）
	（网址：http://www.zjgsupress.com）
	电话：0571-88904980，88831806（传真）
排 版	杭州彩地电脑图文有限公司
印 刷	浙江全能工艺美术印刷有限公司
开 本	710mm×1000mm 1/16
印 张	17.75
字 数	343千
版 印 次	2023年5月第1版 2023年5月第1次印刷
书 号	ISBN 978-7-5178-5469-2
定 价	72.00元

序
Preface

————

　　2015年11月,在土耳其安塔利亚,习近平主席说:"杭州是历史文化名城,也是创新活力之城,相信2016年峰会将给大家呈现一种历史和现实交汇的独特韵味。"[①]2016年,G20峰会的成功举办,展现了杭州的文化和杭州的韵味,提升了杭州的国际知名度和美誉度,让世界认识了杭州。后G20时代,杭州的国际化步伐加快,推介力度进一步加强。2023年9月,第19届亚运会将在杭州举行,世界的目光将聚焦杭州,这是亚洲规模最大的综合性运动会。亚运会对杭州来说是一个新的机遇,能够让亚洲、让世界更加了解杭州、了解浙江。亚运会不仅是一次大型的体育盛会,也是杭州向世界展示其地域、文化、经济,提振杭州国际知名度乃至中国风范的极佳机会。基于上述思考,我们编写了《走进亚运　体验杭州》(中英双语)。借此盛会,本书将起到两个方面的作用:一方面,可以宣传"中国风范、浙江特色、杭州韵味",推介主办城市杭州,助力杭州城市形象宣传,让世界了解杭州、认识杭州、喜爱杭州。另一方面,在亚运会举办期间,众多外籍人士将来杭州参加或观赏赛事,语言交流方面的障碍及相关文化背景知识的缺乏等因素势必影响他们对杭州的体验和感受,本书可以为外籍人士读懂杭州提供便捷途径。提升杭州的国际化水平,重视外籍人士的诉求,提高他们对

————

[①] 转引自:乔雪峰,夏晓伦.打造创新活力之省［EB/OL］.（2015-12-15）［2023-02-04］.http://it.people.com.cn/n1/2015/1215/c1009-27932644.html.

杭州的满意度，也是亚运会宣传工作的重要组成部分。

"Hangzhou is not only a city known for its long history and splendid culture, but also a city of innovation and vitality. We believe the G20 Summit 2016 will present to you a unique charm into which history and reality blend." said Chinese President Xi Jinping in Antalya, Turkey, in November 2015. The success of this summit in 2016 helps to acquaint the world with the host city of Hangzhou, shows its culture and charm, enhances its international visibility and reputation. In the post-G20 era, Hangzhou has accelerated its internationalization and further strengthened its promotion. In September 2023, the 19th Asian Games, the largest comprehensive games of Asia, will be held in Hangzhou, on which the world will focus, and will know more about this city as well as Zhejiang Province. The Asian Games is not only a grand sports event, but also a great opportunity for Hangzhou to demonstrate to the world its region, culture and economy, and to boost its international popularity. Therefore, the guidebook *Enjoy Asian Games Explore Hosting City* (*Bilingual in Chinese and English*) has been compiled. The book will serve two purposes: On the one hand, by virtue of this grand event, this guidebook aims to promote "Chinese style, Zhejiang characteristics, Hangzhou charm", and raise the international profile of the host city so as to help the world learn about it and fall in love with it; on the other hand, it is considerate to provide English introduction to Hangzhou for the foreigners to understand the host city better, because the barrier of language and the lack of relevant background knowledge will inevitably affect their experience in Hangzhou during the Games. And helping to make Hangzhou more internationalized, catering to the demands of foreign visitors and improving their satisfaction with Hangzhou are important parts of the publicity of this grand event.

《走进亚运 体验杭州》（中英双语）共9章，聚焦杭州的历史、名人、风土人情、文化遗产、风景名胜和创新发展等，用中英双语呈现最值得向世界推荐的杭州。本书首先介绍杭州的概况，然后分章节阐述杭州作为"历史文化之城""旅游之城""美食之城""购物之城""运动休闲之城""创新活力之城""温暖之城"的历史与现实。例如，在"杭州概况"中，"杭州印象"一节围绕古今中外历代名人所描绘的自己心目中的杭州展开叙述，如唐朝白居易的"江南忆，最忆是杭州"，元朝意大利旅行家马可·波罗盛赞杭州是"世界上最美丽华贵之天城"，等等。"历史文化之城"选编"名人故居"一节，在众多资料中选取具有代表性的几位名人，充分说明杭州一直是文人墨客喜欢居住的地方。"旅游之城"按几大旅游景区布局，其中西湖名胜风景区、京杭大运河、良渚古城遗址已被联合国教科文组织正式列入世界遗产名录，彰显了杭州的旅游品质。"民间美食与历史故事"一节讲述美食背后的典故，有助于了解杭州的历史。"购物之城"中，杭州的传统百货与现代购物中心并存。"运动休闲之城"从杭州举办过的各级体育盛会细数到国际博览会，彰显杭州的开放程度。"创新活力之城"推介阿里巴巴等杭州著名企业及创意小镇，展示杭州蓬勃的活力。"温暖之城"描绘了杭州的公共自行车和斑马线前礼让行人等城市的另一道风景。杭州的韵味，不仅在于其5000多年的建城史和源远流长的历史文脉、最美的湖山和作为"人间天堂"的深厚底蕴，也在于不断会聚而来的高层次人才挥洒着的创新活力，在于无数温暖的城市细节，在于其自然、人文、历史之美和中国最强劲的经济脉搏与现代精神。杭州，是人们神往的心灵栖息地。

This bilingual book consists of nine chapters, focusing on Hangzhou's history, celebrities, local customs, cultural heritage, scenic spots and innovative development, presenting in both Chinese and English the worthiest of recommending of this city to the world. First, it introduces the overview of Hangzhou, and then elaborates on its history, culture, tourism, food, shopping, sports and leisure, innovation and vitality, and warmth as well. For example, the section of "Hangzhou Impression" in Chapter One focuses on how celebrities in ancient and modern times describe Hangzhou in their minds, such as Bai Juyi in the Tang Dynasty wrote "the memory of Jiangnan is Hangzhou"; Marco Polo, the famous Italian traveler in the Yuan Dynasty, praised Hangzhou as "the most beautiful and magnificent city in the world"; and so on. In Chapter

Two, City of History and Culture, the section titled "Former Residences of Celebrities" introduces several representative figures from many candidates, fully demonstrating that Hangzhou has always been the habitat loved by literati and personages. Chapter Three, City of Tourism, is about several scenic zones, among which West Lake Scenic Area, Beijing-Hangzhou Grand Canal and Archaeological Ruins of Liangzhu City have been admitted to the World Heritage List by UNESCO, highlighting the quality of tourism in Hangzhou. "Folk Cuisine and Their Historical Stories" in Chapter Four tells the allusions behind the local cuisine, helping to understand the history of Hangzhou. Chapter Five, Paradise for Shopping, introduces traditional department stores along with modern shopping malls. Chapter Six, City of Sports and Leisure, mentions the national and international sports events and expos held in Hangzhou, showing the openness of this city. Chapter Seven, City of Innovation and Vitality, showcases the vitality of Hangzhou with the examples of Alibaba and other famous enterprises as well as creative towns. Chapter Eight, City of Warmth, introduces the public bicycle service and the priority of pedestrians at zebra crossings practised in Hangzhou. The charm of Hangzhou lies not only in its over 5,000 years' history, in its most beautiful landscapes, in the profound heritage of "Paradise on Earth"; it also lies in the innovation and vitality from the continuous influx of high-level talents, in the numerous warm details, in the blending of its picturesque nature, splendid culture and glorious history, as well as in its booming economy and modern spirit. In a word, Hangzhou is the spiritual habitat desired by many people.

在 2023 年亚运会背景下，《走进亚运 体验杭州》（中英双语）一书涵盖杭州自然、历史、文化、经济和社会，将对杭州特色韵味和现代活力的推介与亚运会盛事的宣传融为一体，符合杭州亚运会"心心相融，@ 未来"的主题口号，使外籍人士在享受杭州亚运会盛事的同时，更好地感受杭州韵味。此次亚运会也是杭州提升知名度，走向世界的又一契机。本书在编写过程中，首先体现其信息功能——不仅介绍杭州悠久的历史、文化、自然和人文景观，还展现新时代杭州充满活力的形象；其次体现其向导功能，为设定的目标人群提供所需服务；最后体现其宣传功能，通过阅读传播，实现一种动态的宣传。本书将先面向参与 2023 年杭州亚运会的外籍人士，亚运会闭幕后，将面向所有到杭州旅游、学习和工作的外国友人，实现可持续的动态宣传效果。通过本书，那些来杭州学习、旅游、工作、创业、投资和生活的外籍人士不仅能看到杭州四季的风景，还能感受到这座城市蓬勃的创新力量、飞速的经济发展和悠久多元的文化传承。

As mentioned above, this bilingual book covers the nature, history, culture, economy and society of Hangzhou, integrating its characteristics, charm and vitality with the publicity of the Asian Games, which is in line with the Games' slogan of "Heart to Heart, @ Future", so that foreign visitors can feel its charm better while enjoying the Games. The Asian Games is also a good opportunity to enhance the popularity of the city. The three principles underpinning the compiling of this book are informativeness, guide, and publicity. Firstly, it not only presents a comprehensive introduction to the history, culture, natural and cultural landscape of Hangzhou, but also shows its modern image in the new era. Secondly, it provides guide for the target population. And thirdly, it intends to help more foreign visitors to know better about Hangzhou. This book aims at both foreigners who will participate in the 2023 Asian Games and other foreign people who will travel, study and work in this city, so as to achieve prolonged publicity, and to help those foreigners who study, travel, work, start businesses, invest and live in Hangzhou to feel its amazing innovation, booming economy and long and diverse culture when enjoying the breathtaking scenery in this city.

最后，我们引用时任浙江省委书记袁家军于 2021 年 3 月在接受中国国际电视台专访时对国际运动员和观众说的一番话："浙江省拥有最美的山水、丰厚的文化遗产、创新力和活力十足的经济，尤其是数字经济。我们有仁爱、热心的社会，有美丽的乡村、清澈的水域和绿色的群山。我们有充满创造性和干劲的企业家队伍，有务实高效的政府。更重要的是，我们有聪明、勤劳、友好、美好的人民。在此，我向来自亚洲和世界各地的朋友们表示最热烈的欢迎，欢迎来到杭州，我相信你们的旅行将充实而愉快，非常感谢！"

Finally, we'd like to quote what Yuan Jiajun, Party Secretary of Zhejiang Province at the time, said to international athletes and audiences in an exclusive interview with China International Television in March 2021: "Zhejiang province has the most beautiful landscape, rich cultural heritage, innovative dynamic economy, especially the digital economy. We have loving and warm-hearted society. We have beautiful countryside. We have lucid water and green mountains. We have created a dynamic team of entrepreneurs. We have pragmatic and efficient government, and above all, the intelligent, hardworking, friendly and beautiful people. So I would like to give friends from Asia and the whole world a warmest welcome to the city of Hangzhou. I am certain that you will have a fulfilling trip. Thanks so much."

叶依群　潘　飞　石教旺
浙江科技学院
初稿 2022 年 4 月
终稿 2023 年 4 月

Ye Yiqun Pan Fei Shi Jiaowang
Zhejiang University of Science and Technology
Finished in April, 2022
Final version in April, 2023

目 录
Contents

第三章　旅游之城

Chapter Three
City of Tourism

第四章　美食之城

Chapter Four
City of Gastronomy

第一章　杭州概况

　　杭州是浙江省省会城市，位于中国东南沿海，钱塘江下游，京杭大运河南端，是浙江省的政治、经济、文化、教育、交通和金融中心。得益于长江三角洲的区位优势、京杭大运河和通商口岸的便利，杭州自古以来就是重要的商业、贸易中心，已成为中国最重要的电子商务中心之一。

　　杭州钟灵毓秀，历史悠久，文化底蕴深厚，是古代文人墨客旅居、创作的理想之地，也是当今中国最受欢迎的旅游目的地之一。近年来，随着杭州在经济、城市建设、社会事业等方面的发展，越来越多的年轻人选择来杭就业和生活。从2007年起，杭州连续15年被评为"中国最具幸福感城市"。2016年G20峰会在杭州举办，2023年第19届亚运会将在杭州举办。立足于"后峰会、新亚运、现代化"历史机遇，杭州向城市国际化迈出了坚实步伐。杭州被认为是未来10年中国最具发展潜力的十大城市之一。

Chapter One
Hangzhou Overview

Hangzhou, the capital city of Zhejiang Province, is the political, economic, cultural, educational, transportation and financial center of Zhejiang Province. Thanks to the location advantages of the Yangtze River Delta and the convenience of the Beijing-Hangzhou Grand Canal and trading ports, it has been an important commercial and trade center since ancient times. At present, it has become one of the most important centers of e-commerce in China.

With beautiful sceneries and humanities treasure, a long history and profound culture, Hangzhou is an ideal place for ancient literati to live and create. It is also one of the most popular tourist destinations in China today. In recent years, with the development of economy, urban construction and social utilities, more and more young talents choose to work and live in Hangzhou. Since 2007, Hangzhou has been rated as "the happiest city in China" for 15 consecutive years. G20 summit was held in Hangzhou in 2016, and the 19th Asian Games will be held in Hangzhou in 2023. Based on the historical opportunity of "Post G20 Summit, New Asian Games and Modernization", Hangzhou takes solid steps towards city internationalization. Hangzhou is considered one of the top 10 cities in China with the best potential in development in the next decade.

第一节 历史变迁

　　杭州历史悠久,是中国七大古都之一。萧山跨湖桥遗址的发掘证实,早在 8000 多年前就有人类在此繁衍生息。5000 多年的余杭良渚文化被誉为"文明的曙光"。公元前 222 年,秦于今杭州地域置钱唐县、余杭县。五代十国时期,吴越国(907—978)定都杭州。1129 年(南宋建炎三年),宋室南迁至杭州,并改"杭州"为"临安府"。1138 年(绍兴八年),南宋正式定都临安。1927 年,杭州置市。1949 年 5 月 3 日,杭州解放,杭州市人民政府成立。

Ⅰ History

Hangzhou, one of the seven ancient capitals in China, enjoys a long history. The excavation of the Kuahu Bridge site in Xiaoshan confirms that as early as 8,000 years ago, the place already saw thriving human activities. The Liangzhu culture in Yuhang, which dates back over 5,000 years, is hailed by historians as "the dawn of civilization". In 222 BC, during the Qin Dynasty, Qiantang County and Yuhang County were established in the current location of Hangzhou. During the Five Dynasties and Ten Kingdoms Period, the Wuyue State (907—978) established its capital in Hangzhou. In 1129 (the third year of the Jianyan Reign Period of the Southern Song Dynasty), the Song court moved south to Hangzhou and renamed "Hangzhou" as "Lin'an Prefecture".

In 1138 (the eighth year of the Shaoxing Reign Period), the Southern Song Dynasty officially established its capital in Lin'an. In 1927, "Hangzhou City" was officially established. On May 3, 1949, Hangzhou was liberated and the Hangzhou Municipal People's Government was established.

第二节　自然地理

　　杭州地处长江三角洲南翼、杭州湾西端，是"丝绸之路经济带"和"21世纪海上丝绸之路"的延伸交点。杭州地形地貌复杂多样。西部属浙西丘陵区，主干山脉有天目山等。东部属浙北平原，地势低平，河网密布，湖泊众多，物产丰富，具有典型的"江南水乡"特征。除了美丽的西湖外，京杭大运河和钱塘江也穿城而过。杭州属于亚热带季风气候，夏季高温多雨，冬季温和少雨，四季分明。

Ⅱ Geography

　　Located in the southern wing of the Yangtze River Delta, western tip of the Hangzhou Bay, Hangzhou is the crossing point of the extension of "Silk Road Economic Belt" and "21st Century Maritime Silk Road". Hangzhou has a complex and diverse terrain and landform. The western part belongs to the hilly area of western Zhejiang, with main mountain ranges such as Tianmu Mountain. The eastern part belongs to the North Zhejiang Plain, with a low and flat terrain, dense river networks, and numerous lakes. It is rich in natural resources and has typical characteristics of "water town in Jiangnan". In addition to the beautiful West Lake, the Beijing-Hangzhou Grand Canal and Qiantang River also pass through the city. Hangzhou belongs to the subtropical monsoon climate zone. It is hot and rainy in summer, and mild and dry in winter, with four distinct seasons.

第三节　行政区域

中华人民共和国成立后，杭州的区域范围经历了不断变化。1994 年，杭州升格为副省级城市。目前，杭州市下辖上城、拱墅、西湖、滨江、钱塘、余杭、萧山、临平、富阳、临安 10 个区，建德 1 个县级市，桐庐、淳安 2 个县。全市有 191 个乡镇（街道），其中乡 23 个、镇 75 个、街道 93 个，居委会 1293 个、行政村 1913 个。全市土地面积 16850 平方千米（根据第二次土地利用调查），其中市区面积 8289 平方千米。[①]

Ⅲ Administrative Divisions

After the foundation of the People's Republic of China, the regional scope of Hangzhou has undergone constant changes. At present, under the jurisdiction of the City of Hangzhou are 10 urban districts, namely Shangcheng, Gongshu, Xihu, Binjiang, Qiantang, Yuhang, Xiaoshan, Linping, Fuyang and Lin'an, 1

①杭州日报. 行政区划［EB/OL］.（2015-11-16）［2023-04-06］. http://www.hangzhou.gov.cn/art/2022/7/1/art_1229144714_59060446.html.

county-level city of Jiande, and 2 counties of Tonglu and Chun'an. There are a total of 191 towns (subdistricts), among which are 23 townships, 75 towns, 93 subdistricts, 1,293 neighborhood committees and 1,913 administrative villages. The city covers a total area of 16,850 square kilometers (according to the second land survey), of which the urban area takes up 8,289 square kilometers.

第四节　杭州印象

　　杭州以风景秀丽著称，素有"上有天堂，下有苏杭"的美誉。唐代诗人白居易写道："江南忆，最忆是杭州。"元代来华的三位意大利旅行家马可·波罗（Marco Polo）、鄂多立克（Friar Odoric）、马黎诺里（Marignolli），是第一批为欧洲人描绘"杭州印象"的文化使者。马可·波罗盛赞杭州为"世界上最美丽华贵之城"。鄂多立克说杭州是全世界最大的城市，他对杭州规模和富有程度的描述比起马可·波罗来是有过之而无不及的。马黎诺里在他的《马黎诺里游记》里写道："一个非常有名的地方叫行在（杭州），这里最好、最大、最富饶、人口最多，总之是最绝妙的一个城市。"

IV Impression of Hangzhou

　　Hangzhou is famous for its beautiful scenery, earning the reputation "There is paradise in heaven, and Suzhou and Hangzhou on earth". The poet Bai Juyi in the Tang Dynasty wrote, "the memory of Jiangnan is Hangzhou." Marco Polo,

Friar Odoric and Marignolli, three Italian travelers in the Yuan Dynasty, were the first cultural envoys to depict the "impression of Hangzhou" for Europeans. Marco Polo praised Hangzhou as "the most beautiful and magnificent city in the world". Odoric said that Hangzhou was the largest city in the world, and his description of the scale and wealth of Hangzhou was better than that of Marco Polo. In *The Travels of Marignolli*, Marignolli wrote, "A very famous place is called Hang Zai (Hangzhou), which is the best, the largest, the richest and the most populous city. In a word, it's the most wonderful city."

第二章 历史文化之城

杭州历史文化内涵博大精深。几千年来，以西湖文化、运河文化、钱塘江文化为代表的杭州文化，在开放中融合，在创新中发展。西湖文化撷跨湖桥文化、良渚文化、吴越文化、南宋文化、明清文化、民国文化等各个时期文化之精华，集山水文化、园林文化、宗教文化、建筑文化、名人文化、民俗文化、丝绸文化、茶文化、饮食文化之广博，体现了杭州文化精致、和谐、典雅的特色；运河文化集水利文化、商贸文化、物产文化、水景文化、戏曲文化、庙会集市文化于一身，体现了杭州文化开放、兼容的特色；钱塘江文化犹如滚滚钱塘潮，是杭州人大气、开放的象征和标志。[1]

① 杭州市人民政府. 历史文化［EB/OL］.（2015-11-16）［2023-04-06］. http:// www.hangzhou.gov.cn/art/2022/7/1/art_1229144714_59060445.html.

Chapter Two
City of History and Culture

Hangzhou is proud of its profound historical culture. For millenniums, the Hangzhou Culture, as represented by the West Lake, Grand Canal, and Qiantang River cultures, has featured a fusion in the opening to the outside world and progress in creation and innovation. By absorbing the essence of different cultures, including those of the Kuahu Bridge, the Liangzhu, the Wuyue, the Southern Song, the Ming and Qing and the Republic of China, the West Lake Culture integrates the richness of landscaping, gardening, religion, architecture, celebrity, folkways, silk, tea, and food cultures to embody the exquisiteness, harmony and elegance of Hangzhou culture; while the Canal Culture features a blending of indigenous cultural elements in water conservation, trade and commerce, local specialty, water-scape, traditional opera and temple fair, reflecting the openness, inclusiveness and closeness to life of Hangzhou culture; The Qiantang River Culture, like the surging tide of the river, symbolizes the broad-mindedness and open spirit of Hangzhou natives.

第一节　博物馆和美术馆

　　杭州是一座具有丰富的历史、旅游及文化资源的城市，拥有大大小小博物馆和美术馆近百个。其中最具代表性的有浙江省博物馆、中国茶叶博物馆、中国丝绸博物馆、中国京杭大运河博物馆、中国杭帮菜博物馆、浙江美术馆、韩美林艺术馆、富春山馆等。

Ⅰ Museums and Art Galleries

Hangzhou is a city rich in historical, tourist and cultural resources, with nearly 100 museums and art galleries. Among them, the most representative are Zhejiang Provincial Museum, China National Tea Museum, China National Silk Museum, The Beijing—Hangzhou Grand Canal Museum, Hangzhou Cuisine Museum, Zhejiang Art Museum, Han Meilin Art Gallery, Fuchun Mountain Museum, etc.

★ 浙江省博物馆

　　浙江省博物馆始建于 1929 年，初名"浙江省西湖博物馆"，经过 90 多年的发展，它已成为浙江省内规模最大的综合性人文科学博物馆，形成了包括孤山馆区、名人故居、古代文物保护科研基地等在内的集收藏、研究、保护、展示和教育等于一身的多功能的新格局。

　　浙江省博物馆馆藏文物及标本 10 万余件，文物品类丰富，年代序列完整。其中，河姆渡文化遗物，良渚文化玉器，越文化遗存，越窑、龙泉窑青瓷，五代两宋佛教文物，汉代会稽镜，宋代湖州镜，南宋金银货币，历代书画和金石拓本，历代漆器，等等，都是极具地域特色及学术价值的珍贵历史文物。

★ Zhejiang Provincial Museum

Zhejiang Provincial Museum was founded in 1929, named the West Lake Museum of Zhejiang Province at that time. Over the past nine decades, it has developed into the largest comprehensive humanities museum in Zhejiang, including Gushan branch, former residences of celebrities, and cultural relics protection and scientific research base, and so on. It forms a new pattern of multi-functions of collection, research, exhibition and education.

Zhejiang Provincial Museum has a collection of more than 100,000 cultural relics and specimens, with rich categories and complete chronological sequences. Among them, there are remains of Hemudu culture, jade of Liangzhu culture, remains of Yue culture, celadon of Yue kiln and Longquan kiln, Buddhist relics of the Five Dynasties and the Song Dynasty, Kuaiji mirror of the Han Dynasty, Huzhou mirror of the Song Dynasty, gold and silver coins of the Southern Song Dynasty, calligraphy and painting and stone rubbings of all dynasties, and lacquer ware of all dynasties, which are all precious historical relics with great regional characteristics and academic value.

★ 中国茶叶博物馆

中国茶叶博物馆是我国唯一以茶和茶文化为主题的国家级专题博物馆。目前，中国茶叶博物馆分为 2 个馆区：双峰馆区位于龙井路 88 号，1991 年 4 月对外开放；龙井馆区位于翁家山 268 号，2015 年 5 月对外开放。两馆的占地面积共约 12.2 万平方米，建筑面积共约 1.3 万平方米，集文化展示、科普宣传、科学研究、学术交流、茶艺培训、互动体验及品茗、餐饮、会务、休闲等服务功能于一体，是中国与世界茶文化的展示交流中心，也是茶文化主题旅游综合体。

★ China National Tea Museum

China National Tea Museum is the one and only national museum focusing on tea and tea culture. It consists of two branches: Shuangfeng Branch (No. 88, Longjing Road) opened in April, 1991 and Longjing Branch (No. 268, Wengjiashan) opened in May, 2015, covering an area of 122,000 square meters and a building area of 13,000 square meters. With the multiple functions such as cultural display, popular science publicity, scientific research, academic exchange, tea art training, interactive experience, as well as tea tasting, catering, conference and leisure, etc., China National Tea Museum is not only the exhibition and exchange center of tea culture between China and the world, but also the tourism complex centering on tea culture.

★ 中国丝绸博物馆

位于杭州西子湖畔玉皇山下的中国丝绸博物馆是国家一级博物馆、中国最大的纺织服装类专业博物馆，也是全世界最大的丝绸专业博物馆，现占地面积 42286 平方米，建筑面积 22999 平方米。中国丝绸博物馆于 1992 年 2 月 26 日建成开放，2004 年 1 月 1 日起对公众实行免费开放。2015 年又开启了改扩建工程，2016 年 9 月以全新的面貌呈现给国内外参观者。

中国丝绸博物馆展示了中国 5000 多年的丝绸历史及文化。博物馆内藏有自新石器时代起各朝代与丝绸有关的历史文物，特别是出土于"丝绸之路"沿途的汉唐织物、北方草原的辽金实物、江南地区的宋代服饰、明清时期的官机产品以及近代旗袍和像景织物等。此外，还有众多的民族文物和现代文物。

近年来，中国丝绸博物馆与世界各地的学术机构加强合作，成立了"国际丝路之绸研究联盟"，开展了大量的合作项目，正在让精美的丝绸和博大的丝绸文化走向世界。

★ China National Silk Museum

China National Silk Museum, situated by the side of the West Lake, is one of the first state-level museums in China, covering an area of 42,286 square meters and a building area of 22,999 square meters, which was opened on February 26th, 1992. Since January 1st, 2004, it has provided free entry for public. In 2015, the museum started an extension and renovation project. In September, 2016, after a year of arduous work, the museum was reopened to visitors at home and abroad with a new look.

The museum displays over 5,000-year history and culture of Chinese silk. It has a collection of historical relics related to silk in all dynasties from the Neolithic Age, especially the relics from the Han and Tang Dynasties, which were unearthed along the Silk Road, objects from the Liao and Jin Dynasties in the northern grasslands, costumes from the Song Dynasty in the south of the Yangtze River, official machinery products from the Ming and Qing Dynasties, and cheongsam and landscape fabrics in modern time. In addition, there are numerous ethnic and modern cultural relics.

In recent years, the museum has cooperated with academic institutions around the world, and founded the International Association for the Study of Silk Road Textiles, which has undertaken a large number of international cooperation, and will let the exquisite silk as well as the profound silk culture take on the world.

★ 中国京杭大运河博物馆

中国京杭大运河博物馆，位于杭州拱墅区运河文化广场南侧，毗邻大运河南端终点标志——拱宸桥。博物馆投资1亿多元人民币，建筑面积10000多平方米，展览面积5000多平方米，分序厅以及"大运河的开凿与变迁""大运河的利用""运河畔的城市""运河文化"4个展厅。目前收集、展出的上千件文物和史料，充分展示了大运河在中华民族发展历史中的地位和作用。

中国京杭大运河博物馆不是一座单纯的、普通意义上的博物馆。它一方面是一个全方位、多角度反映和展现运河自然特性、人文精华等的大型博物馆，另一方面又是运河文物、文献资料等的征集和收藏中心，以及运河文化的研究和展示中心，同时结合运河文化广场功能又是运河旅游的中心枢纽和游客综合服务中心。

★ The Beijing-Hangzhou Grand Canal Museum

The Beijing-Hangzhou Grand Canal Museum of China is located in the south of Canal Culture Square, Gongshu District, Hangzhou, adjacent to the southern end of the Grand Canal—Gongchen Bridge. The museum, with an investment of more than 100 million yuan, has a construction area of more than 10,000 square meters and an exhibition area of more than 5,000 square meters, including a preface hall and four exhibition halls. They are "The Construction and Change of the Grand Canal", "The Utilization of the Grand Canal", "The City by the Canal" and "Canal Culture". Thousands of cultural relics and historical materials collected and exhibited so far fully demonstrate the position and role of the Grand Canal in the history of the development of the Chinese nation.

The Grand Canal Museum of China is not just an ordinary museum. On the one hand, it is a large-scale museum which reflects and displays the natural characteristics and humanistic essence of the canal in all directions and from different perspectives. On the other hand, it is the collection center of the canal cultural relics and documents, etc., the research and demonstration center, as well as the central hub of canal tourism and comprehensive service center for tourists by combining with the canal cultural square function.

★ 中国杭帮菜博物馆

中国杭帮菜博物馆坐落在南宋皇城大遗址旁的江洋畈生态公园内。博物馆毗邻西湖，与钱塘江风景串联成片，共包括 10 个展区、20 个历史事件的场景复原、大量的文字图片史料、历代文物陈列，梳理了上溯至良渚文化、秦至南北朝时期等不同历史阶段杭帮菜传承和发展的肌理脉络。

博物馆的亮点是展示了 300 多款仿制菜肴和小吃。在其中一个展板上有二十四节气的应季小吃，它们与某一特定的天文事件或一些自然现象相匹配。

除了展区，博物馆还设有体验区和经营区。体验区体现了杭帮菜饮食文化的参与、交流、互动、学习的特征。经营区为杭帮菜饮食文化的进一步延伸。在以 40 位杭州历史名人的事迹美文来命名和修饰的包厢中，可以细细品尝正宗的杭州菜肴，回味杭州 2000 多年的历史文化变迁，以及杭州城市的市井百态，饮食风格，在与这些历史名人的超时空对话中，感知他们的艺术魅力和人格魅力。

★ Hangzhou Cuisine Museum

China Hangzhou Cuisine Museum is located in Jiangyangfan Ecological Park next to the Ruins of the Southern Song Dynasty Imperial City. The museum, adjacent to the West Lake, connected the scenery of the West Lake with that of the Qiantang River. It consists of 10 exhibition areas, 20 restored scenes of historical events, a large number of texts, pictures and historical documents, and the exhibitions of cultural relics in all ages, which sort out the history of the inheritance and development of Hangzhou cuisine in different historical stages, such as the Liangzhu Culture, the Qin Dynasty, and the Northern and Southern Dynasties.

The highlight of the museum is the display of over 300 duplicated dishes and snacks. On one of the displays there are seasonal snacks of twenty-four solar terms, each of which matches a particular astronomical event or some natural phenomena.

Besides exhibition areas, there are an experience area and a business area. The audience experience area reflects the characteristics of participation, communication, interaction and learning of Hangzhou cuisine culture. The business area is a further extension of Hangzhou cuisine culture. In the separate dining rooms named and decorated by the articles glorifying the deeds of 40 historical celebrities in Hangzhou, you can savor and appreciate the authentic Hangzhou cuisine, relive the historical and cultural changes of Hangzhou during the past more than two thousand years, as well as everyday life and food styles of Hangzhou city. By conversing with these historical celebrities beyond time and space, you can perceive their artistic and personality charm.

★ 浙江美术馆

浙江美术馆坐落于杭州市南山路西子湖畔，毗邻万松岭，占地面积35000平方米，建筑面积32000平方米。拥有各种规格的展厅14个，其中恒温恒湿展厅6个，展厅面积9000平方米，库房区面积3000平方米。另有中央大厅、天光长廊、国际学术报告厅、多功能厅、鉴赏厅、贵宾室、美术图书文献中心、儿童美术天地、美术书店、美术材料用品商店、咖啡吧等多种配套设施。

浙江美术馆2009年8月正式向公众开放，自开馆以来，一直坚持"重在当代、兼顾历史，立足浙江、面向世界"的立馆方向和"公共性、多元性、开放性"的学术宗旨，以"中国风"作为自己的风格追求，成功举办了"浙江历史文化重大题材美术作品大展""神州国光——黄宾虹艺术展""米罗作品展""煌煌大观——敦煌艺术展""东西贯中——吴冠中艺术回顾大展""杭州·中国画双年展""杭州纤维艺术三年展"等一大批优秀展览，并围绕浙江近现代美术史展开一系列学术研究计划，在国内外产生重要影响。2009年，成为全国美术馆专业委员会首批会员馆。2011年，成为国际现当代美术馆协会成员馆。2015年，成为国家重点美术馆。

★ Zhejiang Art Museum

Zhejiang Art Museum, with a coverage of 35,000 square meters and floorage of 32,000 square meters, is located on Nanshan Road, Hangzhou, adjacent to Wansongling and opposite to the West Lake. In the museum, there are 14 exhibition halls of different sizes, taking up 9,000 square meters, including 6 exhibition halls with constant temperature and humidity; the storehouse area takes up 3,000 square meters. Besides, the museum is equipped with multiple supporting facilities such as the Central Hall, Skylight Corridor, International Academic Hall, Multi-Functional Hall, Assessment and Appreciation Hall, VIP Room, Literature Center for Art Books and Documentations, Children's Fine Arts World, Arts Bookstore, Store of Arts Materials and Supplies, and Cafe. The museum, on behalf of the nation, is dedicated to the exhibition, display, solicitation, and collection of art works and art literatures, with which it aims to provide and present academic research, education promotion, international exchanges and public cultural services.

Since its opening to public in August 2009, Zhejiang Art Museum has always followed the direction of "focusing on contemporary era, giving the consideration to history, keeping a foothold in Zhejiang, and facing the World" and the guidance of the academic principle of "publicity, variety and sociability". With a pursuit of "Chinese style", Zhejiang Art Museum has successfully hosted numerous excellent exhibitions such as "Major Exhibition of Arts Works on Important Historical and Cultural Subjects in Zhejiang Province" "Glory on the Divine Land Art Exhibition of Huang Binhong" "Exhibition of Works by Miro" "Great Landscape of Splendid Art Exhibition of Dunhuang" "Across the East and the West Art Review Exhibition of Wu Guanzhong" "Hangzhou Biennial Exhibition of Chinese Painting" and "Triennial Exhibition of Fiber Art in Hangzhou", exerting important influence at home and abroad. It became one of the first members of Committee of Art Museums in China (CAMC) in 2009. In 2011, it became a member of International Committee for Museums and Collections of Modern Art, and in 2015 a key national art museum.

★ 韩美林艺术馆

坐落在西湖边植物园腹地的韩美林艺术馆，是一处与著名艺术家韩美林先生相关的集收藏、展览、研究、公共教育与对外交流于一体的艺术空间。

2005 年 10 月 19 日，韩美林艺术馆落成并对外开放，成为杭州文化发展中不可或缺的艺术亮点。2011 年，韩美林艺术馆完成二期扩建，此后日益成为杭州的一处文化地标和艺术高地。2019 年，在艺术馆三期开馆之际，韩美林先生再次捐赠 500 件艺术作品，充分彰显了他对杭州这座城市的深厚情愫，体现了艺术家的无私大爱。

扩建后的韩美林艺术馆共设 7 个展厅，包括足迹、雕塑厅、公教厅、绘画厅、工艺厅、综合艺术厅、学术研究厅，展品 2000 余件，全面系统地展示了韩美林先生的艺术成就，以及多方面的艺术才华和无限的创造力。

★ **Han Meilin Art Gallery**

Located inside Botanical Garden next to the West Lake, Hangzhou, Han Meilin Art Gallery is an art space related to famous artist Han Meilin, which integrates collection, exhibition, research, public education and foreign exchange.

On October 19, 2005, Han Meilin Art Gallery in Hangzhou was completed and opened to the public, which became an indispensable art highlight in the cultural development of Hangzhou. In 2011, the second phase of expansion was completed, and the gallery increasingly became a cultural landmark and art highland in Hangzhou. In 2019, when the third phase was opened, Mr. Han Meilin donated 500 pieces of works of art a second time, which fully demonstrates his deep affections for the city of Hangzhou and his selfless love as an artist.

After expansion, the whole art gallery is composed of 7 exhibition halls, including Archives, Sculpture Hall, Public Education Hall, Painting Hall, Arts and Crafts Hall, General Hall and Academic Research Hall. There are more than 2,000 exhibits, which comprehensively and systematically show the artistic achievements, various artistic talents and unlimited creativity of Mr. Han Meilin.

★ **富春山馆**

坐落在富春江畔的富春山馆，是杭州市富阳区博物馆、美术馆、档案馆"三馆合一"的古典建筑群，是矗立在现实版《富春山居图》上的新的文化坐标。作为浙江省的重大公共文化设施，富春山馆由著名建筑设计师、普利兹克奖获得者王澍亲自设计。2017 年 12 月 23 日，富春山馆正式开馆。同日，"乾隆与董家父子书画特展""'公望富春'首届中国山水画大展""'家在富春江上'富阳区美术书法摄影精品展"也分别在馆内开幕。富阳区博物馆的常设展览主题为"家在富春江上"，分"山水富阳""千年古县""东吴源流""造纸名乡""鱼米之乡""黄金水道""人杰地灵"7个单元，以叙事的方式，向观众展示悠远、凝重、丰厚的富阳历史和瑰丽多姿的富春文化。

富春山馆以山水为主题来体现山水可游可居的意境，巧妙地融合了城市山水文化，并通过富阳建筑语言展示了富春江山水文化和地域文化的内涵，成为富阳乃至杭州的地标性建筑。

★ **Fuchun Mountain Museum**

Located on the Fuchun River, Fuchun Mountain museum is a classic building group of Fuyang District Museum, Art Gallery and Archive, which is a new cultural coordinate standing on the realistic version of *Dwelling in the Fuchun Mountains*. As a major public cultural facility in Zhejiang Province, Fuchun Mountain Museum was designed by Wang Shu, a famous architect and winner of the Pritzker Architecture Prize. On December 23, 2017, Fuchun Mountain Museum was officially opened. On the same day, the Exhibition of the Calligraphy and Paintings by Emperor Qianlong and Junior and Senior Dong, the First Grand Exhibition of Chinese Landscape Painting of Gongwang Fuchun, and the Fine Arts and Calligraphy and Photography Exhibition of Fuyang District with the Theme "Home on the Fuchun River" were opened respectively in it. The standing theme of Fuyang District Museum is "home on the Fuchun River", which is composed of seven units: Fuyang Landscape, A Thousand-year-old Ancient County, Dongwu Source, Famous Paper-making Township, Fish-and-rice Town, Golden Waterway and Outstanding People, by which a long, dignified and rich history of Fuyang and magnificent Fuchun culture in a narrative way are displayed to audience.

Fuchun Mountain Museum embodies the artistic conception of landscape which is favorable for travelling to or living in with the theme of landscape, skillfully integrates the urban landscape culture, and displays the connotation of the landscape culture and regional culture of the Fuchun River through Fuyang architectural language. It has become the landmark building of Fuyang and even Hangzhou.

★ 杭州国家版本馆（中国国家版本馆杭州分馆）

杭州国家版本馆又名文润阁，位于杭州市余杭区瓶窑镇文润路 1 号，总建筑面积 10.31 万平方米，是集图书馆、博物馆、档案馆、展览馆等多种功能于一体的综合性场馆。杭州国家版本馆采用宋韵园林建筑风格，因地制宜，随山就势，突出江南色彩、宋韵元素、浙江特色。作为国家文化种子基因库和版本资源灾备中心，杭州国家版本馆将古今中外载有中华文明印记的各类版本资源纳入收藏范围，承担中华版本保藏的重要任务。

杭州国家版本馆包括主书房、南书房、文润阁、山体库房、附属用房等 13 个单体建筑，其中展览总面积 7000 平方米。设有展示区、保藏区、洞藏区、交流区等区域，于 2022 年 7 月 30 日正式开馆。

截至 2022 年 7 月，杭州国家版本馆收藏有各类版本累计 100 万册（件），内容包含各种语言版本的《共产党宣言》、战国越王州句青铜剑、吴越国时期刊刻的《雷峰塔经》，以及明清时期的各种刻本。截至 2022 年 8 月，杭州国家版本馆推出"潮起之江——'重要窗口'主题版本展""文献之邦——江南版本文化概览""盛世浙学——浙江文化研究工程成果展""千古风流——浙江历史文化名人展"等 4 个实体展厅、1 个版本数字展厅，共展出珍贵古籍、文物、手稿等 5000 余件。

杭州国家版本馆是新时代的文化地标，是国家站在文化安全和文化复兴战略高度上谋划的用以存放保管文明"金种子"的"库房"，也称中华文明种子基因库。

★ China National Archives of Publications and Culture (Hangzhou)

China National Archives of Publications and Culture (Hangzhou), also known as Wenrun Pavilion, is located at No. 1 Wenrun Road, Pingyao Town, Yuhang District, Hangzhou City, with a total floor area of 103,100 square meters. It is a comprehensive venue integrating libraries, museums, archives, exhibition halls and other functions. China National Archives of Publications and Culture (Hangzhou) adopts the garden architecture with "Song Yun" (the Charm of Song Culture), adapts measures to local conditions, follows the mountain, and highlights Jiangnan color, elements of Song culture, and

Zhejiang characteristics. As a gene bank of national cultural seed and the disaster recovery center of bibliological resources, China National Archives of Publications and Culture (Hangzhou) has collected all kinds of bibliological resources with the imprint of Chinese civilization, undertaking the important task of preserving Chinese publications.

There are 13 individual buildings in total, including the main study, the south study, Wenrun Pavilion, the warehouse built along the mountain, and the auxiliary rooms, with a total exhibition area of 7,000 square meters. There is exhibition area, preservation area, cave storage area, communication area and other areas. China National Archives of Publications and Culture (Hangzhou) was officially opened on July 30, 2022.

By July 2022, China National Archives of Publications and Culture (Hangzhou) has a total collection of one million volumes (pieces) of various editions, including *The Manifesto of the Communist Party* in various languages, the Bronze Sword of Zhou Ju, the King of Yue in the Warring States, the Scripture of Leifeng Pagoda engraved in the Wuyue period, and various engravings in the Ming and Qing Dynasties. By August 2022, four physical exhibitions and one digital exhibition had been launched, and more than 5,000 pieces of precious ancient books, cultural relics and manuscripts were exhibited. The four physical exhibitions are respectively "The Tidal Bore of the Qiantang River: The Bibliological Exhibition of Zhejiang as 'A Showcase of China'", "A Realm Noted for Its Books: An Overview of Bibliological Culture in Jiangnan", "Flourishing Zhejiang Studies: Zhejiang Cultural Research Project Achievement Exhibitions", and "Amorous Through the Ages Zhejiang Historical and Cultural Celebrities Exhibition".

China National Archives of Publications and Culture (Hangzhou) is a cultural landmark in the new era. It is a "warehouse" designed by the state on the strategic height of cultural security and cultural rejuvenation to store and preserve the "golden seeds" of civilization, also known as the seed gene bank of Chinese civilization.

★ 南宋德寿宫遗址博物馆

南宋德寿宫遗址博物馆位于杭州市上城区,总用地面积约2.1万平方米,建筑面积约1.2万平方米,是一座依托德寿宫遗址,以保护、研究、收藏和展示遗址本体及出土文物为主,同时展示南宋历史文化和文物遗产的遗址专题博物馆。2020年底,经国家和浙江省有关部门批准,开工建设。2022年11月22日,正式对外开放。

德寿宫,原为南宋宰相秦桧的旧第,秦桧亡故后收归官有,改筑新宫。1162年,宋高宗移居新宫,并改名"德寿宫"。之后,宋孝宗为表孝敬,将德寿宫一再扩建,时称"北内"或"北宫"。后又因高宗吴皇后、孝宗谢皇后入住,先后易名为慈福宫、寿慈宫。

德寿宫遗址是迄今为止发掘面积最大、规格最高、揭露遗存最丰富的一处南宋皇家宫殿园林建筑遗址。从2001年起,德寿宫遗址历经4次考古发掘,总揭露面积近7000平方米,发现了各历史时期类型丰富的考古遗迹,其中包括宋孝宗时期中轴线上的重华殿及西区慈福宫等重要建筑遗址,能确定德寿宫基址范围的宫墙遗址,揭示南宋皇家园林"鲁石理水"意境的水闸、方池、假山、亭榭等遗址。出土遗物共计6696件(组),其中陶瓷器5784件。另出土砖瓦脊兽等建筑构件368件、石质文物71件、动物骨骼及骨器151件(组)、铜钱207件(组)、金银器等金属文物65件、漆木器34件、料器16件。[①]

德寿宫遗址的发掘,不仅体现了宋代中国园林与建筑的最高水平,也是南宋临安城遗址保护的重要一环,在历史、艺术和科学上具有重要的研究价值。

★ Deshou Palace Site Museum of the Southern Song Dynasty

Deshou Palace Site Museum of the Southern Song Dynasty is located in Shangcheng District with a total land area of about 21,000 square meters and a building area of about 12,000 square meters. It is a site museum based on the site of Deshou Palace, focusing on the protection, research, collection and display of the site itself and unearthed cultural relics, as well as the display of

---

① 南宋德寿宫遗址博物馆现场图文资料。

the history, culture and cultural relics of the Southern Song Dynasty. At the end of 2020, with the approval of the relevant departments of the state and Zhejiang Province, construction began on Deshou Palace Site Museum. On November 22, 2022, Deshou Palace was officially opened to the public.

Deshou Palace was originally the old residence of Qin Hui, the prime minister of the Southern Song Dynasty. After Qin Hui died, it was taken over by the government and a new palace was built on the site. In 1162, Emperor Gaozong moved to the new palace and named it Deshou Palace (palace of virtue and longevity). Then, to show his filial piety, Emperor Xiaozong expanded the Deshou Palace again and again, which was then called the "Beinei" or "Northern Palace". Later, Empress Wu of Gaozong and Empress Xie of Xiaozong lived there successively and changed its name to Cifu Palace and Shouci Palace.

The Deshou Palace site, among the Southern Song imperial palace sites, has the largest excavation area, of the highest quality, and that has yielded the richest trove of relics to date. Since 2001, the Deshou Palace site has undergone four archaeological excavations with a total exposed area of nearly 7,000 square meters. As a result, abundant archaeological relics of various historical periods have been found, including the foundations of Emperor Xiaozong's Chonghua Hall, located along the central axis of the palace grounds; Cifu Palace, in the western section of the site; the palace wall; and the water gates, rectangular pools, artificial hills, and pavilions characteristic of the Southern Song imperial palace gardens, which were known for their use of stacked stone and water. Altogether, 6,696 relies have been found, 5,784 of them being ceramics. Also found were 368 pieces of bricks, tiles, and roof-ridge sculptures, 71 stone relics, 151 animal bones bone implements, 207 bronze coins, 65 gold/silver articles, 34 pieces of lacquered wood, and 16 pieces of glassware.

The excavation of the Deshou Palace site is not only the embodiment of the refined quality of Chinese garden and architecture in the Song Dynasty, but also an important link in the preservation of the site of Lin'an City in the Southern Song Dynasty, which has important research value in history, art and science.

第二节　名人故居

杭州物华天宝，人杰地灵，自古名人辈出，同时也吸引了众多名人客寓或定居，留下了许多故居（旧居）。这些故居（旧居）既是杭州传统建筑、近现代建筑发展的缩影，更是杭州悠久历史、灿烂文化的精华所在。

Ⅱ Former Residences of Celebrities

Rich in natural treasures, Hangzhou is a remarkable place with outstanding people. Since ancient times, men of talent have come out in succession in large numbers. At the same time, it has attracted many celebrities to live or settle down, thus many former residences (old houses) are left behind and preserved. These former residences (old houses) are not only the miniature of the development of traditional and modern architecture of Hangzhou, but also the essence of long history and splendid culture of Hangzhou.

★ 胡雪岩故居

胡雪岩故居，位于杭州市河坊街、大井巷历史文化保护区东部，建于清同治十一年（1872），正值胡雪岩事业的巅峰时期。工程历时 3 年，于 1875 年竣工。落成的故居是一座富有中国传统建筑特色又颇具西方建筑风格的美轮美奂的宅第，整个建筑南北长东西宽，占地面积 7200 平方米，建筑面积 5815 平方米。胡雪岩故居从建筑到室内家具陈设，用料之考究，堪称清末中国巨商第一宅。宅内有芝园、十三楼等亭台楼阁。其中有 2 顶罕见的红木官轿值得一看。

　　胡雪岩（1823—1885），杭州人，祖籍安徽绩溪。少年时入杭州一钱庄当伙计，后在浙江巡抚王有龄的扶持下，自办阜康钱庄。又因力助左宗棠有功，受朝廷嘉奖，封布政使衔，赐红顶戴、紫禁城骑马，赏穿黄马褂。在其事业鼎盛时，胡雪岩除经营钱庄外，兼营粮食、房地产、典当，还进出口军火、生丝等，后又创办胡庆余堂国药号，成为富甲一时的红顶商人。

★ Hu Xueyan's Former Residence

Hu Xueyan's Former Residence is located in Hefang Street and the east of Dajing Lane Historical and Cultural Conservation Area, Hangzhou. It was built in the 11th year of the reign of Emperor Tongzhi in the Qing Dynasty (1872), when Hu Xueyan was at the peak of his career. The project lasted 3 years and was completed in 1875. It is a magnificent residence with Chinese traditional architectural characteristics and western architectural style. The whole building is long from north to south and wide from east to west, covering an area of 7,200 square meters and a construction area of 5,815 square meters. Exquisite materials are used from the architecture to the interior furnishings, and it can be called the first residence of a Chinese businessman in the late Qing Dynasty. There are many pavilions in it, such as Zhiyuan, the 13th Building, and so on. There are two rare mahogany official sedans worth seeing.

Hu Xueyan (1823—1885) is a native of Hangzhou, whose ancestral home is Jixi, Anhui Province. He became an apprentice in a bank in Hangzhou from his boyhood and later set up his own bank Fukang Bank with the help and support of Wang Youling, the governor of Zhejiang. And because of his contribution to Zuo Zongtang, he was praised by the imperial court and awarded the title of the imperial envoy, enjoying the honor and treatment of wearing official hat with red tassel on the top, riding the horse in the Forbidden City, and wearing the yellow mandarin jacket. In his heyday, besides running the bank, Hu Xueyan engaged in business of grain, real estate, pawnbrokers, import and export of munitions, raw silk, etc. Later, he founded Huqingyutang, a Chinese medicine company, and became a wealthy Red Caped Honored Businessman at that time.

★ 章太炎故居

章太炎故居位于杭州市余杭仓前老街，包括故居本体、游客服务中心、章太炎先生生平展、专题展厅、章太炎研究中心和国学讲堂等部分。故居总面积近 2700 平方米，其中故居本体建筑面积 811 平方米，坐北朝南，共四进一弄，由轿厅、正厅、内堂、书房、避弄等组成，为晚清时期建筑。章太炎在此出生成长，度过了他青少年时代的 22 个春秋，投身革命后也曾几度回家探亲、避难。故居前三进为历史场景的再现，展示了章太炎青少年时期故居的风貌；第四进辟为展厅，以多种传统与现代相结合的手法展现了章太炎波澜壮阔的一生。

故居 2006 年被国务院公布为全国重点文物保护单位，2013 年被公布为浙江省爱国主义教育基地。

章太炎（1869—1936），原名学乘，字枚叔，后易名炳麟，号太炎。浙江余杭仓前人。是中国近代伟大的民主革命家、思想家、国学大师。一生"七被追捕"，"三入牢狱"，三次流亡海外，为推翻清朝帝制，肇建共和，厥功至伟。一代文豪鲁迅赞其为"有学问的革命家"，"是先哲的精神，后生的楷范"。周恩来总理称其为"一代儒宗"。

章太炎文思学理博大精深，一生著述宏富，举凡小学、经学、佛学、哲学、文学、史学、医学等无不涉及，堪称现代中国学术的伟大奠基者。

★ Zhang Taiyan's Former Residence

Zhang Taiyan's Former Residence is located in Cangqian old street, Yuhang, Hangzhou City, including the former residence itself, a tourist service center, an exhibition hall of Mr. Zhang Taiyan's life, a special exhibition hall, a research center of Zhang Taiyan and a lecture hall of traditional Chinese studies. The total area of the residence is nearly 2,700 square meters, of which the main building area of the former residence is 811 square meters. It was built in the late Qing Dynasty, facing south with the back to the north, with four rows composed of a sedan chair hall, a main hall, an inner hall, and a study, and a side alley. Zhang Taiyan was born and grew up here and spent 22 years of his youth. After joining the revolution, he came home several times to visit relatives and take refuge. The first three rows of the former residence are the representation of historical scenes, showing the style of the former residence of Zhang Taiyan in his youth; the fourth row is an exhibition hall, which shows his magnificent life by combining a variety of traditions and modernity.

In 2006, the residence was listed as a historical and cultural monument under state protection unit by China's State Council. In 2013, it was also listed as a Provincial Patriotic Education Base in Zhejiang.

Zhang Taiyan (1869—1936), formerly known as Xuecheng, courtesy name Meishu, later renamed Binglin, and Pseudonym Taiyan, was born in Cangqian, Yuhang District, Zhejiang Province. He is a great democratic revolutionist, thinker and master of Chinese studies in modern China. During his lifetime, he had been chased seven times, put into jail three times, and forced to exile abroad three times. He had achieved remarkable success in his effort to overthrow the imperial monarchy of the Qing Dynasty and to build a Republic. Lu Xun, a great writer, praised him as "a learned revolutionist", presenting "the spirit of previous philosophers and the model for later generations". Premier Zhou Enlai called him "a great master of Confucianism".

Zhang Taiyan's learning is broad and profound and during his lifetime, he had produced voluminous writings covering topics in linguistics and philosophy, Confucian classics, Buddhism, philosophy, literature, history, and medicine, etc. He can be rated as the great founder of modern Chinese academy.

★ 盖叫天故居

盖叫天故居位于杭州西湖赵公堤，又名燕南寄庐，系京剧表演艺术家盖叫天于 20 世纪 30 年代置地构筑。外观白墙青瓦，为典型的江南民居建筑风格，内部由门厅、正厅（百忍堂）、后厅（艺人之家）、左右厢房（盖叫天纪念馆）、佛堂等建筑组成，是一独特、完整的私家宅园。故居内陈列着盖老生前遗物 200 余件，展示了盖老的从艺经历及艺术成就。于 2003 年 10 月 1 日对外开放。

盖叫天（1888—1971），原名张英杰，河北省保定高阳县人。幼时因生活所迫而学戏，13 岁到杭州，在拱宸桥"天仙戏院"学唱老生，15 岁改学武生。后以武戏闻名天下，被誉为"燕北真好汉，江南活武松"，开创了独具特色的盖派艺术。

★ Gai Jiaotian's Former Residence

Gai Jiaotian's Former Residence, also named as Yannanjilu, is located at Zhaogong Causeway across the West Lake, Hangzhou. It was built by the Peking Opera artist Gai Jiaotian in the 1930s. With white walls and green tiles, it is a typical architectural style of folk houses in the south of the Yangtze River. Inside, it is composed of hall, main hall (Hall of Patience), back hall (Home of artists), left and right wing-rooms (Gai Jiaotian Memorial Hall) and Buddhist hall. It is a unique and intact private garden. More than 200 pieces of his relics are displayed in his former residence, showing his art studying experience and artistic achievements. It was opened to the public on October 1, 2003.

Gai Jiaotian (1888—1971), formerly known as Zhang Yingjie, was born in Gaoyang County, Baoding, Hebei Province. In his childhood, he was forced to learn drama for living. At the age of thirteen, he came to Hangzhou and learned to sing the part of an old gentleman in Chinese operas at the Goddess Theatre in Gongchen Bridge. When he was fifteen, he changed to play martial role. Later he was famous for playing the martial role and was hailed as "a true hero in the north of the Yanshan mountain, and a living Wu Song in the south of the Yangtze River", creating a unique art of Gai School.

★ 郁达夫故居

郁达夫故居，又名风雨茅庐，位于杭州市大学路场官弄 63 号，是 1933

年4月郁达夫为暂避国民党的政治迫害，从上海举家移居杭州时购置的寓所。故居是一座典型的中式平房别墅，由郁达夫自己设计。分正屋与后院两部分，3间正屋坐北朝南，过去主要为客厅与卧室，目前主要作为郁达夫生平事迹的陈列展览室，展室正门郁达夫塑像上方悬挂着著名学者马君武所写的"风雨茅庐"牌匾。与正屋砖墙相隔的是后院，有平屋3间，过去为书房与客房，现为郁达夫书稿作品陈列地和书房、卧房场景还原地，院内有假山点缀，林木参差，环境幽雅。1936年郁达夫离开杭州后，就再没有回来居住。其后故居产权几经易手，新中国成立后由政府置换回收。1986年4月，被列为杭州市文物保护单位。2015年8月，正式对外开放，成为纪念郁达夫的一处重要场所。

郁达夫（1896—1945），浙江富阳人，中国现代著名小说家、散文家、诗人。他是新文化运动的重要代表人物，也是一位为抗日救国而殉难的爱国主义作家。他以笔为枪，将爱国主义思想与现代文学创作风格巧妙融合，创作出一篇篇"战斗檄文"，号召全民族对日本军国主义奋起反击。

★ **Yu Dafu's Former Residence**

Yu Dafu's Former Residence, also known as the "Wind and Rain Cottage", is located at No. 63 Changguan Lane, Daxue Road, Hangzhou. It was purchased by Yu Dafu when he moved to Hangzhou from Shanghai in April 1933 to escape the political persecution by the Kuomintang. The former residence is a typical Chinese bungalow villa designed by Yu Dafu himself and consists of two parts, the main room and the backyard. The three main rooms, facing south, mainly used to be a living room and bedrooms, but now they are mainly used as exhibition halls for Yu Dafu's life stories. Above the statue of Yu Dafu at the main entrance of the exhibition hall, there is a plaque with the inscription of "Wind and Rain thatched cottage" by the famous scholar Ma Junwu. Separated from the brick walls of the main house is the backyard, with three one-storey houses, which used to be the study and the guest room, but now are exhibited with Yu Dafu's manuscript works and the restored study and bedroom. The courtyard is dotted with artificial hill, full of jagged trees and have a quiet and elegant environment. After Yu Dafu left Hangzhou in 1936, he never came back. Afterwards the property had different owners and was replaced and recovered by the government after liberation. In April 1986, it was listed as a cultural relic protection unit in Hangzhou. It was officially opened to the public in August 2015 and has become an important place to commemorate Yu Dafu.

Yu Dafu (1896—1945), a native of Fuyang, Zhejiang Province, was a famous novelist, proser and poet in modern China. He was an important representative of the New Culture Movement and a patriotic writer who died for the sake of resisting Japan and saving the country. He used his pen as a gun, dexterously integrated his patriotic thoughts into the creation style of modern literature, and produced pieces of works to call on the whole nation to fight against the Japanese militarism.

★ 黄宾虹故居

黄宾虹故居是著名画家黄宾虹的旧居，位于杭州市西湖栖霞岭 31 号。黄宾虹自 1948 年秋移居此处，曾作西湖山水画多幅，称"愿作西湖老画工"。1955 年 3 月病逝后，家属将其先前作品及收藏 10000 余件全部捐献国家。1959 年 9 月，故居辟为画家黄宾虹先生纪念室。纪念室系独门小院，庭院呈方形，园中央置黄宾虹全身汉白玉雕像一座，四周伴以松、竹、梅等林木。展览厅设于 2 层楼房内，楼下画室陈列画家用的红木画桌、文房四宝、木质沙发等；楼上作品陈列室 165 平方米，展出画家具有代表性的山水、花鸟画 12 幅。遗物陈列室展出画家年谱、著作、手稿等。

黄宾虹（1865—1955），近现代画家，擅画山水。6 岁时，临摹家藏的沈廷瑞（樗崖）山册，曾从郑珊、陈崇光等学花鸟。精研传统与关注写生齐头并进，早年受新安画派影响，以干笔淡墨、疏淡清逸为特色，为"白宾虹"；80 岁后以黑密厚重、黑里透亮为特色，为"黑宾虹"。

★ Huang Binhong's Former Residence

Huang Binhong's Former Residence is located at No. 31, Qixia Ridge by the West Lake. Huang Binhong moved here in the autumn of 1948 and had painted many landscape paintings of the West Lake, claiming "willing to be an old painter of the West Lake". After his death in March 1955, his family donated more than 10,000 pieces of his previous works and collections to the country. In September 1959, his former residence was used as the National Memorial Hall of Mr. Huang Binhong. The memorial room is a small detached house with a square courtyard. In the middle of the garden is a white marble statue of Huang Binhong, surrounded by trees like pines, bamboos and plums. The exhibition hall is located inside a two-story building. Displayed in the studio downstairs are the mahogany painting table, four treasures of the study and wooden sofa. Displayed in the artworks showroom upstairs which is 165 square meters are 12 pieces of his representative landscape paintings and flower and bird paintings. Other things like his chronologies, writings and manuscripts are displayed in the relic exhibition room.

Huang Binhong (1865—1955) is a modern and contemporary painter, good at landscape painting. At the age of six, he began to facsimile paintings from Shen Tingrui (Chu Ya) landscape books which was the collection of his home. He learned to paint flowers and birds from Zheng Shan, and Chen Chongguang, etc. He made an intensive study of tradition and focused on sketching at the same time. In his early years, influenced by the "Xin'an School of Painting", his painting was characterized by dry brush and light ink, thinness and purity, and thus he was nicknamed "White Binhong". After he was eighty years old, his painting was characterized by black dense and thick ink, black and brightness, and therefore he was nicknamed "Black Binhong".

★ 钱学森故居

钱学森故居位于杭州市上城区马市街方谷园 2 号，占地面积约 867 平方米。房子为木结构，主色调为老红色，是一个三进民居，由两个天井相连，还有一个后花园。故居属于杭州市文物保护点，2011 年 12 月 1 日正式对外开放。

　　一楼正厅匾额上,"克勤克俭"4个大字,是钱家的家训。二楼突出了"家"的温馨和亲切,书房中安静摆放的笔墨纸砚,更是有着"江南书香门第"的独特气韵。在陈列室中,有钱学森家20世纪50年代在上海使用的木质碗柜,还有很多生活用品。

　　钱学森(1911—2009),吴越王钱镠第33世孙,生于上海,祖籍浙江省杭州市临安。世界著名科学家、空气动力学家、中国载人航天奠基人、中国科学院及中国工程院院士、中国"两弹一星"功勋奖章获得者,被誉为"中国航天之父""中国导弹之父""中国自动化控制之父"和"火箭之王"。

★ **Qian Xuesen's Former Residence**

Qian Xuesen's Former Residence is located at No. 2, Fanggu Garden, Mashi Street, Shangcheng District, Hangzhou City, covering an area of about 867 square meters. The house is constructed of wood with the main color—dark red. It is a three-row dwelling house connected by two patios, and there is a garden in the back of the house. The former residence is the cultural relic protection site of Hangzhou, opened officially to the public on December 1, 2011.

Hung above the main hall on the ground floor is a plague with the inscription of the four big characters "Ke Qin Ke Jian" (diligent and frugal), which is the motto of Qian Family. The second floor highlights the warmth and friendliness of "home". In the study owned by Qian Xuesen, pen, ink, paper and inkstone are quietly placed, which presents the unique charm of "Jiangnan scholarly family". Displayed in the showroom are wooden cupboards used by Qian family when they were in Shanghai in the 1950s, and many household items as collections.

Qian Xuesen (1911—2009) is the son of the 33rd generation of Qian Liu, King of the Wuyue State. He was born in Shanghai, and his ancestral home was Lin'an, Hangzhou City, Zhejiang Province. He is a world-famous scientist, an aerodynamicist, and a founder of manned spaceflight in China. He is an academician of Chinese Academy of Sciences and Chinese Academy of Engineering, and the Merit Medalist of China's "Two Bombs and One

Satellite". He is widely regarded as "Father of Aerospace in China", "Father of Missile in China", "Father of Automation Control in China" and "King of Rockets".

★ 沙孟海故居

沙孟海故居位于杭州市龙游路 15 号，距西湖仅几步之遥。属于杭州市文物保护单位。沙孟海故居是一座中西结合式的花园别墅，建于 20 世纪 20 年代，砖木结构，屋顶直立的烟囱和突出的门呈楼裙样式，具英式乡间别墅风格。房子的取材是简朴而牢固的青砖，原来的小园里种着几棵火红的石榴树，石榴花盛开的时候，衬得房子十分雅致，故又被称为"若榴花屋"（其实，"若榴花屋"最早是沙孟海和弟弟沙文求、沙文威于 1926 年在上海戈登路 715 号租住的一所小房子，搬到杭州龙游路后沙老十分怀念早年在上海的经历，就把新宅也命为此名）。

沙孟海（1900—1992），书法家、篆刻家，毕业于浙东第四师范学校，曾为浙江大学中文系教授，1963 年起在浙江美术学院（现为中国美术学院）兼课，1979 年起为书法、篆刻专业研究生导师。曾担任西泠印社社长。代表作品有《印学史》《沙孟海书法集》《沙孟海标准草书集》《中国书法史图集》等。沙老学问渊博，识见高明，于语言文字、文史、考古、书法、篆刻等均深有研究。沙孟海是中国当代书坛巨擘，现代高等书法教育的先驱之一。1992 年，沙老先生逝世于杭州。

★ Sha Menghai's Former Residence

Sha Menghai's Former Residence is located at No. 15, Longyou Road, Hangzhou, just a few steps away from the West Lake. It is the cultural relic protection unit of Hangzhou. Sha Menghai's former residence is a garden villa with the combination of Chinese and Western style, built in the 1920s. It is structured of brick and wood in a style of an English country villa with upright chimney on the roof and protruding door in the style of skirt building. It is made of a kind of plain but solid black brick. Once there were several red pomegranate trees planted in the small garden. When the pomegranate flowers were in full bloom, the house looked very elegant against the red flowers, so it is also called "Pomegranate house". (Actually, "Pomegranate House" is the name of a small house rented in Shanghai in 1926 by Sha Menghai and his two younger brothers Sha Wenqiu and Sha Wenwei, which is located at No. 715 Gordon Road. After moving to Longyou Road in Hangzhou, Mr. Sha is very nostalgic for the life experience in Shanghai in the early time, so he named the new house after it.)

Sha Menghai (1900—1992), a calligrapher and seal engraver, graduated from Zhedong No. 4 Normal School. He was once a professor in Chinese Department of Zhejiang University. From 1963 he had been teaching part-time in Zhejiang Academy of Art (now known as China Academy of Art), and from 1979, he had been a tutor of graduate students majoring in calligraphy and seal cutting. He once served as president of Xiling Seal Art Society, and his representative works include *History of Seal Studies*, *Collection of Sha Menghai's Calligraphy*, *Collection of Standardized Cursive Script of Sha Menghai*, *Catalogs of Chinese Calligraphy History*, etc. Sha Menghai has profound knowledge, broad insight, and has made a deep study on language, history, archaeology, calligraphy, seal cutting and so on. Sha Menghai is a great master of Chinese contemporary calligraphy and one of the pioneers of modern higher calligraphy education. In 1992, Mr. Sha passed away in Hangzhou.

★ 潘天寿纪念馆

潘天寿纪念馆位于杭州市上城区南山路212号，原是潘天寿先生晚年的居所。这是一幢建于20世纪40年代的2层青砖老楼，建筑面积331平方米，外观质朴、厚重，既有传统特色，又有鲜明现代感。大门左侧的围墙上，镶嵌着6块1米见方的黑色花岗石，上有著名书法家沙孟海书写的"潘天寿纪念馆"金色大字。

纪念馆收藏了潘天寿各个时期的代表作共120幅，是收藏潘天寿作品最多、最集中的地方，也是目前国内学术品位较高的一座名人纪念性美术馆，历年来举办过多次国内国际高水平学术研讨会和学术展览。

潘天寿（1897—1971），画家、教授，浙江宁海人，毕业于浙江省立第一师范学校。潘天寿精于写意花鸟、山水，偶作人物，兼工书法，尤擅指墨。画风沉雄奇险，苍古高华。其画大气磅礴，具有慑人的力量感和强烈的现代意识，与吴昌硕、齐白石、黄宾虹并称为 20 世纪"中国画四大家"。一生著述丰富，对艺术思想、美术教育、画史画论、诗书篆刻等均有深入研究，并建立了一套完整的迄今影响最大的中国画教学体系，被称为现代中国画教育的奠基人。

★ **Pan Tianshou Memorial Museum**

Pan Tianshou Memorial Museum is located in No. 212, Nanshan Road, Shangcheng District, Hangzhou, where Pan Tianshou lived in his remaining years. It is an old two-story brick building of the 1940s with a construction area of 331 square meters. Its appearance is simple but stately, with both traditional characteristics and distinct modern sense. The wall on the left side of the gate is inlaid with six one-square-meter black granite. Six golden characters "Pan Tian Shou Ji Nian Guan" (Pan Tianshou Memorial Museum) written by the famous calligrapher Sha Menghai are respectively engraved in each granite.

The memorial museum houses 120 pieces of Pan Tianshou's representative works in each period of his life, which is the place with the largest and most concentrated collection of Pan Tianshou's works. It is also a celebrity memorial art museum with high academic grade in China at present, where many high-level national and international academic symposiums and exhibitions have been held over these years.

Pan Tianshou (1897—1971) is a painter and professor from Ninghai, Zhejiang Province, who graduated from Zhejiang Provincial No.1 Normal School. He is proficient in painting flowers and birds, and landscapes. He paints figures occasionally. He is also skilled at calligraphy, and especially excellent at finger painting. His painting style is serene and precipitous, unsophisticated and lofty. His paintings are grand and majestic with an overwhelming sense of strength and strong modernistic style. He is known as one of "The Four Masters of Chinese Painting" together with Wu Changshuo, Qi Baishi and Huang Binhong. He has written numerous books in his lifetime and studied profoundly on art concept, art education, art history and theory, poetry, calligraphy and seal cutting. He has established an integrated and most influential educational system of Chinese painting and is regarded as the founder of modern Chinese painting education.

★ 题襟馆

题襟馆又名隐闲楼，建于民国初年，属中式花园别墅，位于杭州孤山南麓、西泠印社的最高处，面积约 70 平方米，砖木结构。房子依山取势，坐北朝南，古朴典雅，为吴昌硕在杭州的"创作别墅"。这是上海题襟馆书画会在杭州的艺术活动场所，所以叫"题襟馆"。

吴昌硕（1844—1927），湖州安吉人，晚清、民国时期著名国画家、书法家、篆刻家，"后海派"代表，西泠印社首任社长，与厉良玉、赵之谦并称"新浙派"的 3 位代表人物，与任伯年、蒲华、虚谷合称为"清末海派四大家"。

他集诗、书、画、印于一身，融金石书画于一炉，被誉为"石鼓篆书第一人""文人画最后的高峰"，在绘画、书法、篆刻上都是旗帜性人物，在诗文、金石等方面均有很高的造诣。吴昌硕热心提携后进，齐白石、王一亭、潘天寿、陈半丁、赵云壑、王个簃、沙孟海等均得其指授。

★ Tijin Guan

Tijin Guan (Insciption Hall) , also known as Yinxian Lou, is a Chinese style garden villa,built in the early years of the Republic of China. It is located at the top of Xiling Seal Art Society at the southern foot of Gushan Hill in Hangzhou. It covers an area of about 70 square meters and has a brick and wood structure. The house is situated on the mountain, facing south, simple and elegant, which is Wu Changshuo's "creation villa" in Hangzhou. Art activities of Shanghai Tijin Guan Calligraphy and Painting Association are held here, so it is called "Tijin Guan".

Wu Changshuo (1844—1927), from Anji County, Huzhou, is a famous Chinese painter, calligrapher and seal engraver in the late Qing Dynasty and in the era of the Republic of China. He is the representative of the "Post Shanghai School" and the first president of Xiling Seal Art Society. Wu Changshuo, Li Liangyu and Zhao Zhiqian are collectively known as the three representatives of the "New Zhejiang School"; and together with Ren Bonian, Pu Hua and Xu Gu, they four are collectively known as the "Four Masters of the Shanghai School in the Late Qing Dynasty".

He is a poet, calligrapher, painter, and seal engraver, and excellent at engraving, calligraphy and painting. He is hailed as "The First Person in Engraving Seal Character in the Stone Drum", "The Last Peak of Literati Painting". He is a flagship character in painting, calligraphy and seal cutting, and has high attainments in poetry, engraving and other aspects. Wu Changshuo was happy to guide and help younger painters such as Qi Baishi, Wang Yiting, Pan Tianshou, Chen Banding, Zhao Yunhe, Wang geyi, Sha Menghai, etc.

★ 司徒雷登故居

司徒雷登故居位于杭州市天水桥耶稣堂弄 1—3 号，是一幢占地面积约 239 平方米的白墙红窗 2 层小楼，尽管被附近 7 层高的居民楼环绕，但从白的墙体、朱红的门窗、高挑的房檐及门廊上的柱子，还是能够看出当年的气派。据说，这幢建筑是 1878 年司徒雷登的父亲司徒尔来杭传教时建造的，是目前杭州最古老的传教士住宅。故居仅仅开放了一层的 4 个房间，4 个房间的墙壁上分别展示了司徒雷登早年在杭州的生平事迹、在北京创办燕京大学和在华做大使期间的一些珍贵老照片等图文资料。

司徒雷登（John Leighton Stuart，1876—1962），美国基督教长老会传教士、外交官、教育家。1876 年 6 月生于杭州，父母均为美国在华传教士。1904 年开始在中国传教，曾参加建立杭州育英书院（即后来的之江大学）。1919 年起任燕京大学校长、校务长，1946 年任美国驻华大使，1949 年 8 月离开中国。1962年9月19日，司徒雷登逝于美国华盛顿，终年86岁。

★ **Former Residence of John Leighton Stuart**

Situated at No. 1-3, Jesus Hall Lane, Tianshui Bridge, Former Residence of John Leighton Stuart in Hangzhou is a two-story building with white walls and red windows, covering an area of about 239 square meters. Although surrounded by seven-story residential buildings nearby, the white walls, vermilion doors and windows, high eaves and pillars on the porch still show the style of that time. It is said that this building was built in 1878 when his father Senior Stuart came to Hangzhou for missionary work. It is the oldest missionary residence in Hangzhou at present. Only four rooms on the ground floor are open to the public. On the walls of the four rooms are displayed with some graphic and literature documents about John Leighton Stuart, among which are his life stories in Hangzhou, and some precious old pictures about his foundation of Yenching University in Beijing and during the time when he was an ambassador to China.

John Leighton Stuart (1876—1962) was an American Presbyterian missionary, diplomat, and educator. He was born in Hangzhou in June 1876 when his parents were working as missionaries in China. He began his missionary work in China in 1904 and participated in the establishment of Hangzhou Yuying Academy (later known as Zhijiang University). He was the president and dean of Yenching University from 1919. He served as U.S. Ambassador to China in 1946 and left China in August 1949. Leighton Stuart died on September 19, 1962 in Washington, D.C. when he was 86 years old.

第三节　名家诗作

白居易说："江南忆，最忆是杭州。"中国古代文人雅士，陶醉于江南烟雨，留下了千古不朽的诗篇。东坡居士留下了西湖"水光潋滟晴方好，山色空蒙雨亦奇"的唯美画面，许承祖写出了"就中只觉游鱼乐，我亦忘机乐似鱼"的闲情雅趣。

Ⅲ Poems by Celebrities

Bai Juyi said, "When I recall Jiangnan, Hangzhou brings back the most of my memories." The ancient Chinese literati, who were intoxicated with the misty rain in the south of the Yangtze River, left numerous immortal poems. Dongpo Jushi (Su Shi) left a beautiful picture of the West Lake in his poem, "The brimming waves delight the eye on sunny days; The dimming hills present rare view in rainy haze." Xu Chengzu wrote about the leisure and elegant taste of the West Lake in his poem, "While viewing fish at the harbor I can feel the happiness of the fish, and I also forget the worldly affairs, being happy like the fish."

★ 忆江南

［唐］白居易

江南好，

风景旧曾谙。

日出江花红胜火，

春来江水绿如蓝。

能不忆江南？

★ Memories of the South[①]

[Tang] Bai Juyi

The South of Yangtze, how great!

Its scenery I once knew by heart.

At sunrise, the river-flowers, more red than flames,

In spring the river water, as blue as indigo.

How can I not think of the South of Yangtze?

★ 钱塘湖春行

［唐］白居易

孤山寺北贾亭西，

水面初平云脚低。

几处早莺争暖树，

谁家新燕啄春泥。

乱花渐欲迷人眼，

浅草才能没马蹄。

最爱湖东行不足，

绿杨阴里白沙堤。

---

① CHANG K S. The evolution of Chinese T'zu poetry: from late Tang to Northern Sung[M].
Princeton: Princeton University Press, 1980: 22-23.

★ Walking in Spring by West Lake[①]

[Tang] Bai Juyi

North of Lone Hill Temple, west of the Jia Pavilion,

The water's surface has just smoothed, the foot of the cloud low.

Wherever you go new-risen orioles jostle for the warmest tree:

What are they after, the newborn swallows that peck at the spring mud?

A riot of blossoms not long from now will be dazzling to the eyes,

The shallow grass can hardly yet submerge the horse's hoof.

Best loved of all, to the east of the lake, where I can never walk enough,

In the shade of the green willows, the causeway of white sand.

★ 饮湖上初晴后雨

［宋］苏 轼

水光潋滟晴方好，
山色空蒙雨亦奇。
欲把西湖比西子，
淡妆浓抹总相宜。

★ Drinking at the Lake, First in Sunny, Then in Rainy Weather[②]

[Song] Su Shi

The brimming waves delight the eye on sunny days,

The dimming hills present rare view in rainy haze.

West Lake may be compared to Lady of the West[*],

---

① GRAHAM A C. Poems of the West Lake: translations from the Chinese ［M］. London: Wellsweep Press, 1990: 15.

② 许渊冲. 中国古诗精品三百首：汉英对照 ［M］. 北京：北京大学出版社，2004：395.

Whether she is richly adorned or plainly dressed.

* Xi Shi (482 BC), a beautiful lady born near West Lake.

★ 望海潮

〔宋〕柳 永

东南形胜，
三吴都会，
钱塘自古繁华。
烟柳画桥，
风帘翠幕，
参差十万人家。
云树绕堤沙，
怒涛卷霜雪，
天堑无涯。
市列珠玑，
户盈罗绮，
竞豪奢。

重湖叠巘清嘉，
有三秋桂子，
十里荷花。
羌管弄晴，
菱歌泛夜，
嬉嬉钓叟莲娃。
千骑拥高牙，
乘醉听箫鼓，
吟赏烟霞。
异日图将好景，

归去凤池夸。

★ Watching the Tidal Bore[①]

[Song] Liu Yong

Scenic splendor to the southeast of River Blue

And capital of ancient Kingdom Wu,

Qiantang's as flourishing as e'er.

Smoke-like willows form a wind-proof screen;

Adorned with painted bridges and curtains green,

A hundred thousand houses stand here and there.

Upon the banks along the sand,

Cloud-crowned trees stand.

Great waves roll up like snow banks white;

The river extends till lost to sight.

Jewels and pearls at the Fair on display,

Satins and silks in splendid array,

People vie in magnificence

And opulence.

The lakes reflect the peaks and towers,

Late autumn fragrant with osmanthus flowers,

Lotus in full bloom for miles and miles.

Northwestern pipes play with sunlight;

Water chestnut songs are sung by starlight;

Old fishermen and maidens young all beam with smiles.

With flags before and guards behind you come;

---

① 许渊冲. 宋词三百首：中英文对照 [M]. 北京：中国对外翻译出版公司，2007：346–347.

Drunken, you may listen to flute and drum,

Chanting praises loud

Of the land'neath the cloud.

You may picture the fair scene another day

And boast to the Court where you're in full array.

★ 夏日忆西湖

［明］于　谦

涌金门外柳如烟，

西子湖头水拍天。

玉腕罗裙双荡桨，

鸳鸯飞近采莲船。

★ On a Summer Day Remembering West Lake[①]

[Ming] Yu Qian

Outside Yongjin Gate the willows are like smoke,

On the Lady of the West's lake the water pats the sky.

Arms jade-white and damask-skirted couples wave the oar,

Mandarin duck and drake fly near the lotus-pickers' boat.

★ 西湖泛舟呈运使学士张掞

［宋］欧阳修

波光柳色碧溟蒙，

曲渚斜桥画舸通。

---

① GRAHAM A C. Poems of the West Lake: translations from the Chinese ［M］. London: Wellsweep Press, 1990: 53.

更远更佳唯恐尽，

渐深渐密似无穷。

绮罗香里留佳客，

弦管声来扬晚风。

半醉回舟迷向背，

楼台高下夕阳中。

★ Boating on West Lake: To Zhang Shan, Academician and Fiscal Commissioner[①]

[Song] Ouyang Xiu

Light on the waves, colors of willows,

Veils of sapphire haze,

To winding isles and arching bridges

Our painted skiff makes its way.

The farther we go, the more lovely,

We fear only that it will end;

But on deeper within, the more secret,

And it seems a space without bounds.

In the fragrance of figured satins

Fine guests are brought to stay,

And the sound of harps and piping

Weeps in with evening wind.

Half-drunk then, we turned the boat,

Uncertain of our direction;

---

① STEPHEN O. An anthology of Chinese literature: beginning to 1911 [M]. New York: W. W. Norton & C Inc. , 1996: 687.

There were mansions and terraces high and low
In the light of the evening sun.

★ 晓出净慈寺送林子方
［宋］杨万里

毕竟西湖六月中，
风光不与四时同。
接天莲叶无穷碧，
映日荷花别样红。

★ West Lake in Midsummer[①]
[Song] Yang Wanli

After all it's the West Lake in summer hot,
 Displaying scenes no other scenes have got;
Green lotus leaves stretch so far to the ruddy horizon,
Bathed in sunshine are exceptionally pink lotus blossoms.

★ 送崔十二游天竺寺
［唐］李　白

还闻天竺寺，
梦想怀东越。
每年海树霜，
桂子落秋月。
送君游此地，

① CHEN G. China travel kit series: Zhejiang & Hangzhou ［M］. Beijing: Foreign Language Press, 2004: 191.

已属流芳歇。

待我来岁行，

相随浮溟渤。

★ Seeing off Twelfth Son Cui on His Journey to the India Temple[①]
[Tang] Li Bai

Once more hearing of the India Temple,

Imagining in dreams I long for eastern Yue.

Each year in the frost on the seacoast trees

The cassia buds drop from the autumn moon.

Saying goodbye as you travel to that land,

I'm already of those whose scent has faded from the air.

Look out for me, next year here I come,

In search of you, floating in from the estuary.

★ 浪淘沙（节选）
［唐］刘禹锡

八月涛声吼地来，

头高数丈触山回。

须臾却入海门去，

卷起沙堆似雪堆。

---

① GRAHAM A C. Poems of the West Lake: translations from the Chinese ［M］. London: Wellsweep Press, 1990: 11.

★ Noise of Breakers in the Eighth Month（Excerpt）[①]

[Tang] Liu Yuxi

In the Eighth Month the noise of breakers comes roaring through the land,

The head a dozen yards high butts the hill and turns.

An instant, and it bends round to enter Sea Gate,

Rolling back heaps of sand like heaps of snow.

★ 苏小小墓

［唐］李　贺

幽兰露，

如啼眼。

无物结同心，

烟花不堪剪。

草如茵，

松如盖。

风为裳，

水为佩。

油壁车，

夕相待。

冷翠烛，

劳光彩。

西陵下，

风吹雨。

---

① GRAHAM A C. Poems of the West Lake: translations from the Chinese［M］. London: Wellsweep Press, 1990: 13.

★ Little Su's Tomb[①]

[Tang] Li He

Dew on the hidden orchid
Is like an eye with tears.
Nothing that ties a true-love-knot,
Flowers in mist, can't bear to cut.

The grass like the riding cushion,
The pines like the carriage roof.
The wind is her pendants.
The waters is her skirt,
The coach with polish sides
Awaits in the twilight.
Cold azure candlelight
Struggling to shine.
Beneath western mound
Wind blows the rain.

★ 题临安邸

[宋] 林 升

山外青山楼外楼，
西湖歌舞几时休？
暖风熏得游人醉，
直把杭州作汴州。

---

① STEPHEN O. An anthology of Chinese literature: beginning to 1911 [M]. New York: W. W. Norton & Co Inc. ,1996: 490.

★ At an Inn in Hangzhou[①]

[Song] Lin Sheng

Beyond the hills blue hills, beyond the mansions mansions—

To song and dance on the West Lake when will there be an end?

Idlers fuddled on the fumes of the warm breeze

Will turn Hangzhou that rises into Kaifeng that fell.

[①] GRAHAM A C. Poems of the West Lake: translations from the Chinese [M]. London: Wellsweep Press, 1990: 35.

第四节　商业老字号

杭州历史悠久，拥有世代传承的产品、技艺或服务，具有中华民族特色和鲜明的杭州地方文化特征，具有历史价值和文化价值。2010年1月，杭州市人民政府公布78家首批"杭州老字号"名单。2013年1月，又有"喜得宝""十竹斋""法根"等34家企业被列入第二批"杭州老字号"名单。2016年2月，杭州龙井茶业集团有限公司（注册商标"御"）等44家企业品牌被列入第三批"杭州老字号"名单。[①]杭州老字号品牌中，有40多家为"中华老字号"。

目前，"杭州老字号"分布在六大行业：以"胡庆余堂"为代表的中医中药类、以"王星记"为代表的工美艺术类、以"致中和"为代表的食品加工类、以"解百"为代表的商贸服务类、以"张小泉"为代表的日用制造类、以"楼外楼"为代表的餐饮美食类。老字号企业都有世代传承的独特产品，如"张小泉"的剪刀、"状元馆"的面条、"都锦生"的丝绸等。

IV Time-honored Commercial Enterprises

Hangzhou enjoys a long history, having various kinds of products, skills or services passed down from generation to generation, which have Chinese national characteristics and distinctive local cultural characteristics of

---

① 杭州市人民政府办公厅.杭州市人民政府办公厅关于认定第三批杭州老字号的通知［EB/OL］.（2016-02-04）［2023-04-06］. http://www.hangzhou.gov.cn/art/2016/2/4/art_1093962_3696.html.

Hangzhou, as well as historical and cultural value. In January 2010, Hangzhou Municipal Government announced the first batch of the list of "Hangzhou Time-honored Brand", 78 in total. In January 2013, other 34 enterprises such as Hedepot, Shizhuzhai and Fagen Food were on the second batch of the list of "Hangzhou Time-honored Brand". In February 2016, brands of other 44 enterprises such as "Hangzhou Longjing Tea Group Co., Ltd" (registered trademark: Imperial) were listed in the third batch. Among all those Hangzhou time-honored brands, there are more than 40 listed in "China Time-Honored Brand".

At present, Hangzhou time-honored brands are distributed in six industries: traditional Chinese medicine represented by Huqingyutang, crafts and arts represented by Wangxingji, food processing represented by Zhizhonghe, commercial service represented by Jie Bai, daily manufacturing represented by Zhang Xiaoquan, and catering and gourmet represented by Louwailou, etc. All these time-honored enterprises have their unique products passed down from generation to generation, such as Zhang Xiaoquan scissors, Zhuangyuanguan noodles, and Du Jinsheng silk, etc.

★ 胡庆余堂

清同治十三年（1874），晚清"红顶商人"胡雪岩为"济世于民"开始筹建胡雪岩庆余堂药号，于光绪四年（1878）在大井巷店屋落成并正式营业。胡庆余堂位于美丽的西子湖畔，吴山脚下。它以宋代皇家的药典为本，选用历朝历代的验方，以研制成药著称于世，其成药一直到今天仍为中外人士所喜用。它和北京的同仁堂并称为中国著名的南北两家国药老店。

★ Huqingyutang

Huqingyutang Chinese Pharmacy was prepared to establish in the 13th year of the reign of Emperor Tongzhi of the Qing Dynasty (1874) by Hu Xueyan, a "Red-caped Honored Businessman" in the late Qing Dynasty, to "benefit the world and the people" and was completed and officially opened in Dajing Lane in the 4th year of the reign of Emperor Guangxu (1878). It is located by the beautiful West Lake at the foot of Wushan Hill. Based on the royal pharmacopoeia of the Song Dynasty and by selecting the prescription of the past dynasties, Huqingyutang Chinese Pharmacy is well known to the world by producing Chinese patent drug, which is still favored to this day by people at home and abroad. Huqingyutang and Tongrentang in Beijing are known as the two famous traditional Chinese Pharmacy respectively in the south and north of China.

★ 方回春堂

方回春堂是杭州一家具有 370 余年历史的老字号国医馆。清顺治六年（1649），出身中医世家的杭州人方清怡在清河坊创建了方回春堂。自创立之初，方回春堂就严谨遵从古代良方，精选各地最好的药材，选工尽善尽美，煎虎鹿龟驴各种补胶，依法炮制各种丸散膏丹。尤其是家传的小儿回春丸，救助幼儿无数，名动天下。尤为难得的是，方回春堂敢于冲破传统商业模式的桎梏，积极向世界名牌企业学习，重视对品牌资产的培育和积累，开创了中华老字号焕发新生命的成功之道。

★ Fanghuichuntang

Fanghuichuntang is a time-honored national Chinese farmacy in Hangzhou with a history of more than 370 years. In the sixth year of the reign of Emperor Shunzhi of the Qing Dynasty (1649), Fang Qingyi, a Hangzhou native, born in a family of traditional Chinese medicine, established Fanghuichuntang in Qinghefang. Since its foundation, Fanghuichuntang has strictly followed the good recipe of the ancient time, selected the best medicinal materials from all provinces in China, and used perfect pharmaceutical technology to tisane various kinds of tonics with some ingredients from tiger, deer, turtle, donkey and so on, and make various kinds of pills, powders, creams, and pellets according to prescribed methods. Especially the life-saving pill for children handed down from generations of the family is famous all over the world, which has saved numerous children's lives. What is particularly rare is that Fanghuichuntang dares to break the shackles of the traditional business model and actively learn from the world-famous enterprises and attaches great importance to the cultivation and accumulation of brand equity. As a result, it creates a successful way for Chinese time-honored brands to coruscate a new life.

★ 西泠印社

西泠印社创建于清光绪三十年（1904），由浙派篆刻家丁辅之、王福庵、吴隐、叶为铭等召集同人发起创建，吴昌硕为第一任社长。以"保存金石，研究印学，兼及书画"为宗旨，是海内外研究金石篆刻历史最悠久、成就最高、影响最广的国际性民间艺术团体，有"天下第一名社"之誉。

社址坐落于西湖景区孤山南麓，东至白堤，西近西泠桥，北临北里湖，南接外西湖。占地面积7090平方米，建筑面积1750平方米。主要建筑有柏堂、竹阁、仰贤亭、还朴精庐等，均挂匾披联，室外摩崖凿石林立，名人墨迹触目可见。内建中国印学博物馆，收藏历代字画、印章多达6000余件。

★ Xiling Seal Art Society

Xiling Seal Art Society was initiated and founded in 1904 by a group of seal engravers of Zhejiang School like Ding Fuzhi, Wang Fuan, Wu Yin, Ye Weiming and so on. Wu Changshuo was the first president. For the purpose of "preserving ancient metal with engraved text and praise, and studying sealing, calligraphy and painting", Xiling Seal Art Society is an international folk art society with the longest history, the highest achievement and the most extensive influence at home and abroad, and has a reputation of "The Best Society in the World".

It is located at the southern foot of Gushan Hill in the West Lake Scenic Area, with the Bai Causeway in the east, the Xiling Bridge in the west, the North Inner Lake in the north and the Outer West Lake in the south. It covers an area of 7,090 square meters and a construction area of 1,750 square meters.

The main buildings are Cedar Hall, Bamboo Pavilion, Yangxian Pavilion, and Huaipujing Cottage, etc., each with the plaque over the door and couplets on the pillar of the hall. Outside the buildings are numerous precipices with inscriptions on them, and writings and paintings by celebrities here and there. There is a museum of Chinese sealing inside the building, with a collection of more than 6,000 pieces of calligraphy, paintings and seals of past dynasties.

★ 楼外楼

素以"佳肴与美景共餐"而驰名的杭州楼外楼坐落在秀丽的西子湖畔、孤山脚下。楼外楼创建于清道光二十八年（1848）。

175 年以来，楼外楼走过了艰苦创业、发展繁荣的不平凡的道路，如今已成为集工、商、贸为一体的实业有限公司，并以令人瞩目的经营业绩、丰厚的历史文化跨入了全国名楼的行列。"以菜名楼，以文兴楼"的楼外楼，先后迎来了不计其数的历史名人，孙中山、鲁迅、郁达夫、竺可桢、马寅初、丰子恺、潘天寿、赵朴初等都光临过楼外楼。楼内各餐厅装饰典雅，环境幽美，设施齐全。菜肴不仅注重色、香、味、形、质，而且品种多样，除西湖醋鱼、龙井虾仁、叫花童鸡、宋嫂鱼羹、东坡焖肉等传统名菜外，还有一大批风味特色菜。

★ Louwailou

Located at the bank of the beautiful West Lake and at the foot of Gushan Hill, Hangzhou Louwailou, famous for its "delicious food and beautiful scenery", was founded in the 28th year of the reign of Emperor Daoguang in the Qing Dynasty (1848).

Over the past 175 years, Louwailou has gone through the extraordinary road of hard pioneering and development and prosperity, and now it has become an industrial company limited, which integrates industry, commerce and trade. It has been on the list of the national famous restaurants with its remarkable business performance and profound history and culture. Louwailou becomes famous owing to its dishes and becomes prosperous by its culture. Numerous historical celebrities such as Sun Yat-sen, Lu Xun, Yu Dafu, Zhu Kezhen, Ma Yinchu, Feng Zikai, Pan Tianshou, Zhao Puchu and so on came to dine here successively. The rooms inside the restaurant are elegantly decorated and well equipped with beautiful surroundings. The dishes attach importance not only to color, aroma, taste, shape and quality, but also to variety. In addition to the traditional famous dishes such as West Lake Fish in Sweet Sour Sauce, Fried Shrimps with Longjing Tea, Beggar's Chicken (Baked Chicken), Sister Song's Fish Broth (Braised Fish Soup), Dongpo Pork and so on, there are also a large number of specialities.

★ 张小泉

张小泉股份有限公司是一家集设计、研发、生产、销售、服务于一体的现代生活五金用品企业。"张小泉"品牌始创于明崇祯元年（1628），至今已有近400年的历史。张小泉因其优异的产品质量，屡屡斩获国际大奖，并于1915年获得了巴拿马万国博览会大奖。2006年，张小泉剪刀锻制技艺被国务院列为第一批国家级非物质文化遗产。"张小泉"品牌也是最早一批被商务部评为"中华老字号"的民族品牌。

张小泉人继承和发扬"良钢精作"的祖训和精神，锐意进取，不断突破自我，为海内外消费者带来了家居厨房用品、个人护理用品、园林农艺用品、酒店厨具用品等1000多种优质产品，得到了广大消费者的喜爱与青睐。

★ Zhangxiaoquan

Zhangxiaoquan Co., Ltd. is a modern life hardware enterprise integrating design, research, production, sales, and services. "Zhangxiaoquan" brand was founded in the first year of the reign of Emperor Chongzhen in the Ming Dynasty (1628) and has a history of nearly 400 years. Owing to its excellent product quality, Zhang xiaoquan has won many international awards and in 1915 won Grand Prize of Panama Pacific International Exposition. In 2006, Zhangxiaoquan's scissor forging technology has been listed as the first batch of national intangible cultural heritage by the State Council. "Zhangxiaoquan" brand was also among the earliest batch of "China Time-honored Brand" awarded by the Ministry of Commerce.

All staff in Zhangxiaoquan Co., Ltd. inherit and carry forward the ancestral motto and spirit of "quality steel with exquisite craftsman", forge ahead with determination, constantly break through themselves, and have brought more than 1,000 kinds of high-quality products to consumers at home and abroad, such as household kitchen supplies, personal care supplies, garden agricultural products, and hotel kitchenware supplies, etc., which have won overwhelming popularity and acceptance by consumers.

★ 致中和

浙江致中和酒业公司坐落在山清水秀的国家级风景名胜区——千岛湖湖畔，是我国传统保健酒的专业生产企业、我国最大的五加皮酒生产基地、杭州市优强企业。清乾隆二十八年（1763），安徽大药商朱仰懋以《中庸》中的"致中和"为号，在古建德严州府开设了第一家"致中和酒坊"。这就是致中和的历史发端，从此，致中和开始了近300年的品牌经营与发展。

清光绪二年（1876），致中和五加皮获得新加坡南洋商品赛会金质奖后，举世闻名，开始享誉世界。致中和保健酒问世以来始终受到消费者的青睐。由于外部环境的变化，致中和积极寻求"演变"，2010年5月27日，浙江宋都控股有限公司正式收购了致中和旗下的所有企业。宋都控股是一家拥有30多亿元资产的大型集团企业，经营范围从房地产到致中和保健酒与食品，这标志着"致中和"这个中华老字号品牌正焕发着勃勃生机。

★ Zhizhonghe

Zhejiang Zhizhonghe Wine Co., Ltd., located in Qiandao Lake, a state-level scenic area with beautiful scenery, is a professional manufacturing enterprise of traditional health wine in China, the largest production base of Wujiapi (Cortex Acanthopanacis) wine in China and an excellent enterprise in Hangzhou. In the twenty-eighth year of the reign of Emperor Qianlong of the Qing Dynasty (1763), Zhu Yangmao, a big pharmacist in Anhui Province, set up the first Zhizhonghe Wine Store in Yanzhou, the capital of ancient Jiande, with the name " 致中和 " from *The Doctrine of the Mean*. This is the beginning of the history of Zhizhonghe. From then on, Zhizhonghe embarked on its brand management and development for nearly 300 years.

In the second year of the reign of Emperor Guangxu (1876), Zhizhonghe Wujiapi wine won the gold medal in Nanyang Commodity Competition in Singapore, and became world-famous. Zhizhonghe health wine has been favored by consumers all the time. Due to the changes in the external environment, Zhizhonghe seeked for "evolution" actively. On May 27, 2010, Songdu Holding Co., Ltd. formally acquired all the enterprises of Zhizhonghe. Songdu Holding is a large group enterprise with more than 3 billion assets, whose business ranges from real estate to Zhizhonghe health wine and food. The acquisition marked that Zhizhonghe—China time-honored brand was coruscating its great vitality.

★ 王星记

杭州雅扇自古有名，尤其是南宋定都临安（今杭州）后，制扇工艺更为发达。明清以后，杭扇生产更为兴旺，当时的杭扇，与丝绸、茶叶齐名，被视为"杭产三绝"，现以王星记扇为杭扇代表。

杭州王星记扇庄（杭州王星记扇厂前身）创办于清光绪元年（1875），创始人王星斋，故扇庄又名"王星斋扇庄"。王星记扇子共有15个大类、400多个品种、3000多个花色，其中以黑纸扇和檀香扇最负盛名。黑纸扇制作工序需要86道，工艺精湛，风格别具，再进行泥金剪贴绘画书法等形式的装饰，使画面丰富华丽，十分名贵。其中尤以黑纸真金微楷为世人所称道。檀香扇则采用难度极高的工艺技术——"三花"工艺（拉花、烫花、画花），制作精巧雅致。王星记扇工艺精美，历史上多次作为杭州特产进贡朝廷。王星记扇在国际博览会上屡获殊荣，远销世界各地。现王星记扇仍有艺人在传承发展，扇面新作迭出。王星记扇子以其独特的艺术性和工艺性，成为我国出类拔萃的工艺美术精品。

★ **Wangxingji**

"Hangzhou elegant fan" is famous since ancient times, especially after the Southern Song Dynasty moved its capital to Lin'an (now known as Hangzhou). After the Ming and Qing Dynasties, the production of Hangzhou fans became more prosperous. At that time, Hangzhou fans, along with silk and tea, were regarded as "three unique products of Hangzhou". Now Wangxingji fan is the representative of Hangzhou fans.

Hangzhou Wangxingji Fan Mill (the predecessor of Hangzhou Wangxinji Fan Factory) was founded in 1875, the first year of the reign of Emperor Guangxu of Qing Dynasty. It was founded by Wang Xingzhai, so it is also named as "Wangxingzhai Fan Mill". There are more than 400 varieties of products in 15 categories with more than 3,000 colors, among which black paper fan and sandalwood fan are the most famous. There are 86 procedures in the production of black paper fan, with exquisite craftsmanship and unique style. Then it is decorated in the form of clay and gold scraping, painting and calligraphy, which makes the picture rich, gorgeous and very valuable. It is praised by the world especially for its black paper, real gold and micro regular script. Sandalwood fans are produced with exquisite and elegant techniques, such as drawing, ironing and painting. Wangxingji fan has exquisite craftsmanship and has been paid tribute to the imperial court many times as a special product of Hangzhou in history. Wangxingji fan has won numerous awards in international expositions and has been well sold at home and abroad. With its unique artistry and craftsmanship, Wangxingji fan has become one of the best arts and crafts in China.

★ **都锦生**

都锦生是杭州著名丝绸品牌、中华老字号，1922 年由爱国工业家都锦生在杭州创立。都锦生在继承传统杭州织锦工艺的基础上，不断创新改进，研制出五彩锦绣、经纬起花丝织风景画等工艺，将中国画与西洋画的表现形式通过织锦工艺体现出来，形成特有的艺术风格。

多年来，都锦生丝绸坚持用传统工艺设计生产，通常需要 58 道手工工序。因工艺精湛、色彩瑰丽、质地细腻、手感坚实、民族特色极为丰富，其被誉为神奇的"东方艺术之花"，成为杭州丝绸的杰出代表。

★ **Dujinsheng**

Dujinsheng is a famous silk brand in Hangzhou, and China time-honored brand, which was founded in Hangzhou by the patriotic industrialist Du Jinsheng in 1922. On the basis of inheriting the traditional Hangzhou brocade technology, Dujinsheng has constantly made innovation and improvement, and developed the technique of five-color brocade, and weaving silk landscape painting with warp and weft, and such brocade technologies reflect the expression form of Chinese and Western painting to form a unique artistic style.

Over the years, Dujinsheng silk has been designed and produced by traditional technology. Generally, the product can only be completed through 58 manual processes. Due to characteristics of exquisite workmanship, magnificent color, fine texture, solid in the hand and extremely rich national characteristics, it is known as the magic "Flower of Oriental Art", and has become an outstanding representative of Hangzhou silk.

★ **孔凤春**

孔凤春香粉号由萧山人孔传鸿创建于清同治元年（1862），是中国历史上记载的第一家化妆品企业，是中华"百年老字号"企业。清朝末年，孔凤春"鹅蛋粉"成为皇家贡品，因慈禧专用而久负盛名。从清朝到民国十几年间，孔凤春市场占有率超 50%。1929 年，孔凤春莲花霜、玉堂扑粉在第一届西湖博览会上大放异彩，斩获多项大奖。

孔凤春化妆品一贯以做工考究、膏体细腻、香型独特而深受广大消费者的认可。孔凤春因其"优质、安全、天然"的产品质量而多次荣获国家级、省级优质产品奖，列入"全国亿万民众最喜爱的家用产品""浙江省著名商标"。近几年来，孔凤春加大科技研发投入，开发新产品，已形成了以"孔凤春"成人护理品牌、"妈妈乐"儿童护理品牌为主的产品格局。

★ Kongfengchun

Kongfengchun powder shop, founded in the first year of the reign of Emperor Tongzhi in the Qing Dynasty (1862) by Kong Chuanhong from Xiaoshan (now a district of Hangzhou), is the first cosmetics enterprise recorded in Chinese history and a one-hundred-year-old time-honored enterprise in China. In the late Qing Dynasty, Kongfengchun "goose egg powder" had long enjoyed a good reputation as a royal tribute of the Qing Dynasty, and being exclusively used by Empress Cixi. During the years between the Qing Dynasty and the Republic of China, Kongfengchun had a market share of more than 50%. In 1929, Kongfengchun lotus frost and Yutang powder won a number of awards at the First West Lake Exposition.

Kongfengchun cosmetics have been recognized by consumers for its exquisiteness, delicate paste and unique scent. Kongfengchun products have won the national and provincial "Quality Products Award" many times for its "superior, safe and natural" quality, and have been listed as "the favorite household products of hundreds of millions of people in China" and "the famous trademark of Zhejiang Province". In recent years, Kongfengchun has increased the investment in scientific and technological research and development and developed new products, and has formed a product pattern, with "Kongfengchun" adult care brand and "Mama Le" (Mama happy) child care brand as its representative products.

★ 毛源昌

杭州毛源昌眼镜厂始创于 1862 年，是一家专业生产、经营、加工、销售各类近视眼镜、太阳眼镜、隐形眼镜、老花眼镜的浙江省知名商号，商业部首批认定的"中华老字号"企业。目前已在杭州市区开设 14 家直营门店，全国范围内有近 70 家企业慕名加盟。

毛源昌目前拥有杭州唯一的国家一级高级验光师和数名国家级高级验

光师，拥有国内先进的电脑综合验光仪、红外线验光仪、自动割边机等验光设备和品种齐全的"毛源昌"牌镜架、镜片和隐形眼镜产品。"毛源昌"牌镜架、镜片是浙江省名牌产品。

★ Maoyuanchang

Founded in 1862, Hangzhou Maoyuanchang glasses factory is a well-known firm in Zhejiang Province, specializing in the production, operation, processing and sales of all kinds of myopia glasses, sunglasses, contact lenses and presbyopia glasses. It has been among the first batch of "China Time-Honored Brand" enterprises recognized by the Ministry of Commerce. At present, 14 retail stores have been opened in Hangzhou, and nearly 70 enterprises throughout China have allied themselves to Maoyuanchang enterprise.

At present, Maoyuanchang has employed the only first-class national senior optometrist in Hangzhou and several state-level senior optometrists. It has domestic advanced optometry equipment such as computer integrated optometry, infrared optometry, automatic edge-cutting machine, and a great variety of products such as spectacle frames, lenses and contact lens with Maoyuanchang brand. Maoyuanchang spectacle frames and lens have won the title of "Zhejiang Provincial Brand-name Products".

第五节　知名品牌

杭州深厚的文化底蕴、传统的工匠精神、良好的商务环境及政府的政策支持等为企业的品牌创立和发展提供了丰沃的土壤。近年来，不少杭州本土品牌开始走出国门，影响世界。

V Famous Brands

Hangzhou's profound cultural heritage, traditional craftsmanship, good business environment and favorable policy support from the government provide fertile soil for the establishment and development of enterprises' brands. In recent years, many local brands in Hangzhou have begun to go abroad and influence the world.

★ 吉利汽车

吉利汽车集团隶属于浙江吉利控股集团，总部位于浙江杭州，是中国领先的汽车制造商。经过20多年的建设与发展，吉利在汽车、摩托车、汽车发动机、变速器、汽车电子电气及汽车零部件方面取得辉煌业绩。特别是1997年进入轿车领域以来，凭借灵活的经营机制和持续的自主创新，吉利取得了快速的发展，资产总值超过100亿元，连续4年进入全国企业500强，被评为"中国汽车工业50年发展速度最快、成长最好"的企业，跻身于国内汽车行业10强。

2019 年 4 月，吉利汽车与第 19 届亚运会组委会正式签约，成为杭州亚运会官方汽车服务合作伙伴，并正式启动主题为"科技吉利 悦行亚运"的亚运战略。2021 年 2 月 24 日，吉利和沃尔沃联合官宣，称双方达成了最佳合并方案，在保持各自现有独立公司的基础上，两家汽车公司计划将其动力系统业务合并为一家专注于下一代混合动力系统和内燃发动机的新公司。

★ **Geely Auto**

Geely Automobile Group, a subsidiary of Zhejiang Geely Holding Group and headquartered in Hangzhou, Zhejiang Province, is a leading automobile manufacturer in China. After over 20-year construction and development, it has made brilliant achievements in automobile, motorcycle, automobile engine, transmission, electronics as well as automobile parts. Especially since it entered the car industry in 1997, with its flexible running mechanism and continuous independent innovation, it has achieved rapid development, with a total asset value of more than 10 billion yuan. For four consecutive years, it has been on the list among the top 500 Chinese enterprises and has been rated as "the fastest and best growing enterprise in China's automobile industry in the past 50 years", ranking among the top 10 in the domestic automobile industry.

In April 2019, Geely Auto signed a contract with the Organizing Committee of the 19th Asian Games and became official prestige partner of the 19th Asian Games in Hangzhou, and officially launched the Asian Games strategy with the theme of "Geely Technology, Happy Asian Games". On February 24, 2021, Geely Auto and Volvo Cars announced that they had reached the best combination plan. Retaining independent corporate structures, the two auto companies plan to combine their dynamical system operations into one new company focusing on next-generation hybrid systems and internal combustion engines.

★ 万事利

万事利集团有限公司创办于 1975 年，目前已经发展为一家以丝绸纺织、文化创意为主业，辅以生物科技、资产经营、金融管理等多产业的现代企业集团，拥有全国丝绸行业唯一国家企业技术中心以及多家省级高新技术企业，系中国民营 500 强企业。

集团秉承"让世界爱上中国丝绸"的企业使命，着力挖掘、传承中国丝绸文化，实现了丝绸从"面料"到"材料"再到"载体"的华丽转身，走出了一条"传统丝绸＋移动互联＋文化创意＋高科技＝丝绸经典产业"的转型升级"新丝路"。近几年，集团通过收购法国百年丝绸名企，聘请世界级奢侈品高管，引进跨国设计团队，携手国际一线奢侈品品牌等举措，全面开启"万事利"丝绸品牌的国际化战略。万事利用极致的文化创意与匠心工艺彰显了中国风范，让中国丝绸站在了世界舞台中央。

★ Wensli

Founded in 1975, Wensli Group Co., Ltd. has developed into a modern enterprise group with silk textile and cultural creativity as the main business, supplemented by biotechnology, asset management, financial management and other industries which has the only national enterprise technology center in the silk industry and a number of provincial high-tech enterprises. It is among the top 500 Chinese private enterprises.

Adhering to the corporate mission of "Let the World Fall in Love with Chinese Silk", the group has made great efforts to excavate and inherit Chinese silk culture, realized the gorgeous turn of the silk from "fabric" to "material" and then to "carrier", and created a "New Silk Road" with the transformation and upgrading of "traditional silk + mobile internet + cultural creativity + high technology = classic silk industry". In recent years, the group has fully opened the international strategy of "Wensli Silk" brand through the acquisition of a famous 100-year-old French silk enterprise, the recruitment of world-class luxury executives, and the introduction of the initiatives like multinational design teams, and the cooperation with international luxury brands and so on. With the ultimate cultural creativity and craftsmanship, Wensli has highlighted Chinese style and made Chinese silk stand in the center of the world stage.

★ 西子奥的斯电梯

西子奥的斯是美国联合技术公司旗下奥的斯电梯在华子公司，是中国领先的电梯、自动扶梯及自动人行道制造与服务供应商之一，旗下运营"Otis electric（奥的斯机电）"和"Xizi Otis（西子奥的斯）"两大品牌。

西子奥的斯成立于1997年，旗下拥有在杭州、重庆的两大工厂。经过20多年的高速发展，西子奥的斯已经成为中国著名的垂直升降电梯、自动扶梯和自动人行道制造商和服务供应商，致力于以卓越服务为建筑提供完美品质、绝对安全的全面交通解决方案，成为社会公认的领袖企业。

★ Xizi Otis Elevator

Xizi Otis is the China subsidiary of OTIS elevator of United Technology Corporation of the USA. It is one of the leading manufacturers and service providers of elevators, escalators and moving walkway in China, which owns two brands "Otis electric" and "Xizi Otis".

Established in 1997, Xizi Otis owns two factories with one in Hangzhou and the other in Chongqing. After the rapid development for over 20 years, Xizi Otis has become a famous manufacturer and service provider of elevators, escalators and moving walkway in China. With its excellent service, it is committed to providing comprehensive transportation solutions for architecture with perfect quality and absolute safety, and has become a leading enterprise universally acknowledged.

★ 老板电器

杭州老板实业集团有限公司成立于1979年，是一家以生产厨房家用电器系列产品为主，并涉及房地产、纺织、旅游等领域的现代化大型企业集团。老板集团在企业经营策略、管理模式、企业文化等方面的不断努力、开拓与创新，创造出其独具一格的竞争优势，使得"老板"成为厨电领域中被社会公认的品牌。老板电器拳头产品包括：吸油烟机、燃气灶、消毒柜、整体厨房、炊具小家电等。

40多年的工业实践，使老板集团拥有了一支高素质的工程设计和技术研发队伍，以及一套合理高效的生产管理模式，其产品也因此成为中国消费者协会和建设部推荐产品、部优产品和浙江省名牌产品，"老板"也成为浙江省著名商标，并获得星火计划金奖等众多荣誉。2004年和2005年，"老板"品牌价值连续2年荣登"中国500最具价值品牌"；2005年，老板集团被评为国内首批"标准化良好行为"试点企业，并获得目前最高级别AAA证书。2005年9月1日，老板集团成为油烟机行业中首批获得"中国名牌"的企业之一。

★ Robam

Established in 1979, Hangzhou Robam Industrial Group Co., Ltd. is a modern large-size enterprise group which mainly produces kitchen household appliances, and involves real estate, textile, tourism and other fields as well. With its constant effort, pioneering and innovation in the aspects of enterprise business strategy, management mode, and corporate culture, etc., Robam Group has created a unique competitive advantage of the enterprise, so that "Robam" was identified as a brand name in the field of kitchen household appliances. Its topped products include extractor hood, gas stove, disinfection cabinet, integral kitchen, and small household appliances for cooking, etc.

40-year industrial practice has made it own a large number of high-quality teams in engineering design and technology research and development, as well as a set of reasonable and efficient production management mode. Therefore, Robam products have been listed in "The Recommended Products" by the Chinese Consumer Association and the Ministry of Construction, "Excellent Products", and "Zhejiang Famous Brand Products", rated as "Famous Trademark in Zhejiang Province", and won "Spark Plan Gold Medal" and so on. In 2004 and 2005, the brand "Robam" was listed among "China's 500

Most Valuable Brands". In 2005, Robam Group was rated as one of the first "Standardized Good Behavior" pilot enterprises in China, and obtained the highest AAA-certificate. On September 1, 2005, Robam Group was among the first batch of "China Famous Brand" in the extractor hood industry.

★ 西湖龙井

西湖龙井茶因产于中国杭州西湖的龙井茶区而得名，始产于宋代，明代益盛，是中国十大名茶之一。历史上曾分为"狮"（产地狮峰）、"龙"（产地龙井）、"云"（产地云栖）、"虎"（产地虎跑）、"梅"（产地梅家坞）5个品号，现统称为西湖龙井茶，其中以狮峰龙井为最。西湖龙井茶的品牌有30多个。西湖龙井茶有"四绝"：色绿、香郁、味甘、形美。特级西湖龙井茶扁平光滑挺直，色泽嫩绿光润，香气鲜嫩清高，滋味鲜爽甘醇，叶底细嫩呈朵。

西湖龙井茶与西湖一样，是人、自然、文化三者的完美结晶，是西湖地域文化的重要载体。

★ West Lake Longjing Tea

West Lake Longjing Tea gets its name from the Longjing tea area of the West Lake in Hangzhou, China. It was first produced in the Song Dynasty and became more prosperous in the Ming Dynasty. It is one of the top ten famous teas in China. In history, it was once divided into "Shi" (producing area of Shifeng), "Long" (producing area of Longjing), "Yun" (producing area of Yunqi), "Hu" (producing area of Hupao) and "Mei" (producing area of Meijiawu), which are now collectively referred to as West Lake Longjing Tea, among which Shifeng Longjing Tea is the first and best. There are more than 30 brands of West Lake Longjing Tea. It has "four special characteristics": green color, rich fragrance, sweet taste and beautiful shape. Superior-class Longjing tea is flat, smooth and straight, with a bright green color, a fresh, tender and clear aroma, a refreshing and mellow taste, and delicate and tender leaves like opening flowers.

Like the West Lake, West Lake Longjing Tea is the perfect crystallization of human, nature and culture, and an important carrier of the regional culture of the West Lake.

★ 农夫山泉

农夫山泉成立于 1996 年，是中国最大的包装水供应商，市场占有率排名第一，是中国饮料企业 20 强之一。

多年来，农夫山泉坚持"天然、健康"的品牌理念，从不使用城市自来水生产瓶装饮用水，也从不在饮用水中添加任何人工矿物质。为了保障持续大量的优质天然水供应，农夫山泉独具战略眼光，前瞻性地在中国布局了十大稀缺的优质天然水源，奠定了为消费者提供长期天然、健康服务的基础和能力，形成长期稳定的竞争优势。

农夫山泉不断推陈出新，形成多元化产品矩阵，除饮用水外，已经布局即饮茶、功能饮料、果汁、植物蛋白、咖啡类等品类。

农夫山泉一贯积极投身和倡导社会公益事业。不论是 1998 年长江抗洪，还是 2008 年汶川大地震、2010 年云南大旱，都竭尽所能帮助灾区民众。农夫山泉还多次发起"阳光工程""饮水思源"等公益活动。

★ Nongfu Spring

Founded in 1996, Nongfu Spring is China's largest packaging water supplier, ranking first in the market share and among the top 20 Chinese beverage companies.

For years, Nongfu Spring has strictly adhered to a "natural and healthy" philosophy, never using tap water and never adding artificial minerals to its drinking water. In order to ensure a continuous supply of high-quality natural water, Nongfu Spring has a unique strategic vision and prospectively lays out ten rare high-quality natural water sources in China, laying the foundation and ability to provide consumers with long-term natural and healthy services and form long-term stable competitive advantage.

Nongfu Spring is constantly innovating and diversifying its product offerings. In addition to drinking water, it has launched ready-to-drink tea, functional drinks, fruit juice, plant protein, coffee and other categories.

Nongfu Spring has always been actively involved in and advocating for the social welfare. Whether it is flood fighting in the Yangtze River in 1998, the 2008 Wenchuan earthquake, or the severe drought in Yunnan in 2010, Nongfu Spring does everything it can to help the people in the disaster areas. It also launched some community welfare activities like "Sunshine Project", "Drinking Water with Gratitude for Sources", and so on.

★ 娃哈哈

杭州娃哈哈集团有限公司创建于 1987 年，在创始人宗庆后的带领下，不断开拓，锐意进取，35 年累计销售额 8601 多亿元，利税 1740 亿元，上缴税金 742 亿元。娃哈哈在全国 29 个省市自治区建有 81 个生产基地、187 多家子公司，拥有员工近 3 万人，企业规模和效益连续 20 年处于行业领先地位，位居中国企业 500 强、中国制造业 500 强、中国民营企业 500 强前列。

娃哈哈的产品主要涵盖蛋白饮料、包装饮用水、碳酸饮料、茶饮料、果蔬汁饮料、咖啡饮料、植物饮料、特殊用途饮料、罐头食品、乳制品、医药保健食品等 10 余类 200 多个品种。除食品饮料研发、制造外，娃哈哈还是食品饮料行业少有的具备自行研发、自行设计、自行制造模具及饮料生产装备和工业机器人能力的企业。

近年来，娃哈哈开始了有关健康产品的研发及产业化项目，努力为国人健康做出贡献。同时，大力发展智能制造等高新技术，推动制造行业从"中国制造"迈向"中国创造"。

★ Wahaha

Hangzhou Wahaha Group Co., Ltd. was founded in 1987. Under the leadership of its founder Zong Qinghou, the corporation keeps pioneering and forging ahead. In the past 35 years, the accumulated sales volume has reached more than 860.1 billion yuan, and its profits and taxes are 174 billion yuan with a tax delivery of 74.2 billion yuan. Wahaha has established 81 production bases and more than 187 subsidiaries in 29 provinces and autonomous regions in China, with nearly 30,000 employees. The scale and efficiency of Wahaha has been in the leading position in the industry for 20 consecutive years, ranking among the Top 500 Chinese Enterprises, the Top 500 Chinese Manufacturers and the Top 500 Chinese Private Enterprises.

Wahaha products mainly cover more than 200 varieties of more than 10 categories, such as protein drinks, packaged drinking water, carbonated drinks, tea drinks, fruit and vegetable juice drinks, coffee drinks, plant drinks, special purpose drinks, canned food, dairy products, medical and health food, etc. In addition to food and beverage research and development and manufacturing, Wahaha is one of the few enterprises in the food and beverage industry with the ability of independent research and development, independent design, and independent manufacturing of the molds, beverage production equipment and industrial robots.

In recent years, Wahaha has started the research and development and industrialization of health products, striving to contribute to the health of the Chinese people. Meanwhile, new and high technologies such as intelligent manufacturing will be vigorously developed to promote the transformation of the manufacturing industry from "Made in China" to "Created in China".

★ 苏泊尔

苏泊尔是知名的综合性大众家居用品品牌，公司成立于1994年。创立伊始就率先推出符合国家新标准的压力锅产品，并独创"安全到家"的品牌诉求，使"苏泊尔"牌压力锅一举成为国内压力锅市场的领头羊。从此，"安全到家"的苏泊尔产品文化深入人心，苏泊尔几乎成为压力锅产品的代名词。如今，苏泊尔已经走出厨房，成为涵盖明火炊具、厨房小家电、环境家居电器、厨卫大家电、厨房工具、水杯等领域的综合性家居用品品牌。

"苏泊尔"商标在1999年12月被认定为浙江省著名商标，并于2002年3月被国家工商行政管理总局商标局评为中国驰名商标。

通过在中国市场运营 WMF、KRUPS 等品牌，苏泊尔已进入高端市场；通过推出迷色系列锅具、COCO 料理锅等年轻化产品，苏泊尔越来越受到年轻消费者的喜爱；2019 年，苏泊尔涉足母婴用品领域，推出了"倍爱"系列、"小馋喵"辅食锅等产品。

★ **Supor**

Founded in 1994, Supor is a well-known brand for comprehensive household items. At the beginning of its foundation, it launched pressure cooker products that meet the new national standards and created the original brand appeal of "safety enters home" so that Supor pressure cooker has become the leader in domestic pressure cooker market. From then on, the product culture "safety enters home" was deeply rooted in people's hearts, and Supor almost became a synonym for pressure cooker products. Nowadays, Supor has gone beyond the kitchen and become a comprehensive household brand covering the fields like naked-flame cookers, small kitchen utensils, household appliances for environmental improvement, large home appliances for kitchen and bathroom, kitchen tools, cups and glasses, and so on.

"Supor" was recognized as famous trademark of Zhejiang Province in December 1999, and was rated as well-known trademark of China by Trademark Office of State Administration for Industry and Commerce in March 2002.

Supor has entered the high-end market by operating brands such as WMF and KRUPS in the Chinese market. It is becoming more and more popular with young consumers by launching products like cookers of fancy color series and COCO cooking pots which are targeted for younger consumers. In 2019, Supor set foot in the field of maternal and baby products and launched products such as "Beiai" series and "Xiaochanmiao" complementary food pot.

★ 天堂伞

天堂伞是由杭州天堂伞业集团生产的国内名牌伞，包括雨伞、太阳伞、直杆伞、二折伞、三折伞、四折伞、广告伞、庭院伞、遮阳伞、沙滩伞、工艺伞等多个品种。天堂伞素以"轻、新、牢、美"而著称，产品质量和技术工艺代表了当今世界先进水平，在国内外市场享有很高的声誉和广泛的影响。

公司成立于1984年，总部位于杭州市西湖区西溪路978号，是中国最大的专业雨伞制造商之一。多年来，公司在改革开放政策的指引下，在各级政府的帮助下，不断稳步发展。目前，公司共有员工5100人，拥有6家子公司、2家控股企业、3个大型伞型和雨衣生产基地、1个机械设备制造基地。出口产品生产基地正在筹建中。公司在品牌、质量、技术、市场、规模、效益等方面具有相当稳定的实力优势，先后获得国家级、省级、市级荣誉称号，为地方经济发展做出了重要贡献。

公司精心培育的天堂企业文化，融合了中国传统文化、中国伞文化和浙商文化的精神，成为打造"天堂"品牌的驱动力。

★ Paradise Umbrella

Paradise Umbrella is a famous brand of domestic umbrella produced by Hangzhou Paradise Umbrella Group, including rain umbrellas, sun umbrellas, vertical umbrellas, two-fold umbrellas, three-fold umbrellas, four-fold umbrellas, advertising umbrellas, garden umbrellas, sunshade umbrellas, beach umbrellas, craft decor umbrellas and many other varieties. Paradise umbrella is famous for being "light, new, strong and beautiful", whose quality and technology represent the advanced level in the world today, and it enjoys a high reputation and wide influence in the domestic and foreign markets.

Founded in 1984 and headquartered at No. 978, Xixi Road, Xihu District, Hangzhou City, Hangzhou Paradise Umbrella Group Co., Ltd. is one of the largest professional umbrella manufacturers of China. For years, the company, under the guidance of reform and opening-up policy and with the help of government at all levels, has continuously developed at steady speed. At present, the company has a total staff of 5,100, and 6 subsidiaries, 2 holding enterprises, 3 large-sized production bases of umbrellas and raincoats, and 1 mechanical equipment manufacturing base. Besides, its production base of export products is under preparation. The company, with quite stable advantages in the brand, quality, technology, market, scale and benefit, has been awarded the national, provincial and municipal honorary titles, making important contribution to the local economic development.

The paradise enterprise culture, carefully cultivated by the company, integrates the spirit of Chinese traditional culture, Chinese umbrella culture and Zhejiang business culture, which has become the driving force to build the "Paradise" brand.

★ 顾家家居

1982 年，台州人顾江生在江苏南通创建顾家工坊，传承源自天台的手工技艺，锤炼沙发制作工艺。1996 年，杭州海龙家私有限公司成立。2003 年 6 月，浙江顾家工艺沙发制造有限公司成立，创立"顾家工艺"品牌，成为中国沙发行业的领军品牌。2005 年 7 月，位于杭州下沙经济技术开发区内的顾家工艺沙发工业园全面投产，占地 130000 平方米，内设 120000 平方米现代化标准厂房和国际沙发研发中心，共有 4000 余名熟练技术工人，是亚洲最大的沙发生产基地之一。

2011 年，"顾家工艺"成功升级为"顾家家居"，从一家专门制造沙发的企业发展成集设计开发、生产、销售于一体的规范化企业集团。目前，"顾家家居"旗下的产品已远销 120 多个国家和地区，拥有 6000 多家品牌专卖店。2021 年 1 月，"顾家家居"正式成为第 19 届亚运会官方床垫独家供应商。

★ Kuka

In 1982, Gu Jiangsheng, a native of Taizhou, established Kuka Workshop in Nantong, Jiangsu Province, inheriting the craftsmanship of Tiantai and promoting the sofa manufacturing technology. In 1996, Hangzhou Hailong Furniture Co., Ltd. was established. In June 2003, Zhejiang Kuka Crafts Sofa

Manufacturing Co., Ltd. was established, setting up the brand "Kuka Craft", which becomes the leading brand in China's sofa industry. In July 2005, located in Xiasha economic and technological development zone in Hangzhou, "Kuka Craft" sofa industrial park went into full production, covering an area of 130,000 square meters, with a modern standard workshop of 120,000 square meters and an international center for the research and development of sofa. The company has a total of more than 4,000 skilled workers, and is one of the largest sofa production bases in Asia.

In 2011, Kuka Craft was successfully upgraded to Kuka, developing from a specialized sofa manufacturing enterprise into a standardized enterprise group integrating design and development, production, and sales. At present, Kuka products have been exported to more than 120 countries and regions, with over 6,000 brand stores. In January 2021, Kuka officially became the "exclusive supplier of official mattresses for the 19th Asian Games".

第三章　旅游之城

　　杭州依山傍水，西湖之美自古以来为人赞叹，这令杭州拥有了其他城市艳羡不已的传统文化底蕴和宝贵的旅游资源。

　　杭州市区的西湖风景名胜区风光无限：一湖碧水与三面云山相互辉映，天光云影，长堤卧波，烟柳画桥，舫船往来；沿湖绿荫环绕，花团锦簇，亭台楼阁，美不胜收；群山之间，林泉茂盛，洞窟幽深，古迹遍布；100 多处园林、景点点缀其间，100 多处国家、省、市重点文物保护单位为之增色。春夏秋冬景致不同，昼夜变化多端；晴雨雾雪情韵各异，历代文人赋咏不绝。白娘子与许仙在西湖凄美感人的爱情传说更令杭州陡增神秘色彩。

　　杭州市辖区西南的新安江，支流众多，水流湍急，峡谷、河滩幽远俊秀，晨雾、晚霞轻盈绚丽。千岛湖，由新安江水电站建造后形成，1078 个大小岛屿，宛若天女散花洒落湖中，倩影秀姿，楚楚动人。富春江，水流平稳，夹岸连山妩媚，江上沙洲葱茏。两江风景如画，千岛满湖诗情，素有"新安之水天上来"和"天下佳山水，自古推富春"的赞誉。此外，钱塘江的浩荡大潮，天目山的苍茫林海，良渚文化遗存的璀璨奇绝，京杭大运河的古韵悠扬……无不令人心驰神往，流连忘返。

Chapter Three
City of Tourism

Hangzhou is surrounded by mountains and rivers. The beauty of the West Lake has been praised by people since ancient times, which makes Hangzhou possess the traditional cultural deposits and valuable tourism resources that other cities cannot match.

West Lake Scenic Area in downtown Hangzhou displays enchanting scenery: A lake of clear water and cloud mountains on three sides reflect each other, with sky light and cloud shadow, long embankment lying wave, smoke-like willows and painted bridges, and boats coming and going. Along the bank of the lake are green shades, flowers and pavilions, which is a feast for the eyes. Among the mountains are lush forests, deep caves and monuments everywhere. More than 100 gardens and scenic spots are dotted with them, and more than 100 national, provincial and municipal key cultural relic protection units are added to its luster. Scenery is distinct in spring, summer, autumn and winter and it changes from the day to the night; it shows you different charm and arouses you different feelings in different weather, sunny or rainy, foggy or snowy. The literati of all ages wrote endless odes about it.

The beautiful and touching love story between Lady White and Xu Xian in the West Lake adds to the mystery of Hangzhou.

The Xin'an River, located in the southwest of Hangzhou City, has many tributaries and rapid currents. The canyons and river beaches are quiet and handsome, and the morning mist and sunset glow are light and gorgeous. Qiandao or A-thousand-islets Lake, formed after the construction of the Xin'anjiang Hydropower Station, consists of 1,078 islands of all sizes, which look like flowers scattered into the lake by nymphs. Fuchun River has smooth water flow, charming mountains on both sides of its embankment and verdant sandbanks. With the picturesque scenery of the two rivers and the poetic feeling filling the lake, they are eulogized as "the water of Xin'an comes from the sky" and "speaking of the beautiful landscape in the world, Fuchun is the first to be recommended since ancient times". In addition, the vast tide of the Qiantang River, the vast forest of the Tianmu Mountain, the bright and bizarre relics of the Liangzhu Culture, and the ancient charm of the Beijing-Hangzhou Grand Canal, etc. are all so enchanting that make you forget to leave.

第一节　西湖风景名胜区

杭州西湖风景名胜区，位于浙江省杭州市西湖区，分为湖滨区、湖心区、北山区、南山区和钱塘区，总面积达59.04平方千米，其中湖面6.38平方千米，外围保护区面积35.64平方千米。[①]

景区内有国家级、省级、市级文物保护单位60多处和风景名胜100余处，主要有"西湖十景"、"新西湖十景"、灵隐寺、岳王庙、六和塔等。

1985年，杭州西湖风景名胜区被选为"全国十大风景名胜"之一。2007年，杭州西湖风景名胜区被评为"国家AAAAA级旅游景区"。2011年6月24日，"杭州西湖文化景观"正式被列入世界遗产名录。

Ⅰ West Lake Scenic Area

Hangzhou West Lake Scenic Area is located in Xihu District, Hangzhou City, Zhejiang Province. It is divided into Hubin District, Huxin District, Beishan District, Nanshan District, and Qiantang District, with a total area of 59.04 square kilometers, including 6.38 square kilometers of lake surface and 35.64 square kilometers of peripheral protected area.

There are over 60 Chinese national, provincial and municipal cultural relic protection sites and over 100 scenic areas. The main attractions include Ten

---

[①] 西湖西溪管委会. 西湖概况［EB/OL］.（2022-09-01）［2023-04-06］. https://westlake.hangzhou.gov.cn/col/col1598539/index.html.

Views of the West Lake, Ten New Views of the West Lake，Lingyin Temple, General Yue Fei's Temple, Pagoda of Six Harmonies and so on.

In 1985, Hangzhou West Lake Scenic Area was selected as one of the "Top Ten Scenic Spots in China". In 2007, Hangzhou West Lake Scenic Area was rated as "National AAAAA Tourist Attraction". On June 24, 2011, the "West Lake Cultural Landscape of Hangzhou" was officially included in the World Heritage List.

★ 西湖十景

西湖十景形成于南宋时期，基本围绕西湖分布或位于湖上。西湖十景各擅其胜，组合在一起又能代表古代西湖胜景精华。

★ Ten Views of the West Lake

Ten Views of the West Lake was formed in the Southern Song Dynasty, basically located around or on the West Lake. Each of the ten views has its own unique scenery, and when put together, they can represent the essence of the ancient West Lake scenery.

▶ 苏堤春晓

苏堤春晓，西湖十景之一。南宋时，苏堤春晓被列为西湖十景之首，在元代又被称为"六桥烟柳"而列入钱塘十景。

苏堤长2.8千米，纵贯西湖，南起南坪山，北至栖霞岭，沿途种满了桃树、柳树、木兰和木槿。沿堤矗立着6座单跨石拱桥，分别名为映波、锁澜、望山、压堤、东浦、跨虹。苏堤是北宋诗人苏东坡任杭州知州时，疏浚西湖，利用挖出的泥构筑而成的，为纪念苏东坡，故名之以苏堤。

苏堤春晓景观是形容寒冬过后，苏堤报春的美妙景色。春天来了，柳树在微风中轻拂。桃树开满了花，散发着醉人的芬芳。苏堤六桥是享受春天最好的地方。黎明时分，湖面非常宁静，只能听到鸟鸣。天空和桥倒映在湖面上，满树的桃花如笑脸。走在堤道上，可以纵览西湖和周围的山峦；徜徉在如此令人叹为观止的美景中，享受着视觉和听觉的"盛宴"。

▶ **Su Causeway in Spring Dawn**

"Su Causeway in Spring Dawn" is one of the Ten Views of the West Lake. In the Southern Song Dynasty, it was listed as the top of the ten views; and in the Yuan Dynasty, it was also named as "Six Bridges' Smoke Willow" and included on the list of the Ten Views of Qiantang.

Ranged with peach, willow, magnolia and hibiscus trees, the 2.8-kilometer-long Su Causeway spans the West Lake from the Nanping Hill in the south to the Qixia Ridge in the north. Along the causeway stand 6 single-span stone arch bridges by the name of Yingbo (reflecting the waves), Suolang (locking the waves), Wangshan (looking at distant hills), Yadi (causeway ballast), Dongpu (eastern ford), and Kuahong (spanning rainbow). Su Causeway was constructed with the excavated mud dredged from the West Lake when Su Dongpo was the governor of Hangzhou. In memory of Su Dongpo, it was named Su Causeway.

"Su Causeway in Spring Dawn" describes to the wonderful scenery of heralding spring at Su Causeway after the cold winter. When spring comes, willow trees swing slightly in the breeze. Peach trees are full of blooms, giving out intoxicating fragrance. The 6 bridges along the Su Causeway are the best place for enjoying springtime. At dawn, the lake is so serene that only chirps of birds can be heard. Sky and bridges are reflected on the surface of the lake. Peach blossoms are like smiling faces. As you walk on the causeway, with the whole lake and surrounding hills in sight, and stroll among such a breathtaking panorama, it can bring you visual and auditory enjoyment.

▶ **曲院风荷**

曲院风荷即曲院公园（曲院），位于金沙涧河口附近。金沙涧是西湖最大的天然水源。南宋在这里辟有宫廷酒坊，在酒厂旁边的湖里，种有一大片荷花，夏日清风徐来，荷香与酒香四下飘逸，游人身心俱爽，不饮亦醉。

曲院风荷占地 140000 平方米，分为曲院、风荷和滨湖密林区 3 个部分。曲院是西湖景观的地理枢纽，东接岳湖，南邻郭庄，北接竹素园、植物园、岳王庙。

尽管曲院已不再是酒庄，却是观赏盛开的荷花的最佳地点。它的美丽在于它有各种各样的荷花。荷花盛开时节，红莲、白莲、洒金莲等姿态各异。宽阔的荷叶在清澈的湖水中悠闲地散开，低矮的小桥在花丛中蜿蜒曲折。这样的景色让游客流连忘返。

▶ Lotus in the Breeze at Crooked Courtyard

"Lotus in the Breeze at Crooked Courtyard", also named Quyuan Park (Crooked Courtyard), is situated near the mouth of Jinshajian Stream, the biggest natural water supply into the West Lake. In the Southern Song Dynasty, a royal wine workshop was set up here, next to which was a lake with a large area of lotuses. In summer breezes, while aromas of lotus flowers and wine were wafting in the air, the visitors would feel refreshed and intoxicated.

The park covers an area of 140 thousand square meters hectares, subdivided into three sections—crooked courtyard, lotus flower area and waterfront wooded area. Crooked courtyard is the geographic hub of the West Lake landscape, with Yuehu on the east, Guo Zhuang on the south, and the Bamboo Garden, Hangzhou Botanical Garden and General Yue Fei's Temple on the north.

Though no longer a winery, Crooked Courtyard is the vantage spot for viewing lotus in full blossom in summer. The beauty of the park lies in its wide range of lotus flowers with various species. In blooming season, different types of lotus—Red Lotus, White Lotus, Golden Lotus and so on are all in blossom with different postures. Broad leaves spread leisurely on the limpid waters and low bridges zigzag among flowers. Visitors are enchanted by such a view that they don't want to go home.

▶ 平湖秋月

南宋时，平湖秋月被列为西湖十景之三，在元代又被称为"西湖夜月"而列入钱塘十景。

每当清秋气爽，西湖湖面平静如镜，皎洁的秋月当空，月光与湖水交相辉映，颇有"一色湖光万顷秋"之感，故题名"平湖秋月"。

今天的平湖秋月作为西湖十景之一，有固定景址，但在南宋时，泛指人们泛舟湖上，在习习凉风中浏览秋夜月景。康熙三十八年（1699），圣祖巡幸西湖，御书"平湖秋月"匾额，从此，景点固定。现如今的平湖秋月观景点位于白堤西端，背倚孤山，面临外湖。在那里你可以品茶赏月，或沿着湖边的小路漫步，或在树林里找个地方，悠闲地坐在树荫下，什么都不想，却什么都感受得到。

▶ Autumn Moon over the Calm Lake

In the Southern Song Dynasty, "Autumn Moon over the Calm Lake" was listed as the third of the Ten Views of the West Lake. In the Yuan Dynasty, it was also called "West Lake Night Moon" and listed as the Ten Views of Qiantang.

It refers to a wonderful scenery in autumn with refreshing air, smooth water like a mirror, and bright moon in the sky. As the moonlight and lake water reflect each other, there will be a feeling of "boundless lake in autumn", so it is entitled "Autumn Moon over the Calm Lake".

As one of the Ten Views of the West Lake, today the Autumn Moon over the Calm Lake has its fixed location, but in the Southern Song Dynasty it generally referred to the nightview in autumn when people went boating on the lake appreciating the bright moon and enjoying the cool breeze. In the 38th year of the reign of Emperor Kangxi (1699), Emperor Kangxi visited the West Lake and inscribed four characters " 平湖秋月 " (Ping Hu Qiu Yue/Autumn Moon over the Calm Lake) in a plaque. Since then, the scenic spot was fixed. Nowadays the scenic spot of "the Autumn Moon over the Calm Lake" is located at the west end of Bai Causeway, with its back against Gushan and facing the outer lake. It is a nice location where you can appreciate the moon and sip the tea, or take a stroll along the lakeside path, or find a place in the wood, sitting idly under the tree without thinking but feeling everything.

▶ 断桥残雪

断桥位于杭州市西湖白堤的东端，背靠宝石山，面向杭州城，是外湖和北里湖的分水点。现存的断桥，是1921年重建的拱形独孔环洞石桥，长8.8米，宽8.6米，单孔净跨6.1米。

断桥残雪是西湖上著名的景色，以冬雪时远观桥面若隐若现于湖面而著称，是冬季赏雪胜地。

虽然断桥的名字可以追溯到唐朝的诗歌，但断桥之所以出名，是因为它源自中国民间最著名的爱情故事之一——《白蛇传》。据载，一条白蛇化身为一个美丽的女孩，雨中在断桥上遇到了许仙，两人相爱了，他们用的伞成了爱情的象征。由于这个爱情故事，断桥吸引了无数游客，其传奇美誉也传遍了中国各地，成了恋人们的首选之地。无论晴雨，你都可以在桥上欣赏四季的湖景。不论哪个季节，断桥上的景色都令人惊叹，当冬天的雪在阳光下融化的时候，这一景观尤为出色。

▶ Lingering Snow at the Broken Bridge

Broken Bridge is located at the eastern end of Bai Causeway across the West Lake, backed by Baoshi Hill (Precious Stone Hill) and facing the downtown of Hangzhou. It is the watershed point of the Outer Lake and the North Inner Lake. The existing broken bridge is an arched stone bridge with a single aperture rebuilt in 1921, with a length of 8.8 meters, and a width of 8.6 meters. The net span of the aperture is 6.1 meters.

"Lingering Snow at the Broken Bridge" is a famous scenery of the West Lake. It is named after the scene where the bridge is partly visible on the surface of the lake seen from the distance when it is snowing. It is a good place to enjoy snow in winter.

Although the name Broken Bridge can date back to poetry of the Tang Dynasty, why the bridge becomes so famous up to now is because it is from one of the best-known love stories in Chinese folklore—*Legend of White Snake*. According to the story, the beautiful girl who was actually a white snake came across Xu Xian on the bridge on a rainy day, and then they fell in love with each other. Therefore, the umbrella they used became the symbol of their love. Thanks to the love story, Broken Bridge attracts numerous visitors, whose legendary reputation spread all over China, and it has become the first tourist destination especially for lovers. Whether it is rainy or shiny, you can enjoy the lake views from the bridge in all seasons. No matter which season it is, the scenery on the bridge is amazing, and it is particularly gorgeous when the snow begins to melt in the sun in winter.

▶ 花港观鱼

花港观鱼地处西湖西南，三面临水，一面倚山，是一个占地20多万平方米的大型公园。西山大麦岭后的花家山麓，有一条清溪流经此处注入西湖，故称花港。南宋时，内侍卢允升在花家山下建造别墅，称"卢园"，园内栽花养鱼，池水清冽，景物奇秀。之后，卢园荒废，此景亦衰。清康熙南巡时，在苏堤映波桥和锁澜桥之间的定香寺故址上，重新砌池养鱼，筑亭建园，勒石立碑，题有"花港观鱼"4个字。

花港观鱼是以花、港、鱼为特色的风景点。春天大片梨花盛开，鱼儿戏水在荷叶间，划一只小船至湖中庭院间，观花赏鱼。秋天，花港观鱼是赏枫的最佳地点。

花港观鱼的艺术布局充分利用了原有的自然地形条件，景区划分明确，各具鲜明的主题和特点。在空间构建上，开合收放，层次丰富，景观节奏清晰，跌宕有致，既曲折变化，又整体连贯，一气呵成。它的最大特色还在于把中国园林的艺术布局和欧洲造园艺术手法巧妙统一，中西合璧，而又不露斧凿痕迹，使景观清雅幽深、开朗旷达、和谐一致。

▶ Viewing Fish at Flower Harbor

"Viewing Fish at Flower Harbor" is located in the southwest of the West Lake with waters on three sides and a mountain on one side. It is a large park covering more than 200,000 square meters. A clear stream flows into the West Lake through the foot of Huajiashan which is behind Damailing in Xishan, so it is called Hua Gang (Flower Harbor). In the Southern Song Dynasty, an internal minister Lu Yunsheng built a villa at the foot of the Huajiashan, which was named "Lu Garden" after him. Flowers were planted and fishes were farmed in the villa which is full of clear water and wonderful scenery. Later, with the desert of Lu Garden, this view also declined. In the Qing Dynasty, when Emperor Kangxi made his journey to the south of China, on the former site of Dingxiang Temple between Yingbo Bridge and Suolan Bridge on the Su Causeway, he ordered to rebuild ponds to raise fish, built pavilions and gardens, and erected a stone tablet where he inscribed four characters "Hua Gang Guan Yu" (Viewing Fish at Flower Harbor).

"Viewing Fish at Flower Harbor" is a scenic spot featuring flowers, harbors and fishes. In spring when pear flowers are in blossom and fishes are swimming in the water among the lotus leaves, you can paddle a boat among the courtyards in the lake, viewing flowers and fishes. In autumn, it is the best place for viewing maple trees.

The original natural topographic condition is fully used in the artistic layout of "Viewing Fish at Flower Harbor", where each scenic spot is clearly divided with its distinct theme and characteristic. In terms of spatial composition, there are closed and open spaces, as well as narrow and wide spaces. The gradation is plentiful and the rhythm of the landscape is clear with ups and downs, and twists and turns. The whole space is coherent and consistent. The most distinctive feature of "Viewing Fish at Flower Harbor" is that it skillfully unifies the artistic layout of Chinese gardens with the artistic techniques of European gardens, combining Chinese and Western elements without showing any traces of chisel work, making the landscape elegant and serene, wide and bright, and harmonious and consistent.

▶ 柳浪闻莺

柳浪闻莺是位于西湖东南岸、清波门处的大型公园，占地约21万平方米，分友谊、闻莺、聚景、南园4个景区。南宋时，这里是京城最大的御花园，称聚景园。当时园内有会芳殿和三堂、九亭，以及柳浪桥和学士桥。清代恢复柳浪闻莺旧景。有"柳洲"之名。其间黄莺飞舞，竞相啼鸣，故有"柳浪闻莺"之称。

公园布局开朗、清新、雅丽、朴实，柳丛衬托着紫楠、雪松、广玉兰及碧桃、海棠、月季等异木名花，草坪辽阔无垠，鲜花姹紫嫣红，亭台楼阁展现出古老的浪漫风格，鸟儿翩翩起舞，青草葱翠欲滴。这里是欣赏西子浓妆淡抹的观景佳地，临水眺望，视野开阔，空气清新，令人心旷神怡。

公园东南辟为群众游园文娱活动场所，建起了露天舞台，成为杭州市民和八方游客晨间锻炼、假日休闲和节日庆典的好去处。每到夏秋季节，这里又是人们消暑纳凉的"夜花园"。

▶ Orioles Singing in the Willows

"Orioles Singing in the Willows" is a large park located at Qingbo Gate on the southeast bank of the West Lake, covering an area of about 210,000 square meters. It is composed of four scenic spots—You Yi (Friendship), Wen Ying (Listening to Orioles Singing), Ju Jing (Gathered Scenery), and Nan Yuan (South Garden). In the Southern Song Dynasty, it was the largest imperial garden of the capital, called Jujing Garden, where there were Huifang palace, three halls, nine pavilions, as well as Liulang Bridge and Xueshi Bridge. In the Qing Dynasty, the former scene of "Orioles Singing in the Willows" was restored, therefore it got its name—Liuzhou (Willow Sandbar). In the park, orioles are flying and singing constantly, so it is named "Orioles Singing in the Willows".

The layout of the garden is wide and bright, pure and fresh, elegant and simple. Willow cluster provides a perfect foil for different types of exotic trees and famous flowers such as phoebe serrulate, cedar, magnolia grandiflora, flowering peach, crabapple, rose and so on. In the garden, there are vast and boundless lawns, colorful flowers, pavilions with ancient romantic styles, flying birds and fresh green grasses. It is a good place for enjoying the beauty of the West Lake. Viewing from the bank of the waters, you will feel refreshed with broad view and fresh air.

The southeastern part of the park has been transformed into a place for cultural and recreational activities with an open-air stage, which has become a good place for morning exercises, leisure time activities and festival celebration for Hangzhou citizens and tourists from all over the world. In summer and autumn, it becomes a "night garden" for people to enjoy the cool.

▶ 三潭印月

三潭印月是杭州西湖十景之一，被誉为"西湖第一胜境"。三潭印月是西湖中最大的岛屿，与湖心亭、阮公墩鼎足而立合称"湖中三岛"，犹如我国古代传说中的蓬莱三岛，故又称"小瀛洲"。俯瞰整个小瀛洲犹如一个硕大的"田"字。小瀛洲上有"开网亭""闲放台""先贤祠""迎翠轩""花鸟厅""我心相印亭""曲桥""九狮石"等园林建筑点缀其间，绿树掩映、花木扶疏。湖岸垂柳拂波，水面亭榭倒映；园林富于空间层次变化，造成"湖中湖""岛中岛""园中园"的境界。

岛南湖中建有 3 座微型石塔，造型优美、别致，都是上尖下小，中间镂刻成一个空心的球，像一只宝葫芦。每年中秋节的晚上，月亮最圆最亮的时候，正好照在湖的中心。这时候在 3 个石塔里点起明亮的灯火，再把每个石塔的每一个小圆洞蒙上透光的白纸。这样，灯光倒映在湖水里，就像一个个圆圆的月亮，真月和假月其影难分，夜景十分迷人，故得名"三潭印月"。此时，明月如盘，月色溶溶，波光粼粼。成千上万的人到西湖来赏月、划船，笑语声声，犹如"人间天堂"。

▶ Three Pools Mirroring the Moon

"Three Pools Mirroring the Moon", one of the Ten Views of the West Lake, is praised as the "Top One Scenic Spot of the West Lake". It is the largest isle in the West Lake. Together with Huxin Pavilion (Mid-Lake Pavilion) and Ruan Gong Islet, the three islands in the lake are called "Three Islands in the Lake", just like the three islands of Penglai in the ancient Chinese legend, so it is also called "Small Yingzhou Isle". Overviewed, the whole isle is like a big shape of the character " 田 " (field). There are "Kaiwang Pavilion", "Xianfang

Platform", "Ancestral Temple", "Yingcui Veranda", "Huaniao Hall", "Mind-to-Mind Pavilion", "Curved Bridge", "Nine-lion Carved Stone" and other gardens interspersed in "Small Yingzhou Isle" with exuberant growth of trees and flowers; the weeping willows on the lakeshore are brushing the waves, and the pavilions are reflected in the water; the garden is rich in spatial level changes, resulting in the realm of "lake in lake", "island in island" and "garden in garden".

To the south of the island, three miniature stone pagodas are built in the lake, which are beautiful and unique in shape, with sharp top and small bottom, and a hollow ball carved in the middle, looking like a treasure gourd. On the evening of the Mid-autumn Festival when the moon is the roundest and brightest, the moon lights over the center of the lake. At this time, lights are lit inside the three pagodas, and then the small round hole of each pagoda is covered with transparent white paper. As the lights are reflected in the lake, they look like three round moons, which doesn't seem different from the real one, thus it is named "Three Pools Mirroring the Moon". At this moment, the bright moon is like a plate, the moonlight falls on the whole lake and the water is sparkling. Thousands of people come to the West Lake to enjoy the moon and row the boats, talking and laughing, just like in paradise.

▶ 双峰插云

双峰即南高峰、北高峰，分别位于西湖之西南、西北。两峰遥相对峙，绵延相距约5000米。南高峰临近西湖，峰高约257米；北高峰海拔约314米，灵隐寺坐落于此处。峰顶时隐时现于薄雾轻岚之中，望之如插云天，因而得名。

双峰插云为西湖十景之一。宋、元时称为"两峰插云"，清康熙帝南巡，改题为"双峰插云"，建景碑亭于灵隐路洪春桥畔。

虽然双峰插云从古至今观测的地点和方式迭经变化，但南、北高峰都是西湖山水中极富登临价值的胜景这一点至今未变。西湖综合保护工程全面完工后，人们在拓宽的金沙涧水边观景亭上，可以重新欣赏到双峰插云景观。南高峰临近西湖，登山途中，峻岩显露，绝壁峥嵘。登上山巅向东俯瞰，西湖全景历历在目，不是画图，胜似画图。北高峰是灵隐寺的坐山，从寺西侧上山，石磴多至数千级，盘折回绕三十六弯，沿途山溪清流回转，林木重叠。

▶ Twin Peaks Piercing the Clouds

"Twin peaks" refers to the Southern Peak and the Northern Peak, which are respectively located in the southwest and northwest of the West Lake. The two Peaks face each other at a distance of more than 5 kilometers. The Southern Peak is near the West Lake, with a height of 257 meters. The Northern Peak has an altitude of 314 meters, where Lingyin Temple is seated. Seen from the distance the peaks are disappearing and appearing amidst the thin mist and light haze like piercing the sky, so it is named "Twin Peaks Piercing the Clouds".

"Twin Peaks Piercing the Clouds" is one of the Ten Views of the West Lake. In the Song and Yuan Dynasties, it was called "Two Peaks Piercing the Clouds". Emperor Kangxi of the Qing Dynasty toured the south and changed the name to be "Twin Peaks Piercing the Clouds", and the stele pavilion of this spot is built beside Hongchun Bridge on Lingyin Road.

Although the places for and ways of the observation of "Twin Peaks Piercing the Clouds" have changed since ancient times, the Southern Peak and the Northern Peak are always being the most beautiful scenic spots for ascending the peak of mountain and appreciating the scenery. After the completion of the comprehensive protection project of the West Lake, people can enjoy the view of "Twin Peaks Piercing the Clouds" landscape again in the widened viewing pavilion beside Jinshajian Stream. The Southern Peak is near the West Lake. On the way to it, the steep rocks are exposed and the cliffs are towering. Looking east from the peak, you can see the panoramic view of the West Lake. The Northern Peak is the sitting mountain of Lingyin Temple, so you can reach the mountain from the west side of the temple by walking up thousands of stone steps with thirty-six bends. Along the way, the streams are clear and the trees are overlapped.

▶ 雷峰夕照

雷峰塔坐落在西湖南岸的夕照山上，建于五代，是吴越国王钱弘俶为庆祝黄妃得子而建，初名黄妃塔。清时重建，因夕阳西照，塔影横空，彩霞披照，景象十分瑰丽，康熙御题此景为"雷峰夕照"，为西湖十景之一。雷峰塔之所以远近闻名，与民间传说《白蛇传》有很大的关系。相传，法海和尚曾将白娘子镇压在塔下，并下咒语："若要雷峰塔倒，除非西湖水干。"

1924年9月25日，雷峰塔因塔砖被盗挖过多，加以塔址附近汪庄造屋打桩引起巨大震动而轰然倒塌。自此之后，西湖十景也因雷峰塔的消失而残缺经年。1999年7月，浙江省委、省政府做出了在原址上重建雷峰塔、恢复"雷峰夕照"景观的决定。2000年12月26日，雷峰塔重建工程正式奠基。2001年10月25日，举行了重建落成典礼。

雷峰新塔通高71米，五面八层，依山临湖，蔚然大观。在夕阳西下时分登上塔顶，余晖近在眼前，可观夕阳下的西湖美景。雷峰新塔是继承与创新、历史与现代、自然与文化完美结合的典范。

▶ Sunset Glow at Leifeng Pagoda

Leifeng Pagoda, located on the Evening Glow Hill by the southern shore of the West Lake, was built in the Five Dynasties by Qian Hongchu, King of the Wuyue State, in celebration of the son who was born by his favorite concubine Huang, so it was named Huangfei Pagoda at first. It was reconstructed in the Qing Dynasty. In the setting sun, the pagoda bathed in the evening glow looked radiantly beautiful, therefore Emperor Kangxi inscribed the character "Lei Fei Xi Zhao" (Sunset Glow at Leifeng Pagoda). Leifeng Pagoda is so famous because it is closely related to the *Legend of White Snake*. According to legend, monk Fahai once suppressed the white lady under the pagoda, casting a spell:

"Leifeng Pagoda will never fall unless the West Lake becomes dry."

On September 25, 1924, Leifeng Pagoda collapsed due to excessive brick excavation and huge vibration caused by building and piling in Wangzhuang nearby. Since then, the Ten Views of the West Lake has been missing for years due to the disappearance of Leifeng Pagoda. In July 1999, Zhejiang provincial party committee and provincial government made the decision to rebuild Leifeng Pagoda on the original site and restore the landscape of "Sunset Glow at Leifeng Pagoda". On December 26, 2000, the foundation stone was officially laid for the reconstruction of Leifeng Pagoda. A ceremony for the completion of the reconstruction was held on October 25, 2001.

With a height of 71 meters, new Leifeng Pagoda has five sides and eight floors. Facing the West Lake and backing against the mountain, it looks spectacular. After you reach the top of the pagoda in the setting sun, the sunlight is close at hand, and you can overlook the beauty of the West Lake in the setting sun. Leifeng Pagoda is a model of the perfect combination of inheritance and innovation, history and modernity, and nature and culture.

▶ 南屏晚钟

南屏晚钟指南屏山净慈寺傍晚的钟声。南屏山在杭州西湖南岸，玉皇山北，九曜山东。主峰高百米，林木繁茂，石壁如屏，北麓山脚下是净慈寺，傍晚钟声清越悠扬。

南屏晚钟是宋代西湖十景中问世最早的景点，源于北宋著名画家张择端画过的一幅《南屏晚钟图》。相传康熙皇帝在净慈寺寺门外建一碑亭，上刻"南屏晚钟"4个字。

清朝末年，铜钟在战乱中消失，钟声沉寂。直到1984年10月，净慈寺在日本佛教界的相助下，重铸铜钟。1986年11月21日，中日佛教界400多人欢聚净慈寺，举行了隆重的大梵钟落成法会，108记雄浑有力的钟声回荡在西湖上空，绝响百年的南屏晚钟重新响起。这口铜钟悬挂在净慈寺重建的两层三檐的钟楼内，高3.6米，直径2.3米，重10吨。铜钟造型古朴，外面铸有《大乘妙法莲华经》，6.8 万余字，铸造精致。每敲一下，余音袅袅，长达 2 分钟，十分浑厚动听。

▶ Evening Bell Ringing at Nanping Hill

"Evening Bell Ringing at Nanping Hill" refers to the evening bell in the Jingci Temple at Nanping Hill. Nanping hill is located by the south bank of the West Lake, to the north of the Yuhuang Mountain, and east of the Jiuyao Hill. The main peak is 100 meters high with luxuriant forests and huge rocks. At the northern foot of the hill is the Jingci Temple, where the evening bell sounds clear and melodious.

"Evening Bell Ringing at Nanping Hill" was the earliest of the Ten Views of the West Lake in the Song Dynasty, originating from a painting entitled *A Picture of Evening Bell Ringing at Nanping Hill* by a distinguished artist Zhang Zeduan in the Northern Song Dynasty. Legend has it that outside the gate of the Jingci Temple, Emperor Kangxi built a stele pavilion with four characters " 南屏晚钟 " (Nan Ping Wan Zhong/Evening Bell Ringing at Nanping Hill) inscribed on it.

At the end of the Qing Dynasty, the bronze bell disappeared in the chaos of wars，so is it with the ringing of bell. Until October 1984, with the help of the Japanese Buddhist circle, the bronze bell was recast. On November 21, 1986, more than 400 people from the Buddhist circles in China and Japan gathered at the Jingci Temple to hold a grand ceremony for the inauguration of the Big Buddha Bell. 108 vigorous and powerful bell tones echoed above the West Lake, which shows that the evening bell at Nanping Hill rang again after about a hundred years. Being hung inside the two-story, three-eave bell tower rebuilt in the Jingci Temple, the bell stands 3.6 meters high, 2.3 meters in diameter and weighs 10 tons. The shape of the bell is of primitive simplicity. Outside is exquisitely engraved with *The Lotus Sutra of Mahayana*, which contains more than 68,000 Chinese characters. Once the bell is rung, the sound is lingering, lasting as long as 2 minutes, which is solemn and beautiful.

★ 新西湖十景

1984 年，杭州日报社、杭州市园林文物管理局、园林与名胜（现更名为风景名胜）杂志社、浙江电视台、杭州市旅游总公司 5 家单位联合发起举办"新西湖十景"评选活动。全国各地有 10 万余人参加，共提供 7400 余条西湖景点名，最后评选出 10 处景点，被称为"新西湖十景"。

★ Ten New Views of the West Lake

In 1984, Hangzhou Daily Agency, Hangzhou Municipal Administration Bureau of Landscape and Cultural Relics, The Gardens and Places of Interest Journal Agency (now renamed as Scenic Spots Journal Agency), Zhejiang TV Station and Hangzhou Tourism Corporation jointly sponsored the activity of selecting Ten New Views of the West Lake. More than 100,000 people from all over the country participated, providing more than 7,400 West Lake scenic spot names, and finally 10 were selected and named the "Ten New Views of the West Lake".

▶ 吴山天风

吴山天风，新西湖十景之一，位于西湖东南面。吴山高 94 米，景秀、石奇、泉清、洞美。山上有城隍阁，秀出云表，巍然壮观。吴山是西湖南山延伸进入杭州城区的尾部，春秋时期，这里是吴国的南界。由紫阳、云居、金地、清平、宝莲、七宝、石佛、宝月、骆驼、峨眉等十几个山头形成西南—东北走向的弧形丘冈，总称吴山。吴山不高，但由于插入市区，其东、北、西北多俯临街市巷陌，南面可远眺钱塘江及两岸平畴，上吴山有凌空超越之感，且可尽览杭州江、山、湖、城之胜，"吴山天风"由此而得名。

▶ Heavenly Wind over Wushan Hill

"Heavenly Wind over Wushan Hill" is one of the Ten New Views of the West Lake, located in the southeast of the West Lake. Wushan Hill is 94 meters high with beautiful scenery, strange rocks, clear springs and beautiful caves. On the top of the hill, there is Chenghuang Pavilion, piercing the clouds, majestic and spectacular. Wushan Hill is the rear part of the South Mountain of the West Lake extending into the downtown area of Hangzhou. During the

Spring and Autumn Period, it was the southern boundary of the State of Wu. The boundary are formed by a dozen hills from southwest to northeast like Ziyang, Yunju, Jindi, Qingping, Baolian, Qibao, Shifo (Stone Buddha), Baoyue, Luotuo (Camel), E'mei and so on, which forms a shape of curve. These hills are called Wushan Hill in general. Wushan Hill is not high, but as it lies in the urban area, you can overlook the streets and alleys from its eastern, northern and northwestern parts. From the southern part you can overlook the Qiantang River and the horizontal areas on both sides. On the top of the hill you will feel like being high in the air, with rivers, mountains, lakes, and the city beneath you. "Heavenly Wind over Wushan Hill" is hence named.

▶ 玉皇飞云

玉皇山介于西湖与钱塘江之间，海拔 239 米，凌空突兀，衬以蓝天白云，更显得山姿雄峻巍峨。每当风起云涌之时，伫立山巅登云阁上，耳畔但闻习习之声，时有云雾扑面而来，飞渡而去。湖山空阔，江天浩渺，此景此境被命名为"玉皇飞云"，以其壮阔、崇高而入选新西湖十景。

▶ Flying Clouds over Jade Emperor Hill

Located between the West Lake and the Qiantang River, Jade Emperor Hill is 239 meters above sea level. The mountain is towering against the blue sky and white clouds, which makes it more majestic. When the wind rises and the clouds surge, standing in the pavilion on the top of the mountain, you can hear the sound of the wind, and feel the cloud and mist blow on your face and fly away. With spacious lakes and mountains and vast rivers and sky, this view is named "Flying Clouds over Jade Emperor Hill", which is selected into the Ten New Views of the West Lake for its magnificence and nobility.

▶ 黄龙吐翠

黄龙吐翠是新西湖十景之一，在杭州栖霞岭北麓的曙光路，护国仁王寺遗址处，顺山路步行至茂林修竹深处，就可看到隐藏着道教洞天福地的黄龙洞古迹。南宋以来这里作为西湖上五大祀龙点之一而享有盛名，清杭州二十四景中的"黄山积翠"一景即指此。杭州西湖名胜风景区管委会将集宗教文化、人文文化与寺观园林景观为一体的黄龙洞辟建为仿古游乐园，冠名"黄龙吐翠"。

► **Yellow Dragon Cave Dressed in Green**

"Yellow Dragon Cave Dressed in Green", ranked in the Ten New Views of the West Lake, is located at the Shuguang Road at the northern foot of Qixia Ridge, at the site of the Huguo Renwang Temple[①]. Walking along the mountain road to deep part of the forest full of lush trees and tall bamboos, you can see the historic site of Huanglong Cave, which was once the blessing-spot for Taoism. Since the Southern Song Dynasty, it has enjoyed a great reputation as one of the five sites for worshiping the dragon around the West Lake. One of the 24 scenic spots of Hangzhou in the Qing Dynasty—"Yellow Hill Dressed in Green" refers to this scene. Administration Committee of Hangzhou West Lake Scenic Area broke ground and built Huanglong cave, which integrates religious culture, humanistic culture and temple landscape, into an antique amusement park, and named it "Yellow Dragon Cave Dressed in Green".

► **九溪烟村**

九溪烟树是新西湖十景之一，俗称"九溪十八涧"，位于西湖西边群山中的鸡冠垅下。北接龙井，南贯钱塘江。源发翁家山杨梅岭下，途中汇入清湾、宏法、唐家、小康、佛石、百丈、云栖、清头和方家九溪，曲折隐现，流入钱江。十八涧系指细流之多，流泉淙淙。九溪与十八涧在八觉山下的溪中溪餐馆前汇合，一路重峦叠嶂，茶园散布，峰回路转，流水潺潺，山鸟嘤嘤。晴天秀色可餐，阴天烟云缥缈。

► **Nine Creeks in Misty Forest**

"Nine Creeks in Misty Forest" is one of the Ten New Views of the West Lake, commonly known as "Nine Brooks and Eighteen Dales". It is located at

---

①Huguo Renwang: Buddha to protect the country.

the foot of Jiguanlong (Jiguan Ridge) among the mountains to the west of the West Lake with the Longjing Village in the north and the Qiantang River in the south. Originating from Wengjiashan at the foot of Yangmeiling (Yangmei Ridge), with twists and turns it passes through nine creeks which are Qingwan, Hongfa, Tangjia, Xiaokang, Foshi, Baizhang, Yunqi, Qingtou and Fangjia, and finally flows into the Qiantang River. "Eighteen Dales" refers to the numerous trickles with gurgling water. Nine brooks and eighteen dales meet in front of the Xizhongxi Restaurant at the foot of Bajue Hill. Along the road, there are endless mountains, scattered tea gardens, winding turns, whispering waters, and bird chirps. It looks so beautiful on sunny days and dimly discernible in the mist on cloudy days.

▶ 满陇桂雨

满陇桂雨是杭州新西湖十景之一。满觉陇，又称满陇，位于杭州西湖以南，南高峰与白鹤峰夹峙下的自然村落中，是一处山谷。五代后晋天福四年（939）建有圆兴院，北宋治平二年（1065）改为满觉院，满觉意为"圆满的觉悟"，地因寺而得名。

满觉陇沿途山道边，植有 7000 多株桂花，有金桂、银桂、丹桂、四季桂等品种。每当金秋时节，珠英琼树，百花争艳，香飘数里，沁人肺腑。如逢露水重，往往随风洒落，密如雨珠，人行桂树丛中，沐"雨"披香，别有一番意趣，故被称为"满陇桂雨"。

▶ Sweet Osmanthus Rain at Manjuelong Village

"Sweet Osmanthus Rain at Manjuelong Village" is one of the Ten New Views of the West Lake. Manjuelong, also known as Manlong, is located in the south of the West Lake in Hangzhou. It is a valley through the natural village between the Southern Peak and the White Crane Peak. Yuanxing Garden was built in the fourth year of Tianfu in the Later Jin Dynasty (939) and was changed to be Manjue Garden in the second year of the reign of Emperor Zhiping in the Northern Song Dynasty (1065). Manjue means "perfect consciousness" and the place got its name from the temple.

By the side of the mountain roads along Manjuelong, there are more than 7,000 osmanthus trees, including golden osmanthus, silver osmanthus, red osmanthus and four-season osmanthus, etc. In autumn when the osmanthus flowers are in full blossom dispalying their best charm, with the fragrance floating in the air, you will be extremely enchanted and deeply moved. When there is heavy dew, osmanthus flowers will often sprinkle with the wind. Since the falls of the flowers are as dense as raindrops, when you are walking among the osmanthus bushes, you will be soaked up in the "rain", and wrapped in fragrance, which is a different kind of fun, so it is called "Sweet Osmanthus Rain at Manjuelong Village".

▶ 阮墩环碧

阮墩环碧，新西湖十景之一。阮墩即阮公墩，是位于西湖中的一座绿色小岛。阮公墩北依孤山，南眺三潭印月，西望苏堤，东临湖心亭。站在小岛上可环顾西湖，水阔天空，群山环抱着秀美的西子，各个景点依稀可辨。

该岛是清嘉庆五年（1800）浙江巡抚阮元主持疏浚西湖后，以浚湖淤泥堆积而成，故后人称为"阮公墩"。又因其泥软地低，常为湖水浸漫，俗呼其为"阮滩"。阮公墩成岛后，树木葱茏，芳草萋萋，天真未凿，远远望去如碧玉环绕，故世人称之"阮墩环碧"。

▶ Ruan Gong Islet Submerged in Greenery

"Ruan Gong Islet Submerged in Greenery" is one of the Ten New Views of the West Lake. Ruan Dun, also called Ruan Gong Dun (Ruan Gong Islet) is a small green island located in the West Lake. Ruan Gong Islet is adjacent to Gushan Hill in the north, "Three Pools Mirroring the Moon" to the south, Su Causeway to the west and Huxin Pavilion to the east. Standing on the island and looking around the West Lake, you can see boundless waters and numerous mountains surrounding the West Lake, with each scenic spot faintly distinguishable.

The island was formed by accumulated silt in the fifth year of the reign of Emperor Jiaqing in the Qing Dynasty (1800), when Ruan Yuan, governor of Zhejiang Province presided over dredging the West Lake, so it was called "Ruan Gong Islet" by later generations. And because of its soft mud and low ground, it was often flooded by the lake water, so it was commonly called "Ruan Tan" (Ruan Shoal). After Ruan Gong Islet became an island, it is full of luxuriant trees and grass, which forms a wonderful natural landscape. Seen from afar, it looks as if it were surrounded by jasper, so it is called "Ruan Gong Islet Submerged in Greenery" by the world.

▶ 龙井问茶

龙井问茶,新西湖十景之一,是走访龙井茶文化的著名景点。西湖龙井茶主要产于西湖区龙井村地带,龙井村的茶不仅汇茶之色、香、味、形四绝于一身,而且集名山、名寺、名湖、名泉和名茶之五名于一体。

西湖龙井茶叶有狮、龙、云、虎、梅之别,以狮峰山和龙井村的茶叶为最优,其中奥妙,唯有亲去龙井村品茗问茶方可悟出,因此就有了"龙井问茶"之趣说。龙井泉水清澈甘洌,龙井茶更负盛名,人们争先前来探寻,构成了独特的龙井茶文化。

▶ Enjoying Tea at Longjing Village

"Enjoying Tea at Longjing Village", one of the Ten New Views of the West Lake, is a famous scenic spot for experiencing the Longjing tea culture. West Lake Longjing Tea is mainly produced in Longjing Village. Longjing tea not only integrates the four unique features—color, aroma, taste and shape of the tea, but also integrates the five fames—famous mountain, famous temple, famous lake, famous spring and famous tea.

West Lake Longjing Tea is divided into "Shi" (producing area of Shifeng), "Long" (producing area of Longjing), "Yun" (producing area of Yunqi), "Hu" (producing area of Hupao) and "Mei" (producing area of Meijiawu). Among them, tea from Shifeng Hill and Longjing Village are the best. Only when you go to drink tea in Longjing Village can you comprehend the profoundity and subtlety of the tea, so there is a saying—"Enjoying Tea at Longjing Village". Clear and sweet Longjing spring water, better-known Longjing tea, and people's coming to seek one after another constitute the unique Longjing tea culture.

▶ 虎跑梦泉

虎跑梦泉位于西湖之南，大慈山定慧禅寺内。虎跑之名，因梦泉而来。传说唐代高僧性空住在这里，后来因水源短缺，准备迁走。有一天，他在梦中得到指示：南岳衡山有童子泉，当遣二虎移来，日间果见二虎跑翠岩做穴，石壁涌出泉水。"虎跑梦泉"由此得名。

虎跑的水纯净无菌，分子密度高，表面张力大，水满碗口而不溢，被誉为"天下第三泉"。西湖龙井、虎跑水，素称"西湖双绝"。在此观泉、听泉、品泉、试泉，其乐无穷。

▶ Dreaming of Tiger Spring at Hupao Valley

"Dreaming of Tiger Spring at Hupao Valley" is located to the south of the West Lake, in the Dinghui Temple of Daci Hill. Hupao is named after a dearm of spring. Legend says that in the Tang Dynasty an eminent monk named Xing Kong lived here, and later, due to water shortage, he was ready to move away. One day, he got a sign from the immortal in a dream: There was a Tongzi Spring in Mount Heng in southern China, and you can send two tigers here. During the daytime of the following day, two tigers were seen running into a cave in a green rock, and the spring water gushed out of the rock wall; hence "Dreaming of Tiger Spring at Hupao Valley" gets its name.

Spring water in Hupao valley is pure and sterile with great density of the molecule and high surface tension, and the water will not overflow when it fills the bowl. Tiger Spring is hailed as "the third spring in the world". Hupao Spring Water, together with West Lake Longjing Tea has always been called "two unique features of the West Lake". It is a great joy to view, listen to, taste, and try the spring water here.

▶ 云栖竹径

云栖竹径是新西湖十景之一。云栖竹径是指云栖坞里林木茂盛的山坞景观——深山古寺，竹径磬声。今天的云栖坞，翠竹成荫，溪流叮咚，清凉无比。

云栖竹径，四季皆含画意。春天，竹笋破土，草长莺飞，一片盎然生机；夏日，老竹新篁，丝丝凉意；秋天，黄叶绕地，古木含情；冬日，林寂鸣静，飞鸟啄雪。蝉鸣声声的炎夏暑期，是云栖竹径一年中的最佳时节。行走在"一径万竿绿参天，几曲山溪咽细泉"的幽幽山道上，犹如潜泳在竹海碧波之中。

▶ Bamboo-lined Path at Yunqi

"Bamboo-lined Path at Yunqi" is one of the Ten New Views of the West Lake. The view of "Bamboo-lined Path at Yunqi" refers to the scenery of Yunqi dock with luxuriant trees, where there is an ancient temple in the remote mountain and you can hear the sound of the inverted bell along the bamboo-lined path. In today's Yunqi dock, with densely growing bamboos and tinkling brooks, you will feel extremely cool and refreshing.

"Bamboo-lined Path at Yunqi" is picturesque in every season. In spring, it is full of vitality with bamboo shoots growing out of the earth, grasses growing tall and the nightingales flying in the air. appearing on the branches. In summer, new shoots grow out of the old bamboo, and there comes a cool breeze. In autumn, the ground is paved with yellow leaves, and old trees are rustling in the air. In winter, the woods are tranquil and the birds are pecking at the snow. Hot summer is the best time of the year when cicadas are chirping constantly. Walking on the faint mountain road with towering bamboos and drinking brooks is like snorkelling in green waves in the sea of bamboo.

▶ 宝石流霞

宝石流霞位于西湖北岸宝石山上。宝石山初名石姥山，曾称保俶山、保所山、古塔山等。这里的山岩呈赭红色，岩体中有许多闪闪发亮的红色矿物质，每当阳光映照，满山流霞缤纷，尤其是朝阳或落日霞光洒沐之时，保俶清秀，披着霞光分外耀目，仿佛数不清的宝石在熠熠生辉，因而被称为"宝石流霞"。

宝石山以其秀丽挺拔的保俶塔、千姿百态的石景以及初阳台上看日出等景观吸引游人。当朝阳的红光洒在山上时，小石块仿佛是熠熠发光的宝石，因此得名"宝石山"。一路循阶而上，宝石山绿荫如盖。登上山顶，南望平湖，水波荡漾；北瞰万亩平畴，楼宇鳞次栉比；东则街衢商埠，充满活力；西有青嶂千叠，一派苍翠遥接晴空。

▶ Precious Stone Hill Floating in Rosy Cloud

"Precious Stone Hill Floating in Rosy Cloud" is located on the Precious Stone Hill (Baoshi Hill) to the northern shore of the West Lake. Precious Stone Hill was firstly named Shilao Hill, once known as Baochu Hill, Baosuo Hill, and Guta Hill (Ancient Pagoda Hill), etc. The rocks here have the color of ember, and there are many shining red minerals in the rock. Whenever the sun shines, the whole mountain is full of rosy clouds. Especially at sunrise and sunset, on the eastern top of the Precious Stone Hill, when the elegant Baochu Pagoda is bathed in the sunlight, it is particularly dazzling and looks as if countless precious stones are shining in full brightness. Therefore, it is called "Precious Stone Hill Floating in Rosy Cloud".

Precious Stone Hill attracts tourists with its beautiful and forceful Baochu Pagoda, varied stone scenery and the sunrise view from Chuyang (Rising Sun) Platform. When the red light of the rising sun falls on the Precious Stone Hill, the small stones seem to shine like gems, hence the name "Precious Stone Hill". Go all the way up the steps, you will find the whole hill is covered with green shade. After you reach the top, seeing down to the south, there is the West Lake with rippling water. To the north, there are numerous patches of plain land with rows of buildings. To the east, there are streets and shops full of vitality. To the west, there are thousands of screen-like mountain peaks connecting the clear sky.

★ 灵隐寺

灵隐寺，中国佛教古寺，又名云林寺，位于浙江省杭州市，背靠北高峰，面朝飞来峰，始建于东晋咸和元年（326），占地面积约87000平方米。灵隐寺开山祖师为西印度僧人慧理和尚。南朝梁武帝赐田并扩建。五代吴越王钱镠命请永明延寿大师重兴开拓，并赐名"灵隐新寺"。

宋宁宗嘉定年间，灵隐寺被誉为江南禅宗"五山"之一。清顺治年间，禅宗巨匠具德和尚住持灵隐，筹资重建，仅建殿堂时间就前后历18年之久，其规模之宏伟跃居"东南之冠"。清康熙二十八年（1689），康熙帝南巡时，赐名"云林禅寺"。

灵隐寺布局与江南寺院格局大致相仿，全寺建筑中轴线上依次为天王殿、大雄宝殿、药师殿三大殿，两边是五百罗汉堂、济公殿、华严阁、大悲楼、方丈楼等建筑。

★ Lingyin Temple

Lingyin Temple, an ancient Chinese Buddhist temple, also known as Yunlin Temple, is located in Hangzhou City, Zhejiang Province, backed by Northern Peak and facing the Feilai Peak (peak flying from afar). It was first built in the first year of Xianhe of the Eastern Jin Dynasty (326), covering an area of about 87,000 square meters. The founder of Lingyin Temple was Huili, a monk from the West India. Emperor Liang Wudi of the Southern Dynasty granted the farmland for its expansion. During the Five Dynasties Period, Qian Liu, King of the Wuyue State made an order to invite Master Yongmingyanshou to reconstruct and expand it, and gave the name "Lingyin New Temple" to it.

During the year of Jiading in the reign of Emperor Ningzong in the Southern Song Dynasty, Lingyin Temple was hailed as one of the "Five Mountains" of Jiangnan Zen Buddhism. During the reign of Emperor Shunzhi of the Qing Dynasty, Monk Jude, the great master of Zen Buddhism became abbot of Lingyin Temple and raised funds to rebuild it. It took eighteen years to build the temple and it became the "crown of the southeast" for its pretty grand scale. In the 28th year of the reign of Emperor Kangxi of the Qing Dynasty

(1689), when Emperor Kangxi toured the south, he named it "Yunlin Temple".

The layout of Lingyin Temple is similar to those of other temples in Jiangnan with the three main temples on the central axis, which are Hall of the Heavenly King, Hall of the Great Hero, and Hall of the Buddha of Medicine in sequence. On both sides there are Hall of 500 Arhats, Hall of Monk Jigong, Huayan Pavilion, Hall of Great Mercy, Office and Rest Hall for Abbot.

★ 岳王庙

岳王庙，又称岳坟、岳飞墓，位于杭州市西湖畔栖霞岭下，建于南宋嘉定十四年（1221），明景泰年间改称"忠烈庙"，元、明、清、民国时兴时废，代代相传一直留存到现在。现存建筑于清康熙五十四年（1715）重建，1918年曾大修，1979年全面整修，更加庄严肃穆。

岳王庙是历代纪念英雄岳飞的场所。岳飞是南宋初期的主要抗金将领，但被秦桧、张俊等人以"莫须有"罪名诬陷为反叛朝廷，陷害至死。岳飞遇害后，狱卒隗顺冒着生命危险，背负岳飞遗体，越过城墙，草草地葬于九曲丛祠旁。21年后，宋孝宗下令给岳飞昭雪，并高价悬赏求索岳飞遗体，用隆重的仪式将其迁葬于栖霞岭下，就是现在岳坟的所在地。南宋嘉泰四年（1204），即岳飞死后62年，朝廷追封其为"鄂王"。

★ General Yue Fei's Temple

General Yue Fei's Temple, also known as Yue Grave or Yue Fei's Tomb, located by the West Lake at the foot of Qixia Ridge. It was built in the 14th year of Jiading in the Southern Song Dynasty (1221), and was renamed the "Martyr Temple" during the years of Jingtai in the Ming Dynasty. It rose and fell during the Yuan, Ming, and Qing Dynasty, and the Republic of China, and was handed down from generation to generation. The existing building today was rebuilt in the 54th year of Emperor Kangxi's reign in the Qing Dynasty (1715). It was overhauled in 1918 and completely renovated in 1979, so it became more solemn and serene.

General Yue Fei's Temple is a memorial to the hero Yue Fei. He was the main general in the early Southern Song Dynasty, but was sentenced to death with unwarranted charge by Qin Hui, Zhang Jun and other treacherous ministers who framed him for rebelling against the imperial court. After Yue Fei was murdered, Jailer Wei Shun risked his life to carry Yue Fei's body, crossed the city wall and buried it hastily beside the Jiuqucong Ancestral Temple. 21 years later, Emperor Xiaozong made an order to exonerate Yue Fei, and search for the body of Yue Fei, and bury it with a grand ceremony under Qixia Ridge, which is now the location of Yue Fei's Tomb. In the 4th year of Jiatai in the Southern Song Dynasty (1204), that is 62 years after the death of Yue Fei, the imperial court entitled Yue Fei "E Wang" (one of official titles in ancient China).

★ 六和塔

六和塔，取佛教"六和敬"之义命名；又名六合塔，取"天地四方"之意。位于浙江省杭州市西湖区之江路 16 号。始建于宋开宝三年（970），塔基原址系吴越王钱弘俶的南果园。钱弘俶舍园建塔原为镇压江潮。

六和塔占地 890 平方米，塔外各层檐角挂有 104 个铁铃。六和塔塔高 59.89 米，内部塔芯为砖石结构，分七层，外部为木结构楼阁式檐廊，八面十三层，每级廊道两侧有壶门，塔内由螺旋阶梯相连，第三级须弥座上雕刻有花卉、飞禽、走兽、仙子等各式图案。清朝乾隆皇帝曾为六和塔每层题字。

1961 年 3 月 4 日，六和塔被国务院公布为第一批全国重点文物保护单位。

★ Liuhe Pagoda (Six Harmonies Pagoda)

Six Harmonies Pagoda is named after the Buddhist meaning of "Six Harmonies and Respect". It is also named "Six Directions Pagoda", meaning "east, west, north, south, heaven (up) and earth (down)". Located at No.16 Zhijiang Road, Xihu District, Hangzhou City, Zhejiang Province. It was first built in the third year of Kaibao in the Song Dynasty (970), whose original site is the Southern Orchard of Qian Hongchu, King of the Wuyue State. Qian Hongchu abandoned his orchard to build the Pagoda with the original purpose of suppressing the river tide.

Covering an area of 890 square meters, the pagoda has 104 iron bells hanging on the eave of each floor. It is 59.89 meters high, and the interior core of the pagoda is masonry structure with seven storeys. The external wooden pavilion-style colonnade has eight sides and thirteen storeys, with pot doors on both sides of each corridor. The interior part of pagoda is connected by spiral staircases, and the pedestal of Buddha's statue on the third floor is carved with various patterns such as flowers, birds, animals and fairies. Emperor Qianlong of the Qing Dynasty had inscriptions inside each floor of Six Harmonies Pagoda.

On March 4, 1961, Six Harmonies Pagoda was announced by the State Council of the People's Republic of China among the first batch of national key cultural relics protection units.

第二节　京杭大运河杭州景区

京杭大运河始建于春秋时期，距今已有 2400 多年的历史。它纵贯河北、山东、江苏、浙江 4 省，北京、天津 2 市，全长 1794 千米，是世界上最长、最大、最古老的运河。2014 年，京杭大运河成功入选世界文化遗产名录，成为中国第 46 个世界遗产项目。[①]

京杭大运河是杭州旅游的一大亮点，也是了解江南和长江下游水乡文化的经典目的地。京杭大运河流经了富庶儒雅的钱塘佳丽地，记录了杭州繁华古都的沧桑沉浮和白墙粉黛的市井百态。大运河在杭州呈现了"流动的中华文明，休闲的天堂画卷"。

---

① 京杭大运河博物馆. 运河遗存［EB/OL］.［2023-04-06］. http://www.canal-museum.cn/culture/millennium_canal.

目前，京杭大运河杭州景区两岸已形成了一条以自然生态景观为核心主轴，以历史街区、文化园区、博物馆群、寺庙庵堂、遗产遗迹为重要节点的文化休闲体验长廊和水上旅游黄金线。景区核心范围为"三大街区、四大园区"及博物馆群。

三大街区包括：桥西历史文化街区、小河历史文化街区和大兜路历史文化街区。四大园区包括：运河天地、运河天地文化艺术园区、浙窑公园和富义仓。博物馆群包括：中国伞博物馆、中国扇博物馆、中国刀剪剑博物馆、手工艺活态馆和杭州工艺美术博物馆。

2013年，随着运河综合保护工程和运河申遗项目的推进，众多运河景点成为市民游客休闲旅游的必去之地。经市民推荐、专家评审、投票选举等多个环节，最后评选出10处景点，被称为"运河十景"，分别为：广济通衢、拱宸邀月、桥西人家、香积梵音、富义留余、武林问渡、凤山烟雨、三堡会澜、龙山塔影、西陵怀古。

Ⅱ Hangzhou Scenic Spot of Beijing-Hangzhou Grand Canal

First dug in the Spring and Autumn Period, Beijing-Hangzhou Grand Canal has a history of over 2,400 years. It runs across four provinces which are Hebei, Shandong, Jiangsu, and Zhejiang Province, and two municipal cities which are Beijing and Tianjin, with a total length of 1,794 square kilometers. It is the longest, largest and most ancient canal in the world. In 2014, the Grand Canal was listed as a World Heritage site, making it the 46th world heritage project of China.

Beijing-Hangzhou Grand Canal is a highlight of tourism in Hangzhou as well as a classic destination for understanding the water-town culture in the regions of the south of the Yangtze River and the lower reaches of the Yangtze

River. The Grand Canal passes through rich and refined Qiantang (Hangzhou) Land, witnessing the vicissitude of the prosperous ancient capital—Hangzhou and the folk customs of the locals living in white-wall and black-tile residences. The Grand Canal in Hangzhou section presents a scroll of "flowing Chinese civilization and paradise for leisure".

At present, the two sides of the Beijing-Hangzhou Grand Canal scenic spot have formed a corridor for culture, leisure and experience, and a golden line of water tourism, with natural ecological landscape as the core axis, and with historical blocks, cultural parks, museum complex, temples and nunneries, heritage sites as the important nodes. The core scope of the scenic area is "three blocks and four parks" and the museum complex.

The three blocks are West Bridge Historic and Cultural Block, Xiaohe Street Historic and Cultural Block and Dadou Road Historic and Cultural Block. The four parks are Canal World, Canal World Culture and Art Park, Zheyao Park and Fuyi Warehouse. The museum complex includes China Umbrella Museum, China Fan Museum, China Knife and Sword Museum, Live Handcraft Exhibition Hall and Hangzhou Arts and Crafts Museum.

In 2013, with the promotion of the comprehensive preservation of the canal and the application of the canal as a cultural heritage site, many scenic spots of the Canal have become must-go destinations for tourists and locals. After the public recommendation, expert evaluation, voting and other steps, 10 scenic spots were selected and named as the "Ten Scenic Spots of the Grand Canal", which are respectively "Guangji Bridge Straddling Tangqi Ancient Town", "Moonlight over Gongchen Bridge", "Residents in West Bridge Historic Block", "Bell Ringing in Xiangji Temple", "Remaining Grain in Fuyi Warehouse", "Ferry in Wulinmen Wharf", "Misty Rain in Fengshan Gate", "Meeting Big Wave in Sanbao Navigation Dock", "Shadow of White Pagoda in Longshan", and "Meditating on the Past of Guotanghang Port in Xixing Ancient Town".

第三节 良渚古城遗址公园

良渚古城遗址位于浙江省杭州市余杭区瓶窑镇，始建于公元前3300年。良渚文化始于5300年前至4300年前，持续了大约1000年。良渚古城是长江下游地区首次发现的新石器时代城址，在陕西神木石峁遗址发现之前，是中国最大的史前城址，一直被誉为"中华第一城"。2019年7月6日，良渚古城遗址被正式列入世界遗产名录。[①]2020年5月，良渚古城遗址入选首批"浙江文化印记"。

良渚古城遗址公园，面积约14.33平方千米，包括城址区、瑶山遗址和外围水利系统遗址。城址总面积约6.31平方千米，人工堆筑总土石方量约717万立方米。宫殿区居于城址中央，地势最为高敞，面积约0.39平方千米，是良渚时期最高统治者居住和活动的主要场所。内城由城墙围合而成，平面略呈圆角长方形，南北长约1910米，东西宽约1770米，面积2.8平方千米（含宫殿区）。外城位于内城外围，由17处断续分布的台地构成半闭合的外郭轮廓，包括居址、作坊和墓葬遗迹，面积约3.51平方千米。[②]

瑶山遗址位于城址外东北方向约5千米的一处山丘顶部，是一处祭坛和高等级墓葬的复合遗址，属于良渚文化早期。瑶山墓地的墓葬均为竖穴土坑墓，分南、北2排埋葬，出土随葬品754件（组），其中玉器共出土678件（组）。

外围水利系统为良渚古城建设之初统一规划的城市水资源管理工程，由谷口高坝、平原低坝、山前长堤的11条人工坝体、自然山体、溢洪道构成，总土方量288万立方米，是中国迄今发现的最早的大型水利工程遗址，

---

① 国家文物局."良渚古城遗址"成功列入《世界遗产名录》[EB/OL].（2019-07-06）[2023-04-06].http://www.ncha.gov.cn/art/2019/7/6/art_722_155889.html.
② 良渚古城遗址公园现场图文资料。

也是目前已发现的世界上最早的低坝系统之一。

良渚古城遗址向人们展示了新石器时代晚期一个以稻作农业为支撑、具有统一信仰的早期区域性国家。通过大型土质建筑、城市规划、水利系统以及不同墓葬形式所体现的社会等级制度，这些遗址成为早期城市文明的杰出范例。

Ⅲ Liangzhu National Archaeological Site Park

Archaeological Ruins of Liangzhu City, first built in 3,300 BC, is located in Pingyao Town, Yuhang District, Hangzhou City, Zhejiang Province. Liangzhu culture dates from 5,300 years ago to 4,300 years ago, with a continuous development of about 1,000 years, which belonged to the archaeological culture of the late Neolithic Age. Liangzhu ancient city is the Neolithic city site first discovered in the lower reaches of the Yangtze River. Before the discovery of Shenmu Shimao site in Shaanxi, it was the largest prehistoric city site in China, and has been honored as the "First City of China". On July 6, 2019, Archaeological Ruins of Liangzhu City were officially inscribed on the World Heritage List. In May 2020, it was selected as the first batch of "Zhejiang Cultural Imprint".

Liangzhu National Archaeological Site Park covers an area of about 14.33 square kilometers, including the area of city site, the area of Yaoshan site and the peripheral water conservancy system.

The total area of the city site is 6.31 square kilometers, and the total amount of man-made earth and stone is about 7.17 million cubic meters. Located in the center of the city site, the palace area was the highest and the most open, covering an area of about 0.39 square kilometers. It was the main residence and activity place for the supreme ruler during the Liangzhu period. The inner city is enclosed by the city walls, whose flat surface looks like a rectangular with rounded corners. It is about 1,910 meters long from north to south and 1,770 meters wide from east to west, covering an area of 2.8 square kilometers (including the palace area). The outer city is located outside the inner city, composed of 17 discontinuous terraces which form a semi-closed outer contour. It covers an area of about 3.51 square meters, including dwellings, workshops and burial relics.

Located at the top of a hill about 5 kilometers northeast of the city site, the Yaoshan site is a compound site of an altar and higher rank tombs, belonging to the early period of Liangzhu Culture. The tombs in Yaoshan Cemetery are all vertical pit tombs, buried in two rows with one in the south and the other in the north. 754 pieces (groups) of burial goods were unearthed, among which 678 pieces (groups) are jadeware.

The Peripheral Water Conservancy System was the uniformly planned urban water resources management project at the beginning of the construction of Liangzhu ancient city. It is composed of the Area of High-dam at the Mouth of the Valley, the Area of Low-dam on the Plain, and the 11 artificial dams of the long embankment in front of the mountain, natural mountain and spillway. The total earth volume is 2.88 million cubic meters. It is the earliest large-scale water conservancy project site discovered in China so far, and one of the earliest low-dam systems in the world.

The Archaeological Ruins of Liangzhu City reveal an early regional state with a unified belief system based on rice cultivation in the late Neolithic period of China. These ruins are an outstanding example of early urban civilization expressed in earthen monuments, urban planning, a water conservation system and a social hierarchy expressed in differentiated burials in cemeteries within the property.

第四节　西溪国家湿地公园

　　西溪国家湿地公园位于杭州市西部，距杭州市中心武林门仅 6 千米，距西湖仅 5 千米。西溪地区始于汉晋，发展于唐宋，繁荣于明清，衰落于民国，复兴于近代。西溪与西湖、西泠并称杭州"三西"。历史上的西溪占地约 60 平方千米，目前西溪湿地总面积约 11.5 平方千米[①]，分为东部湿地生态保护培育区、中部湿地生态旅游休闲区和西部湿地生态景观封育区。西溪湿地是我国罕见的集城市湿地、培育湿地和文化湿地于一体的湿地。它也是全国第一个国家湿地公园。

Ⅳ Xixi National Wetland Park

　　Located at the western part of Hangzhou City, Xixi National Wetland Park is only 6 kilometers from the Wulin Gate in the center of Hangzhou and 5 kilometers from the West Lake. The Xixi area started in Han and Jin Dynasties, developed in Tang and Song Dynasties, prospered in Ming and Qing Dynasties, declined in the period of the Republic of China and rejuvenated in modern times. Along with Xihu (the West Lake) and Xiling (Xiling Seal Art Society), Xixi is well-known as one of the "Three Xi". Xixi wetland once covered an area of 60 square kilometers in history. But now its total area is about 11.5 square kilometers, which include the wetland ecological protection and cultivation

---

① 西溪国家湿地公园. 走进西溪［EB/OL］.［2023-04-06］. http://www.xixiwetland.com.cn/access_xixi.html.

area in the east, the wetland ecotourism and leisure area in the center, and the enclosed incubation area of wetland ecological landscape in the west. Xixi wetland integrates urban wetland, cultivating wetland and cultural wetland into a whole, which is rare in China. It is also the first national wetland park in China.

★ 三堤

三堤指福堤、绿堤和寿堤。汉语中"福""绿（禄）""寿"这三个字意为"财富""繁荣""长寿"。

福堤以 6 座带"福"字的桥连接，因此得名。福堤全长约 2300 米，衔接公园南北 2 个出口，并串联起园区的主要景点，是一条以生态为基调、人文为特色的长堤。

绿堤东西全长 1600 米，宽 7 米，自西向东贯穿核心保护区。两侧植被丰茂，生态良好，景观优美。绿堤寓意西溪国家湿地公园和杭州生态旅游城市相呼应。

寿堤南北全长约 5470 米，宽 4.5 米，是三堤中最长的一条，与长寿之意不谋而合。寿堤两岸水网纵横，古树森森，朴野幽趣，景观天成。

★ Three Main Road

The three main roads are Fudi, Ludi and Shoudi, as in Chinese, the three characters " 福 " (fu), " 禄 "(lu) and " 寿 " (shou) carry the meaning of fortune, prosperity and longevity.

The whole road is connected by six bridges with the Chinese character " 福 " (fu), hence the name "Fudi". It is about 2,300 meters long, connecting the north and south exits of the park and connecting the main scenic spots of the park. It is a long road with ecology as the keynote and humanity as the feature.

Ludi has a total length of 1,600 meters from east to west and a width of seven meters, stretching through the core reserve area from west to east, with lush vegetation, good ecology and beautiful landscape on both sides. Ludi means the coherence of Xixi National Wetland Park and Hangzhou eco-tourism city.

With a total length of 5,470 meters and a width of 4.5 meters, Shoudi is the longest of the three, stretching from south to north, which coincide with the meaning of longevity. Criss-crossing waterways and ancient trees on both sides of Shoudi form an ecological landscape.

★ 西溪十景
Ten Scenic Sports of Xixi Wetland
▶ 秋芦飞雪

西溪有"三雪"，桃为绛雪，芦为秋雪，梅为香雪。秋芦飞雪所处位置在蒹葭深处。四面河流，溪水环绕，东面秋雪滩上芦花摇曳，一经风吹，花白而轻如棉絮，随风飞扬，如漫天飘雪。金秋时节，游客可以泛舟徐徐进入芦苇的世界，也可以登秋雪庵弹指楼，观秋芦遍野，赏芦花胜雪，此乃西溪一绝。

▶ Snow-like Reeds Dancing in Autumn

Xixi has "Three kind of Snow", named respectively as "red snow", "autumn snow", and "fragrant snow", which refers to the scenes when the peaches become pink, the reeds are flying and the plum blossoms are in full bloom. The site of "Snow-like Reeds Dancing in Autumn" is in the depths of Jianjia (reeds), surrounded by rivers and streams. When the reeds are swaying on the "autumn snow beach" in the east of Xixi Wetland, once blown by the wind, the reed catkins, as white and light as cotton wool will sway with the wind, like white snow flying all over the sky. In golden autumn, visitors can either come to the world of reeds by boat, or ascend the fillip floor in "Qiuxue Temple", to enjoy the reed catkins swaying like snow all around, which is the uniqueness of Xixi Wetland.

▶ 火柿映波

柿基鱼塘、桑基鱼塘是几千年来农耕劳作形成的西溪湿地独特地貌。在西溪星罗棋布的池塘的塘基上遍布着大大小小的柿树，光百年以上的老柿树就有 4000 多株。柿树既起着固堤、护堤的作用，同时也构成西溪一道绝佳的风景。尤其到了秋天，天高云淡，风清气爽，柿叶也变红了，这时更有芦荻互为映照，芦白柿红，令人心醉。

▶ Persimmons Mirroring in the Water

Formed after thousands of years of farming, ponds for fish-farming and persimmon-planting, and ponds for fish-farming and mulberry-planting are the unique landforms of Xixi Wetland. The banks of ponds are dotted with persimmon trees in different sizes. There are more than 4,000 old persimmon trees which are over a hundred years old. Persimmon trees not only play a role in reinforcement and protection of the dam, but also constitute a perfect scenery of Xixi Wetland. Especially in autumn, with high sky and clear clouds, and light breeze and cool air, persimmon leaves are turning red. As red persimmon leaves and white reeds reflect each other, how fascinating it is!

▶ 龙舟胜会

自古以来，每年农历端午节，西溪四邻八乡会聚一起举行龙舟胜会，这一传统民俗活动至今长盛不衰。相传清乾隆帝南巡江南，曾在深潭口观赏蒋村龙舟，欣而口敕"龙舟胜会"。自此西溪龙舟声名远播。现在，每年端午龙舟胜会，深潭口和五常河道两岸人声鼎沸，古戏台上戏曲、武术、舞龙舞狮精彩纷呈，水中几百条龙舟来往穿梭，试比高低。这是一项象征西溪人勇猛顽强、百折不挠、追求美好生活的民俗活动。

Dragon Boat Festival

Since ancient times, during the Dragon Boat Festival in the lunar calendar every year, people from the surrounding villages and towns will gather to hold Dragon Boat Festival, and this traditional folk activity has been flourishing up to now. Legend has it that Emperor Qianlong of the Qing Dynasty toured the south of the Yangtze River. Once he watched the dragon boat race at Shentankou, and he was so excited at the race that he praised it as "Dragon Boat Festival". Since then, Xixi dragon boat has enjoyed a widespread reputation. Nowadays, during the annual Dragon Boat Festival, Shentankou and the both banks of Wuchang River are filled with a pleasant hubbub of voices. Traditional Chinese opera, martial arts, dragon and lion dances are played on the ancient stage, and hundreds of dragon boats are moving and completing in the water. Dragon Boat Festival is a kind of folk activity symbolizing the bravery and perseverance of people in Xixi and their pursuit of good life.

▶ 莲滩鹭影

西溪综合保护工程极大地改善并恢复了生态环境，西溪已成了鸟类和各种湿地生物的天堂。莲花滩生态保护区位于西溪腹地，是西溪主要的观鸟区，植被丰茂，绿水环绕，鹭鸟飞翔天际，鸣禽啼啭丛林，生意盎然，野趣纷呈。

▶ Egrets Flying over the Lotus Shallow

The comprehensive protection project of Xixi has greatly improved and restored the ecological environment. Xixi has become a paradise for birds and other kinds of wetland creatures. Located in the hinterland of Xixi, the Lotus Beach Ecological Reserve is the main bird-watching area in Xixi, where there is lush vegetation, flying egrets, and singing songbirds, presenting a picture of vitality and wild interest.

▶ 洪园余韵

以园林为背景，洪园余韵包括洪氏宗祠、钱塘望族、洪园、清平山堂、洪昇纪念馆以及民俗文化展示等人文景观。复原后的洪氏宗祠为游客展示了明末清初洪氏祠堂的基本面貌和洪氏家族文化的概况。宗祠墙上展示的是从南宋高宗建炎年间到明武宗正德年间历代帝王对洪氏家族的诏告，体现了洪氏家族文化的重要地位和代表性。在宗祠两侧建有长廊，从而形成天井，寓意为"四水归堂"，象征着人丁兴旺，家族源远流长。

▶ Lingering Charm of Hongyuan

With the garden as the background, "Lingering Charm of Hongyuan" includes Ancestral Hall of the Hong Family, Qiantang Distinguished Family, Hong Garden, Qingpingshan Hall, Memorial Hall of Hong Sheng and Folk Culture Display, etc. The restored Ancestral Hall of the Hong Family shows the basic appearance of the ancestral hall of the Hong family in the late Ming and early Qing Dynasties and the overview of the culture of the Hong family. The walls of the ancestral hall display the imperial edicts to the Hong family from the reign of Emperor Gaozong of the Southern Song Dynasty to the reign of Emperor Wuzong of the Ming Dynasty, reflecting the important position and representativeness of the culture of the Hong family. Long corridors are built on both sides of the ancestral hall to form a patio, which means "Four Waters Come Together". It is a symbol of a prosperous population and long standing of the family.

▶ 蒹葭泛月

蒹葭泛月位于五常港东御田里。西溪环绕五常，四周一望沙汀水濑，蒹葭弥望。土风淳厚，有黄橙、红柿、紫菱、香茶之美，四时皆宜，宜秋更宜月。秋深蒹葭吐絮，遇风吹，漫天秋雪。月夜泛舟芦港，四望茫无边际，晶光摇曳，皎洁炫目，月明溪动，光漾天际。明人施万于月夜泛舟西溪，写道："白露带蒹葭，月光翻在水。恍若御天风，高歌云汉里。"

▶ Reeds in the Moonlight

"Reeds in the Moonligh" is located on Yutianli Road in the east of Wuchang Port. Xixi surrounds Wuchang with plat sand earth by the water here and there, so that a full view of reeds around is in your sight. The breeze will sweep over your face with the aroma of pure earth. In four different seasons, you can appreciate the different beauty of yellow orange, red persimmon, purple water chestnut, or fragrant tea, of which autumn is the best time for enjoying the moon. In late autumn when the reeds are opening the bolls, as the wind blows, the sky will be filled with bolls like autumn snow. On a moonlit night, while boating in the reed port surrounded by boundless water and reeds, you can see a beautiful and calm scene with swaying crystal light, bright and dazzling moonlight, flowing brook water and rippling light on the horizon. When Shi Wan of the Ming Dynasty boated in Xixi wetland on a moonlit night, he wrote a poem, "The white dew covered the reeds, and the moonlight spread over the water. You will feel like being in the sky and singing in the cloud."

▶ 渔村烟雨

渔村烟雨位于烟水庵的南部，此地多为2层的水乡民居式的木结构建筑。临水而居、错落有致的开放型木结构建筑是渔村传神之处。渔村烟雨的"烟雨"，有柳烟、云烟、炊烟"三烟"之妙，人、烟、水共处，犹如身临仙境。在美丽的渔村里，可以一边享受佳肴，一边品茗赏景，此时此刻，真正轻松悠闲，让人忘了尘世的烦扰。如果有余兴，可以去塘堤漫步，在西溪农家生活原生态展示馆感受当地居民的生活状态，又会增添一番乐趣。

▶ Fishing Village in Misty Rain

"Fishing Village in Misty Rain" is located to the south of Yansui Nunnery, and the buildings are mostly two-story wooden houses with waterside dwelling-style. What makes the fishing village remarkable is a group of open wooden buildings well distributed by the water. "Misty rain" in the fishing village has "three Yan", which are Liu Yan (flying catkins from the willow), Yun Yan (mist from the water), and Chui Yan (smoke from cooking fires). In the beautiful fishing village, you can enjoy delicious meal while sipping tea and enjoying the scenery. At this moment, you can really relax yourself and forget the troubles in the world. If you want to have more fun, you can take a walk in the pond dike and feel the living conditions of the local people in the Xixi Farm-life Original Ecology Exhibition Hall.

▶ 曲水寻梅

西溪湿地内现有梅花3000多株,梅林近67万平方米,种类主要有朱砂、宫粉、绿萼、玉蝶、江梅、美人梅、南京红、长兴红等,主要分布在梅竹休闲区内梅竹山庄和西溪梅墅一带。该区域河道沿岸有许多梅树,水域曲折,河道迂回,便如梅树的枝条一样虬曲。而西溪的梅枝亦苍劲嶙峋、风韵洒落,多变而有规律,呈现出一种很强的力度和线的韵律感。因而形成西溪特有的赏梅方式——水上探梅、摇舟探梅。探,一探在于西溪的梅弯曲于水上,有迎客之势;二探在于船从梅树下经过,梅触手可及;三探在于"振",有寻找、摸索之意,河道曲折,正是乘舟寻梅的意趣。

▶ Searching for Plum Blossom Along Winding Waters

There are more than 3,000 plum trees in Xixi wetland, and the area of plum forest is nearly 670,000 square meters. The main species are cinnabar, palace powder, green calyx, jade butterfly, river plum, beauty plum, Nanjing red, Changxing red and so on. They are mainly distributed in Meizhu Villa and Xixi Meishu inside Meizhu recreational area. There are many plum trees along the river in this area. The water is tortuous and the river is circuitous, which is as twisted as the branches of plum trees. The plum branches are also vigorous and rugged, graceful, and changeable but regular, showing great strength with rhythm of lines. So, in Xixi wetland, there are special ways to appreciate plum, which are searching for plum above water and searching for plum by rowing the boat—"Tan" in Chinese. The first "Tan" means that the plum in Xixi is bending above the water with the sign of welcoming the guests; The second "Tan" is that when you are rowing the boat under the plum tree, plum blossom is within your reach; The third "Tan" is vibration, which has the meaning of searching and groping. As the waters is winding, you will have great fun in searching for plum in a boat.

▶ 高庄晨迹

高庄，又名西溪山庄，俗称西庄。始建于清顺治十四年（1657）至康熙三年（1664）之间，是清代高士奇在西溪的别墅。高士奇，杭州人。其学识渊博，能诗文，擅书法，精考证，善鉴赏，被清人比作李白、宋濂一流人物，所藏书画甚富。康熙二十八年，康熙南巡时，曾临幸西溪山庄，并赐"竹窗"2字和诗1首。现恢复的高庄由高宅、竹窗、捻花书屋、桐荫堂、蕉园诗社等建筑组成，再现了当年康熙临幸高庄的历史场景。

▶ Imperial Mark of Gaozhuang

Gaozhuang, also known as Xixi Villa, commonly known as Xi Zhuang. Built between the 14th year of Emperor Shunzhi (1657) and the 3rd year of Emperor Kangxi (1664) of the Qing Dynasty, was the villa of Gao Shiqi in the Qing Dynasty. Gao Shiqi, a native of Hangzhou, had erudite knowledge, was good at poetry and calligraphy and fine at research and appreciation, and was compared to first-class figures like Li Bai and Song Lian, and had rich collection of calligraphy and paintings. In the 28th year of Kangxi's reign, during his southern tour, Emperor Kangxi visited Xixi Villa and bestowed two Chinese characters " 竹窗 " (Zhu Chuang/Bamboo Window) and a poem. The restored Gaozhuang is composed of buildings such as Residence of Gao Family, Bamboo Window, Twist Flower Study, Tongyin Hall and Banana Garden Poetry Club, reproducing the historical scene of Kangxi's visit to Gaozhuang.

▶ 河渚听曲

"舞台搭建在水面上，人们需坐船头听戏，是江南水乡泽国古已有之的风俗。"鲁迅先生在他的小说《社戏》里面有这样的描述。如今，它被特意开发出来，作为西溪的景境风貌。河渚听曲以河渚街为中心，辐射古荡、蒋村集市及周边区域，着重体现当地作为北派越剧发源地的特殊地位，以及延绵至今依旧生生不息、绚丽多彩的民俗文化。

▶ Listening to Chinese Opera in Hezhu

Lu Xun described in his novel *Village Opera*: "The stage is built on the water, and people need to sit on the prow of the boat to listen to the opera, which is a custom of the waterside towns of the south of the Yangtze River in ancient times." Now, it is deliberately developed as the feature of scene and landscape of Xixi wetland. "Listening to Chinese Opera in Hezhu" is centered on Hezhu Street, extending to the market of Gudang, Jiangcun and surrounding areas, highlighting the local special status as the birthplace of Northern Yue Opera, as well as the vibrant and colorful folk culture that has continued to this day.

第四章　美食之城

　　杭州饮食文化源远流长，最早可追溯到距今 8000—7000 年的跨湖桥文化。唐宋以来，经济繁荣，名人云集。经济、文化的发展也催生了人们对物质、精神享受的要求，特别是在衣、食、住和节庆娱乐等方面，饮食又在其中发挥了重要的媒介作用。尤其是宋室南渡建都临安，杭州成为当时的政治、经济中心，饮食的烹饪技艺也达到了鼎盛。

　　杭帮菜兼收山水之灵秀，博采各大菜系之所长，是中国八大菜系之一浙菜的江南一帜。选料时鲜、制作精细、原汁原味、清淡适口是其最大特点。杭州地处江南水乡，气候温和，喜食鱼虾，菜肴历来注重原汁原味，讲究南北口味交融，烹饪时轻油腻轻调料，口感鲜嫩，口味纯美，色、香、味俱全。

　　曾担任杭州地方官的苏东坡当年感慨道："天下酒宴之盛，未有如杭城也！"[①]历经创新发展的杭帮菜今天依然受到大众喜爱，人们在欣赏杭州美景的同时一定不会错过品尝杭州的美食。

---

① 东方网.长江美食的和美聚会——纪录片《大江之味》美味收官[EB/OL].（2021-10-15）[2023-04-06]. https://caijing.chinadaily.com.cn/a/202110/15/WS6168e12ba3107be4979f2a66.html.

Chapter Four
City of Gastronomy

With a long history, the earliest Hangzhou food culture can be traced back to Kuahuqiao culture about 8,000 — 7,000 years ago. Since the Tang and Song Dynasties, the economy had become prosperous and crowds of celebrities came to Hangzhou. The development of economy and culture also gave rise to people's demands for material and spiritual enjoyment, especially in clothing, food, dwelling, and festivals and entertainment, among which food played an important role as a medium. Especially after the royal family of the Song Dynasty moved to the south and built its capital in Lin'an, Hangzhou became the political and economic center, and at the same time the culinary skills reached its peak.

Hangzhou cuisine is a school of Jiangnan cuisine, one of the eight major Chinese cuisines, which combines the beauty of the landscape and the strengths of the major cuisines, characterized by fresh ingredients, fine cooking, original taste, and mild flavour. Hangzhou is located in the south of the Yangtze River and has a mild climate, so people like to eat fishes and shrimps. The dishes have always laid emphasis on the original flavor and the blend of northern and southern tastes. With less oil and flavouring, Hangzhou dishes taste fresh and tender, pure and tasty, and are good in color, smell and taste.

Su Dongpo who served as a local official in Hangzhou once said, "The feast in the world is not as prosperous as in Hangzhou!" After experiencing innovation and development, Hangzhou cuisine is still popular today. Therefore, people do not want to miss delicious food while enjoying the beautiful scenery in Hangzhou.

第一节　民间美食与历史故事

杭州菜选料讲究、色彩鲜明、味美香醇、清淡适口、造型优美。杭州作为文化之邦，人杰地灵，许多菜都有源远流长的历史、优美动人的传说，在国内外享有盛誉。

Ⅰ Folk Cuisine and Their Historical Stories

Hangzhou cuisine features exquisite ingredients, bright colors, mellow taste, mild flavor and beautiful shape. As a land of culture, Hangzhou is a good place full of outstanding people. With high reputations at home and abroad, many dishes have long history and beautiful legends.

★ 东坡肉

杭州人如果喜欢一个人，就会用一道美食去永远地纪念他。其中最有代表性的就是一道叫"东坡肉"的杭帮菜。苏轼，号东坡居士，是著名的唐宋八大家之一。苏东坡跟杭州非常有渊源，他曾是杭州的"市长"，在位期间勤政爱民。杭州当地百姓知道苏东坡喜欢吃红烧肉，所以都不约而同地给他送红烧肉，苏东坡又把红烧肉分给了当时建造苏堤的民工。杭州百姓为了纪念苏东坡，让这道肥而不腻的东坡肉一直流传至今。

★ Dongpo Pork

When Hangzhou natives like a person, they will make a delicious meal to commemorate him forever. One of the most representative Hangzhou dishes is called "Dongpo Pork". Su Shi, known by his literary name Dongpo Jushi, was one of the Eight Great Masters of the Tang and Song Dynasties, who had a close connection with Hangzhou. He was the "former mayor" of Hangzhou, who worked hard for people. As the local people learned that he liked to eat braised pork in brown sauce, they all gave him this dish. Then Su Dongpo distributed them to the workers who were building the Su Causeway at that time. To commemorate Su Dongpo, this fatty but not greasy Dongpo Pork has been passed down to this day by people in Hangzhou.

★ 龙井虾仁

据传，乾隆微服游西湖时，天下起了小雨，他到一茶农家中避雨。茶农奉上龙井茶，乾隆尝到如此好茶，喜出望外，又不好意思开口向茶农要。于是趁人不注意时抓了一把茶叶，藏在口袋里。

雨过天晴，乾隆辞别了茶农，继续游览西湖。黄昏，乾隆来到一家小酒馆用膳，点了一道清炒虾仁。点好菜后，乾隆口渴，想起口袋里的龙井茶，便取茶给店小二。店小二看到龙袍一角，吓了一跳，拿了茶叶奔进厨房，正在炒虾仁的厨师听说皇帝到了，惊慌之中把茶叶当作葱花撒进虾仁里，店小二又将"茶叶炒虾仁"端给乾隆。饥肠辘辘的乾隆看到此菜虾仁洁白鲜嫩，茶叶碧绿清香，胃口大开，一尝之下，连称：好菜！好菜！

从此，这道慌乱之中炒出来的龙井虾仁，就成为杭州名菜。

★ Shelled Shrimp Cooked with Longjing Tea

Legend has it that one day Emperor Qianlong made a private tour to the West Lake, then it began to rain, so he ran to a tea grower's home to take shelter. The owner served him with Longjing tea, Qianlong found it tasted so good, and he was overjoyed, but felt embarrassed to ask for tea, so he grabbed a handful of tea leaves and hid them in his pocket before someone noticed.

After rain, Qianlong bade farewell to the owner and continued his tour. At dusk, Qianlong dined at a tavern and ordered a dish of fried shrimps. After ordering the dishes, Qianlong felt thirsty and thought of the Longjing tea in his pocket. He took the tea to the bartender. When the waiter saw a corner of the dragon robe, he was frightened and ran into the kitchen with the tea leaves. When the cook heard that the emperor had arrived, he panicked and threw the tea leaves into the shrimps he was cooking as chopped green onion. The waiter then served the "tea-fried shrimps" to Qianlong. As the hungry Qianlong saw the white and fresh shrimps, and green and fragrant tea, his appetite was simulated. After a taste, he praised, "Good dish! Good dish!"

Since then, Shelled Shrimps Cooked with Longjing Tea made in a fluster has become a famous dish in Hangzhou.

★ **西湖醋鱼**

西湖醋鱼来源于叔嫂传珍的传说。古时候有姓宋的两兄弟，其中宋兄已娶妻。当地恶霸赵大官人在去西湖游玩的路上看中了宋家大嫂，想占为己有，于是用奸计将宋兄害死了。

宋家弟弟和宋兄妻子两人到处告状申冤，但最终求告无门，反而被棒打一顿赶出府衙。后来叔嫂担心被恶霸报复决定逃离住所，临行之时，嫂子给小叔子做了一条鱼，口味又酸又甜，寓意是告诉小叔子人生有酸甜苦辣，并告诫小叔子将来日子过得甜美了也不要忘了哥哥的死、嫂嫂的酸。

最后小叔子考取功名，衣锦还乡，并且报了杀兄之仇，但一直没有嫂嫂的音讯。后来无意中尝到了这道醋鱼，记得这是嫂嫂曾经烧制的味道，与嫂嫂相认，并辞官过起了归隐的生活。

★ **West Lake Fish in Vinegar Sauce**

West Lake Fish in Vinegar Sauce comes from the story of a brother-in-law and a sister-in-law. In ancient times, there were two brothers of the Song family, and the elder brother had already got married. One day the local bully Zhao took a fancy to the wife of the elder brother on his way to the West Lake for play, so he wanted to take possession of her, and killed the elder brother with treachery.

The younger brother and his sister-in-law tried to accuse the suspect of his crime and redress grievances for his elder brother, but had nowhere to turn to for help. Instead, they were beaten and driven out of the Yamen (government office in feudal China). Later, they decided to flee from the residence for fear of being retaliated by bullies. Before leaving, the sister-in-law made a fish with a sour and sweet taste for the brother-in-law, with the implied meaning that life is full of "sour, sweet, bitter and spicy tastes" (joys and sorrows), and warned that one day when the younger brother led a good life, he cannot forget the death of his brother and the bitterness of his sister-in-law.

Finally, the brother-in-law got honor and rank, returned home and avenged the murder of his brother, but he had not heard from his sister-in-law. Later, when he happened to eat the dish of fish in vinegar, it reminded him of the taste of the fish cooked by his sister-in-law. In the end, he came to find his sister-in-law, resigned and led a reclusive life.

★ 干炸响铃

干炸响铃又名炸响铃，采用杭郊泗乡生产的薄如蝉翼的豆腐皮，成品色泽黄亮，鲜香味美，脆如响铃。

相传这道名菜与南宋名将韩世忠有关。一天，韩世忠慕名到郊外的一家酒店用餐，不巧的是招牌菜油炸豆腐皮卖完了，一时没有办法做出，而韩世忠却非常想吃这道菜，店老板只能如实相告，说豆腐皮的原料产自泗乡，如果想吃，只能等到明日再来。韩世忠听后立即起身，骑上响铃毛驴，一阵铃响，不到一个时辰，便将豆腐皮取了来。当得知眼前这位就是大名鼎鼎的韩世忠时，厨师非常感动，就特地将菜做成响铃状，以此表达对他的敬佩和感激。

因为是韩世忠骑着响铃毛驴去取来的豆腐皮，杭州厨师便将这道菜取名为炸响铃，并一直流传至今。又因为响铃炸好后特别松脆，入口"哗哗"作响，所以现在又称为干炸响铃。

★ **Dry Fried Ring Bell (Stir-fried Bean Curd Rolls Stuffed with Minced Tenderloin)**

Dry Fried Ring Bell, also known as Fried Ring Bell, is made of the bean curd skin produced in Sixiang, a suburb of Hangzhou. The bean curd skin is as thin as cicada wings. After being fried, it turns yellow and bright. This dish is fresh, fragrant, tasty and as crispy as a ringing bell.

Legend has it that this famous dish is related to Han Shizhong, a famous general in the Southern Song Dynasty. One day, Han Shizhong went to dine in a restaurant outside the city. Unfortunately, the famous deep-fried bean curd skin was sold out but Han Shizhong wanted very much to eat it. The boss explained that the bean curd skin was from Sixiang and you can come to eat the next day. After learning this, Han Shizhong immediately rose to his feet and rode the donkey with the ringing bell. After less than an hour, Han Shizhong came back and took out bean curd skin. Learning that the man was actually the famous general Han Shizhong, the chef was so moved that he specially made the dishes into the shape of a bell to express his admiration and gratitude.

As the bean curd skin was fetched by Han Shizhong on a donkey with ringing bell, the chef named the dish "Fried Ring Bell", and it has been passed down to this day. And because it was very crispy after being fried, while you eat it, there will a crackling sound, thus it is also called "Dry Fried Ring Bell".

★ **春笋步鱼**

杭州知味观经理董顺翔认为,春笋步鱼成为杭州名菜与唐朝诗人白居易有关。长庆二年(822),白居易任杭州刺史。长庆四年清明节,白居易私下到上塘河附近考察农耕情况。午饭时,进入一农夫家中,看见一位奶奶与成年孙子在吃饭,桌上有一碗野笋炒步鱼。在主人的热情接待下,白居易品尝了野笋炒步鱼,感觉其味无穷。回家之后,白居易命令下人如法炮制了这道菜。

经过白居易的宣扬,多年以后,野笋被改成春笋。从此,春笋步鱼成为杭州名菜。

★ Spring Bamboo Shoots Fried with Odontobutis Obscura

Dong Shunxiang, manager of Zhiweiguan restaurant, attributed the popularity of Spring Shoots Fried with Odontobutis Obscura to Bai Juyi, a poet in the Tang Dynasty. In the second year of Changqing (822), Bai Juyi served as the governor of Hangzhou. During the Qingming Festival in the fourth year of Changqing, Bai Juyi went privately to the Shangtang River to investigate the farming situation. At lunchtime, he entered a farmer's house and saw a grandmother having dinner with her grown-up grandson. On the table there is a bowl of stir-fried Odontobutis obscura with wild bamboo shoots. Warmly received by the host, Bai Juyi tasted the dish and felt it very delicious. After returning home, Bai Juyi ordered his servants to cook the same dish.

After being publicized by Bai Juyi, many years later, wild bamboo shoots were changed into spring bamboo shoots. Since then, Spring Bamboo Shoots Fried with Odontobutis Obscura has become a famous dish in Hangzhou.

★ 宋嫂鱼羹

宋嫂鱼羹是杭州的一道传统名菜，创制于南宋淳熙年间，通常将鳜鱼或鲈鱼蒸熟后剔去皮骨，加上火腿丝、香菇、竹笋末、鸡汤等作料烹制而成。

据载，南宋淳熙六年（1179）三月十五日，宋高宗赵构登御舟闲游西湖，命内侍买湖中龟鱼放生。有一卖鱼羹的妇人叫宋五嫂，在西湖边以卖鱼羹为生。高宗吃了她做的鱼羹，十分赞赏，并念其年老，赐予金银绢匹。从此，宋嫂鱼羹声名鹊起，富家巨室争相购食，成了驰誉京城的名肴。

★ Sister Song's Fish Broth (Braised Fish Soup)

Sister Song's Fish Broth is a famous traditional dish in Hangzhou, created in Chunxi period of the Southern Song Dynasty. The soup is usually made by the process of steaming mandarin fish or sea bass, removing the skin and bones and adding seasonings such as shredded ham, dried mushrooms, bamboo shoots and chicken soup.

It is recorded that on the 15th day of the third month of the lunar calendar, the sixth year of Chunxi in the Southern Song Dynasty (1179), Zhao Gou, Emperor Gaozong of the Song Dynasty, took a boat trip to the West Lake and ordered his servant to buy turtles from the West Lake and put them back to the water. At that time, they met with a woman nicknamed Song Wusao who was selling fish soup by the West Lake and lived on it. Gaozong tasted the fish soup and appreciated it very much. Giving consideration to her old age, Gaozong gave her some money and silk. From then on, Sister Song's Fish Broth won its reputation rapidly, and rich and influential people rushed to taste it. Therefore, it became a famous dish throughout the capital city.

★ 葱包桧

杭州风味小吃葱包桧有一个有趣的传说。1142 年，抗金英雄岳飞以"莫须有"的罪名被害于临安大理寺，杭州百姓十分痛恨秦桧夫妇。相传有一天，杭州一家油炸食品店的业主，捏了两个人形的面块比作秦桧夫妇，将他们揿到一块，用棒一压，投入油锅里炸，嘴里还念道："油炸秦桧，油炸秦桧！"人们理解了他的意思，争相购买油炸桧吃。这就是油条的来历，后来在此基础上发展为杭州风味小吃——葱包桧。

★ Shallot Stuffed Pancake

Hangzhou traditional folk snack—Shallot Stuffed Pancake, has an interesting literary quotation. In 1142, the hero Yue Fei was murdered on trumped-up charge in the Dali Temple (ancient government office) of Lin'an. People in Hangzhou hated Qin Hui and his wife very much. Legend has it that one day a shop owner selling fried food in Hangzhou kneaded two human-shaped noodles to be Qin Hui and his wife. He pinched them together, pressed it with a stick and put them into the frying pan, saying, "Fry Qin Hui! Fry Qin Hui!" People understood his meaning and rushed to buy it. This is the origin of Deep-fried Dough Sticks. Later, Shallot Stuffed Pancake based on this, and developed into a Hangzhou flavor.

★ 定胜糕

定胜糕是一道点心，属杭州菜系。色呈淡红，松软清香，入口甜糯，有甜甜的豆沙味。传说是南宋时百姓为韩家军出征鼓舞将士而特制的，糕上有"定胜"两字，后被称为"定胜糕"。

另一个传说是南宋定都临安（今杭州）后，岳飞为保护国土多次领军出征，杭州百姓沿途都会送上定胜糕，盼其胜利归来。这便是岳飞与定胜糕的故事，流传千年。南宋吴自牧所著《梦粱录》亦有相关记载。

★ Dingsheng Rice Cake (Victory Cake)

Dingsheng Rice Cake is a kind of snack of Hangzhou cuisine with light red. It is soft, fragrant, sweet and glutinous, with a sweet taste of bean paste. Legend has it that the cakes were specially made by people in the Southern Song Dynasty to encourage officers and soldiers of the Han army to go to war. There are two characters "Ding Sheng" on the cake, and it was later called Dingsheng Rice Cake.

Another legend is that after Lin'an (now known as Hangzhou) was established as the capital of the Southern Song Dynasty, Yue Fei sent his troops to wars many times to protect the territory. People in Hangzhou would send Dingsheng rice cakes to officers and soldiers along the way, hoping them to return in victory. This is the true story of Yue Fei and Dingsheng Rice Cake, which has been spread for thousands of years. There are also relevant records in *The Record of Mengliang* by Wu Zimu in the Southern Song Dynasty

★ 叫花童子鸡

相传，古时有一个流落到江南的叫花子，一天由于饥寒交迫而昏倒，难友为他偷来一只小母鸡却又苦于缺锅少灶无法烹制，就用泥把鸡包起来放入火堆中煨烤，剥开食用时，竟意外地发现此鸡香气四溢，味道极好。后来这一方法传到酒楼，经厨师的不断改进，终于成了一道传统名菜。

★ Beggar's Chicken (Baked Chicken)

Legend has it that in ancient times there was a beggar who lived in the south of the Yangtze River. One day he fainted because of hunger and cold. His friend stole a little hen for him, but there was no pot and stove to cook it, so he wrapped the hen in mud and roasted it in the fire. When he opened it to taste, out of his expectation, it is so fragrant and delicious. Later, this method was spread to the restaurant. With the continuous improvement by the chef, it finally became a famous traditional dish.

第二节　风味美食

杭州不仅风景秀丽，而且有着悠久的饮食文化，一直以来被称为"天堂美食之府"。除了上文列出的民间美食外，杭州还有其他特色美食。以下分为风味名菜和地方小吃两类介绍。

Ⅱ Special Delicacies

Hangzhou has not only the beautiful scenery, but also a long history of food culture. It has long been called "a paradise for foodies". In addition to the folk cuisine listed in the previous section, there are other special foods in Hangzhou. The following is a list of two kinds of delicious food: famous flavor dishes and local pastry snacks.

★ 风味名菜
Famous Flavor dishes

▶ 杭州酱鸭

杭州酱鸭是杭州当地著名的美食之一，通常选用当年饲养成熟的鸭子为原料，经过复杂的腌制后将腌过的酱油兑 50% 的水放入锅内煮沸，将鸭放入，用勺舀起卤水不断地浇淋鸭身，至鸭表皮成酱红色时捞出沥干，在日光下晒 2—3 天即成。鸭肉中含有较为丰富的烟酸，它是构成人体内 2 种重要辅酶的成分之一。所以酱鸭不仅美味更有保健的作用，深受人们的喜爱。

▶ Hangzhou Seasoned Duck in Soy Sauce

Hangzhou Seasoned Duck in Soy Sauce is one of the famous local cuisines in Hangzhou, with the well-bred duck as raw material. After being pickled in a series of complex process, the duck will be put into the pot with boiled mixed water which is composed of 50 percent of water and 50 percent of soy sauce which had been used for pickling the duck. Then the duck was constantly sprinkled by the brine in the pot till the surface of the duck became dark brown. Then it was taken out and drained, and dried in the sun for 2 to 3 days. Duck meat is rich in niacin, which is one of the two important coenzymes in the human body. Hence, Hangzhou Seasoned Duck in Soy Sauce is not only delicious but also has the function of health care. It is very popular with people.

▶ 蜜汁火方

蜜汁火方为杭州传统名菜。烹调时，选用金华火腿质地最好的中腰峰雄爿，用冰糖水浸蒸熟，衬以莲子，缀以樱桃、青梅、桂花等精制而成。其特点是色泽鲜艳，汤汁浓稠，咸甜适中，易于消化，特别受老人的欢迎。

▶ Braised Ham in Honey Sauce

Braised Ham in Honey Sauce is a famous traditional dish of Hangzhou. The main ingredient is lumbar crest of Jinhua ham which is the best part of the ham. After being dipped the water with dissolved crystal sugar, it was steamed until it's ready to eat. Then it was laid out on the plate with lotus seeds, cherry, green plum, osmanthus and so on. This dish has bright color and thick soup, and is neither too sweet nor too salty, easy to digest, and especially popular with the elderly.

▶ 蟹汁鳜鱼

蟹汁鳜鱼是杭州南方大酒店研制的，采用活鳜鱼和蟹粉为原料烹制而成，是一道富有江南风味特色的新佳肴。它造型生动、雅致，鱼肉入味滑嫩，蟹肉洁白鲜美，且上桌淋汁，食趣盎然，曾荣获全国烹饪大赛金奖。

▶ Mandarin Fish in Crab Sauce

Mandarin Fish in Crab Sauce is developed by Hangzhou Nan Fang Hotel. It is made of living mandarin fish and crab powder, and is one of the new delicacies with characteristics of Jiangnan flavor. The dish has vivid and elegant shape, with the tender flesh of fish and white and delicious flesh of crab. In addition, it will bring you great fun as it is being drenched in juice on the table. This dish has won the gold medal in the National Cooking Contest.

▶ 蟹酿橙

用鲜活湖蟹肉和橙汁为原料烹制而成的蟹酿橙原系南宋名菜，后经挖掘研制成功后深受国内外宾客的赞扬，曾获第三届全国烹饪大赛金奖，并已入选《中国名菜谱》。此菜色艳味美，风味独特，既有烹饪古籍《山家清供》上所要求的"新酒、菊花、香橙、螃蟹"之美，又因染历史特色而带有时代气息。

▶ Fried Crab Meat Steamed Inside Orange

Fried Crab Meat Steamed Inside Orange, made of fresh lake crab meat and orange juice, is once a famous dish in the Southern Song Dynasty. After being studied and developed continuously, it was praised by domestic and foreign guests. It has won the gold medal in the Third National Cooking Contest, and has been selected into *Chinese Recipes*. This dish is colorful and delicious, having a unique flavor. It has the beauty of the "new wine, chrysanthemum, orange, and crab" required by the ancient book *Shan Jia Qing Gong*, and it also has the flavor of the times because of its historical characteristics.

▶ 清汤鱼圆

清汤鱼圆或称清汤鱼丸,是一道浙江名菜,在全国第二届烹饪大赛和第一届全国青工技能大赛中均获金奖。早在清代,杭州人袁枚所著的《随园食单》"水族有鳞单"中就有记载。经过历代厨师的不懈努力、继承和发展,这道菜的技术水平提高了,足以代表浙菜的发展方向。其特点是清淡,鲜嫩,外观上汤清见底,洁白鱼丸浮于汤面,圆润柔滑,富有弹性,与浅黄色口蘑、绿色菜心相配,给人神清气爽的感觉。

▶ Fish Balls in Light Soup

Fish Balls in Light Soup is a famous dish in Zhejiang. It has won the gold medal respectively in the Second National Cooking Contest and the First National Youth Workers Competition. Early in the Qing Dynasty, it was listed among the "scaly aquatic creatures" in *Shuiyuan Food List* written by Yuan Mei, a native of Hangzhou. After the unremitting efforts, inheritance and development by successive generations of chefs, the technical level of this dish has been improved well enough to represent the future of Zhejiang cuisine. It tastes light and tender and the soup is crystal clear. The smooth and elastic round white fish balls floating on the surface of the soup is a good match for light brown mushrooms and green vegetables, which gives you a refreshing feeling.

▶ 番茄虾仁锅巴

番茄虾仁锅巴是 1956 年浙江省认定的 36 种杭州名菜之一,虾仁玉白鲜嫩,锅巴金黄松脆,番茄红润酸甜,色泽艳丽,享有"天下第一菜"的誉称。烹调时,选用粳米或糯米制成锅巴并炸脆后盛在荷叶碗里,将鲜虾仁勾芡下锅并倒进番茄汁另行装碗。上菜时将番茄虾仁汁倒在锅巴上,锅巴遇汁立即炸裂，发出"吱吱"响声，随之香气四溢，故此菜又叫"平地一声雷"。它既是佐酒佳肴，又能充当点心。

▶ Fried Rice Crust with Tomato and Shrimp

Fried Rice Crust with Tomato and Shrimp is one of the 36 famous Hangzhou dishes recognized by Zhejiang Province in 1956. The shelled shrimp is jade white and tender, the fried rice crust is golden and crisp, and the tomato is rosy, sour and sweet, all of which makes a gorgeous color. This dish enjoys the reputation of "the best dish in the world". To make it, firstly you should choose japonica rice or glutinous rice to be made into rice crust, then fry it, and put it in a bowl paved with a lotus leaf. Secondly, fry the fresh shrimps thickened with starch, and then pour tomato juice into it. When it's ready, take it out and put into another bowl. As the dish is being served, the tomato and shrimp juice will be poured onto the crispy rice. At that moment, the crispy rice will immediately burst, and there will be a squeak followed by the aroma of overflowing, so this dish is also called "a thunder from the ground". It not only goes well with the wine, but also serves as a snack.

▶ 火蹱神仙鸭

火蹱神仙鸭是杭州传统名菜。烹调时，将金华火腿蹱和本地老鸭（麻鸭）置于大砂锅内，再放入调料，密封锅盖，用文火炖烧而成。该菜原汁原汤，既有较高的营养价值，又鲜美可口。

▶ Pig Knuckle Stewed with Duck

Pig Knuckle Stewed with Duck is a traditional Hangzhou dish. To make it, firstly you should put the knuckle of Jinhua ham and local old duck (Mapo duck) in a large casserole, add seasonings, seal the lid of the pot, and simmer it. The dish is not only highly nutritious, but also very delicious.

▶ 虎跑素火腿

虎跑素火腿为杭州传统素食名菜，因它经常在虎跑供应而得名。烹调时，选用杭州泗乡的优质豆腐皮，加上白糖、绍酒、素油、姜汁和红曲粉等调味品，经模型压制，上笼蒸熟即成。此菜色泽酱红，形如火腿，柔中带韧，鲜甜清香，既是有名的素菜，又是携带方便的旅游食品。

▶ Hupao Vegetarian Ham

Hupao Vegetarian Ham is a famous traditional vegetarian dish in Hangzhou. It is so named because it is often served in Hupao. For cooking, you can use high-quality tofu skin from Sixiang of Hangzhou, and then add sugar, Shaoxing wine, vegetable oil, ginger juice and red koji powder and other condiments into it. After being pressed in a mold, it is then steamed. Red in color, shaped like a ham, soft and tough, fresh, sweet and fragrant, this dish is not only a famous vegetarian dish, but also an easy-taking trip snack.

▶ 油焖春笋

油焖春笋是一道颇具杭州特色的传统风味菜肴，属浙菜系。它选用杭州郊区清明前后出土的短壮、皮薄、肉厚、质嫩的春笋为原料，剥净切成寸段状入锅，以重油、重糖煸炒，再用小火焖透的烹饪方法，使笋块充分吸收调味品。成菜色泽红亮，鲜嫩爽口，略有甜味，既可佐酒又可下饭，为杭州传统名菜。

▶ Braised Spring Bamboo Shoots

Braised Spring Bamboo Shoots is a traditional dish with Hangzhou characteristics, which belongs to Zhejiang cuisine. It is made of short, strong, and tender bamboo shoots with thin skin and thick flesh, which are unearthed before Tomb-sweeping Day. After being stripped and cut into inch segments, it will be put into the pot and stir-fried with heavy oil and sugar, and then be stewed thoroughly with a small fire to make the bamboo shoots fully absorb the seasoning. The dish is red and bright in color, tender and refreshing, and a bit sweet. It is a traditional famous dish in Hangzhou, going well with either wine or rice.

▶ 西湖莼菜汤

西湖莼菜汤又称鸡火莼菜汤，是杭州的一道特色名菜。该菜品选用西湖莼菜、火腿丝、鸡脯丝烹制而成。此汤，莼菜翠绿，火腿绯红，鸡脯雪白，色泽鲜艳。西湖莼菜汤不仅因味道清香，营养丰富，富含胶质、维生素而被人赏识，而且有"莼羹鲈脍""莼鲈之思"的典故。这2个词早在《世说新语》中就已出现，成为表达思乡之情的成语。

▶ West Lake Water Shield Soup

West Lake Water Shield Soup, also known as Water Shield Soup Cooked with Chicken and Ham, is a famous special dish in Hangzhou. This dish is made of West Lake water shield, shredded ham and chicken breast. The soup is bright in color with its green water shield, crimson ham and white chicken breast. Water shield soup is appreciated by people not only for its delicate flavor, good nutrition, and rich colloid and vitamin, but also for the allusions of "Water Shield Cooked with Perch" and "the Thought of Water Shield Cooked with Perch", which are selected early in *A New Account of Tales of the World*, and have become idioms to express homesickness.

★ 地方小吃
Local Pastry Snacks

▶ 虾爆鳝面

虾爆鳝面是浙江省杭州市奎元馆的特色传统名食。烹调时，选用粗壮的鲜活黄鳝，斩头截尾剔骨后切成鳝片，用素油爆，荤油炒，麻油浇，直至鳝片黄脆；取鲜活大河虾洗净，加蛋清上浆，清炒至白嫩；精制面条下锅烧后，不粘不糊；用原汁煮面，使面条吸入鳝鱼的香味，汁浓面鲜。虾爆鳝面为奎元馆的宁式名面。

▶ Noodles with Quick-Fried Eel Shreds and Shelled Shrimps

Noodles with Quick-Fried Eel Shreds and Shelled Shrimps is a famous traditional dish in Kuiyuanguan Noodles Restaurant in Hangzhou, Zhejiang Province. For cooking, firstly, choose sturdy and fresh eel, cut off its head and tail, eliminate its bone, and cut the flesh into slices. Secondly, stir-fried with vegetable oil, fried them with meat oil, and poured sesame oil over them until they become golden and crisp. Thirdly, Clean the fresh river prawns, dress them with egg white, and fry them till they become white and tender. Fourthly, the refined noodles are boiled in water till they become neither sticky nor pasty. Finally put the cooled noodles into the wok where the juice of eel slices are still left so that the noodles can inhale the fragrance of the eel. Therefore, the noodles are palatable with thick soup. Noodles with Quick-Fried Eel Shreds and Shelled Shrimps is the famous pastry snack with Ningbo style in Kuiyuanguan Noodles Restaurant.

▶ 片儿川

片儿川是杭州奎元馆的名点，也是杭州的风味小吃。烹调时，选用瘦猪肉片，配以笋片和雪菜，与面条同烧而成。此面肉片鲜嫩，雪菜笋片色泽翠白分明，食之鲜美爽口。

▶ Pian'er Chuan Noodles

Pian'er Chuan Noodles is a famous pastry snack in Kuiyuanguan Noodles Restaurant, and also a flavor snack of Hangzhou. For cooking, lean pork slices, bamboo shoots and pickled mustard greens are chosen to be cooked with noodles. The noodles are fresh and tender, with a sharp contrast in color between green pickled mustard greens and white bamboo shoots, and taste delicious and refreshing.

▶ 知味小笼

知味小笼是杭州知味观的风味小吃。烹调时，选用发酵精白面粉做皮，用鲜肉或鲜肉拌虾仁或鸡肉拌火腿末做馅，在馅料中加入特制肉皮冻，包好后放入特制小蒸笼用急火蒸制而成，可分别称为鲜肉小笼、虾肉小笼、鸡火小笼。这些小笼包子汁多香鲜，皮薄滑韧，口味各异。

▶ **Zhiwei Steamed Buns**

Zhiwei Steamed Buns is a flavor snack of Zhiweiguan Restaurant in Hangzhou. To make it, you can use fermented white flour as skin, and fresh pork, or fresh pork and shrimps, or chicken and chopped ham as stuffing, and then add a kind of special pigskin jelly into it. After the buns are made, they will be put into a kind of tailored small steamer and steamed with a sharp fire. With those three different kinds of stuffing, the steamed buns are respectively called Steamed Buns Stuffed with Fresh Pork, Steamed Buns Stuffed with Shrimps and Steamed Buns Stuffed with Chicken and Ham. They are all very juicy and tasty, with thin and smooth skin, but in different flavor.

▶ **猫耳朵**

猫耳朵是杭州知味观的传统风味小吃。用 500 克上白面粉可制成 900 多个面瓣，再配上鸡丁、火腿丁、香菇、干贝、笋片等作料烹制而成。该小吃面瓣形如猫耳朵，十分精巧，火腿丁像玛瑙，鸡丁似琥珀，汤鲜味美，十分可口。

▶ **Cat-ear Shaped Pasta**

Cat-ear Shaped Pasta is a traditional flavor snack in Hangzhou. To make it, 500 grams of refined white flour are made into more than 900 flour petals, which will be cooked with diced chicken, diced ham, mushrooms, dried scallops, bamboo shoots and other seasonings. The flour petals are shaped like cat's ears with great delicacy. The diced ham is like agate, and the diced chicken is like amber. Along with its soup, this snack is quite tasty.

▶ **南方迷宗大包**

南方迷宗大包选用精白面粉经发酵后做皮，用鲜猪前腿肉、肉皮冻（或用豆沙或用麻芯或用青菜）等做馅，包成后上大笼用急火蒸成。一般 500

克面粉只能做9只大包。它吸取南、北方各种包子的特点，由于它无宗无派，故称迷宗大包。迷宗包子洁白饱满，吃起来松软，富有弹性，价廉物美，实为快餐食品中的佼佼者。

▶ Southern Big Steamed Stuffed Buns Without Sect

To make Southern Big Steamed Stuffed Buns Without Sect, refined white flour is used. As the skin of the buns, the flour should be fermented at first. Fresh fore hock and pigskin jelly (or mashed red bean or mashed sesame or the greens) are used as stuffing. After the buns are made, they will be put into a big steamer and steamed with a sharp fire. Generally, 500 grams of flour can only be made into 9 large buns. It draws the characteristics of all kinds of steamed buns in the north and south of China. As it has no sect, it is called the Big Steamed Stuffed Buns Without Sect. This kind of steamed stuffed bun is the best of the fast food, which is white and plump, soft and elastic, and cheap but excellent.

▶ 吴山酥油饼

吴山酥油饼选用精白面粉为原料，加入食油和成油面，经造型后入油锅炸成。食时，加上细绵白糖。成品起酥，层层叠叠，色泽金黄，脆而不碎，油而不腻，又香又甜，入嘴即化。此饼在吴山一带常有供应，相传清乾隆游吴山时曾品尝过。民间称它为"吴山第一点"。

▶ Wushan Crispy Cake

To make Wushan Crispy Cake, you should select refined white flour as raw material, mix it with cooking oil, and fry it after being molded. When eating, you can add some soft white sugar. Wushan Crispy Cake is crispy and golden, with layer upon layer. It's crispy but not broken, oily but not greasy, fragrant and sweet, and soft and fluffy. It is often available in Wushan area. Legend has it that Emperor Qianlong of the Qing Dynasty once tasted it during his tour to Wushan Hill. It is called "the first pastry snack of Wushan" among the people.

▶ 菜卤豆腐

菜卤豆腐的特色为豆腐软如海绵，卤味鲜香。制作时，将豆腐切成 3 厘米见方的块，取砂锅一只，用竹篾垫底，然后放上豆腐，加上盐和清水，用大火烧涨再转小火煮至豆腐出现蜂窝孔时，捞出沥干水分。将腌雪菜卤过滤煮沸，加入滤干的老豆腐，再煮约半小时定味后即成。

▶ Marinated Tofu

Marinated Tofu is as soft as sponge and tastes quite delicious. To make it, you should cut tofu into small pieces with 3 square centimeters. Then put them into a casserole with bamboo strips padded at the bottom, add some salt and water, and cook it with a high fire till it is boiling. Then turn to a small fire till there are honeycomb holes inside tofu. After that, take them out and drain them. Filter the brine of the pickled potherb mustard and boil it. Finally, put the drained tofu inside it and continue to boil for about half an hour. Marinated Tofu is ready now.

▶ 桂花年糕

桂花年糕是杭州也是江南地区经典的小吃，入口清香，吃后齿颊留香，美味可口，用来待客也很有面子。桂花年糕是一款家常美味点心，主要原料有糯米粉、大米粉等。制作时，将糯米粉、大米粉放入盆内拌匀，加入糖，倒入适量水，拌成松散的糕粉。这道点心健康营养美味，既可当早餐，也可做下午茶小点。

▶ Osmanthus Rice Cake

Osmanthus Rice Cake is a classic snack in Hangzhou and the south of the lower reaches of the Yangtze River. It is fragrant and has a lingering taste after you eat it. It is delicious and you will gain face by treating it to your guests. Osmanthus rice cake is a home-cooked delicious dish. The main ingredients are glutinous rice flour, indica rice flour and so on. To make it, you should put glutinous rice flour and rice flour into a bowl and mix them well, add some sugar, pour an appropriate amount of water, and mix them into loose powder.

This healthy and nutritious snack can be had not only for breakfast but also for afternoon tea.

▶ 西湖藕粉

西湖藕粉是杭州地区名产之一，风味独特，富含营养，旧时是贡粉，为皇家提供。藕是荷花在地下的茎，经特别加工制成的藕粉，呈薄片状，质地细滑，色泽白中透红。食用时只需先用少量冷水调和，再用开水冲调成糊状即可。冲泡后的藕粉晶莹透明，口味清醇，具有一定的营养价值。

▶ Lotus Root Powder of West Lake

Lotus Root powder of West Lake is one of the famous specialties in Hangzhou with unique flavor and high nutrition. In the old times, it was used to be "tribute powder" for the royal family. Lotus root is the underground stem of lotus, whose powder is flaked, smooth, pink and white after being processed in a special way. Before eating, you just need to mix and stir with a small amount of cold water, and then flushed with boiled water to make it mushy. After being brewed, it looks translucent and transparent, tastes smooth and mellow, and has fair nutritive value.

▶ 杭州春卷

春卷，又称春饼、薄饼，是中国民间传统节日食品，流行于中国各地，江南等地尤盛。杭州春卷是杭州人过年时餐桌上少不了的美食。杭州人还喜欢现做春卷，在薄面皮子里卷上冬笋、韭芽等时令菜蔬，再用微火油炸至金黄色，外酥内嫩，又称为"炸春"。除供自己家食用外，也是老底子宴请宾客的最高规格食品。

▶ Hangzhou Spring Rolls

Spring Rolls, also called Spring Pancakes or Pancakes, are traditional food for Chinese festivals, popular in all parts of China and especially prosperous in Jiangnan and other places. Hangzhou Spring Rolls are indispensable food on the dinner table for people in Hangzhou during the Spring Festival. People in Hangzhou like to make Spring Rolls by themselves. Seasonal vegetable like winter bamboo shoots and leek sprouts are rolled inside the thin pasta, and then fried in a low fire till they become golden. They are crispy outside and tender inside, and also called "Fried Spring". Besides serving for their own family, it is also the highest standard for people in Hangzhou to treat their guests in old times.

第三节　知名餐馆

杭州拥有众多特色美食和风味小吃，正是因为杭州拥有许多历史不同、风格各异的餐馆。

Ⅲ Famous Restaurants

Hangzhou boasts so many distinctive delicacies and snacks, just because there are so many restaurants with different histories and styles in Hangzhou.

★ 楼外楼

楼外楼坐落在西湖边、孤山脚下，是杭州历史最悠久的饭店之一，已有 170 多年的历史。楼外楼是由清朝贵族于 19 世纪 40 年代建造的。许多外国贵宾访问杭州时都曾在这里用餐。周恩来、陈毅、贺龙等多位名人也曾到此就餐。

招牌菜：西湖醋鱼、东坡肉、叫花鸡、龙井虾仁、宋嫂鱼羹等

地址：杭州市孤山路 30 号

★ Louwailou Restaurant

Louwailou Restaurant, located by the West Lake and at the foot of Gushan Hill, is one of the oldest restaurants in Hangzhou with a history of more than 170 years. It was built in 1840s by a noble in the Qing Dynasty. Many foreign guests have dined there while visiting Hangzhou, and many Chinese leaders have also been to the restaurant for dinning, including Zhou Enlai, Chen Yi, He Long, and so on.

Signature dishes: West Lake Fish in Vinegar Sauce, Dongpo Pork, Beggar's Chicken (Baked Chicken), Shelled Shrimps with Longjing Tea, and Sister Song's Fish Broth (Braised Fish Soup), etc.

Address: No.30, Gushan Road, Hangzhou City

★ 知味观

知味观是杭州老字号餐饮名店，创办于 1913 年，是杭州知名度极高的餐饮企业。知味观拥有正宗的杭帮菜肴和独特的风味名点，其人气和楼外楼不相上下。知味观菜肴风味各异，不管是哪里的人都能在此找到喜欢的美食。知味观也招待过很多重要人士。知味观在杭州有很多分店，最受欢迎的是西湖边的知味观总部。当你在湖边用餐时，你可以享受到很好的环境和美妙的景色。

招牌菜：龙井虾仁、西湖醋鱼、叫花童鸡、西湖莼菜汤、知味小笼包、猫耳朵

地址：杭州市仁和路 83 号（近东坡路）

★ Zhiweiguan Restaurant

Zhiweiguan Restaurant is a time-honored restaurant in Hangzhou, established in 1913, which is a well-known catering enterprise in Hangzhou. With authentic Hangzhou cuisine and unique pastry snacks, it is as popular as Louwailou Restaurant. The dishes have different flavors, and you can find your favorite food here no matter where you are from. It has also hosted a lot of

VIPs. Zhiweiguan has a number of branches in Hangzhou, the most popular of which is its headquarters near the West Lake. While you are dining by the lake, you can enjoy the nice dining environment and the wonderful view outside.

Signature dishes: Shelled Shrimps with Longjing Tea, West Lake Fish in Vinegar sauce, Beggar's Chicken (Baked Chicken), West Lake Water Shield Soup, Zhiwei Steamed Buns, Cat-ear Shaped Pasta, etc.

Address: No,83, Renhe Road, Hangzhou City (near Dongpo Road)

★ 奎元馆

奎元馆是杭州一家很知名的以面条为主的老字号餐馆，于 1867 年创办。奎元馆经营的面食品种达百种之多，但最负盛名的要数片儿川和虾爆鳝面。

奎元馆的面条都有自己的特色，其选用最好的面粉专人制作。面条要做到下水后烧而不糊，韧而滑口，吃起来有筋。面上的配料也十分讲究，汤是用肉骨头熬出来的，加上点碧绿的葱花，喷香鲜爽，让顾客吃得痛快、舒坦。

1996 年，著名武侠小说家金庸先生在杭州留下了半年内"三顾奎元馆"的佳话。金庸先生一时兴起，在留言簿上写下了"杭州奎元馆，面点天下冠"的题词。

招牌面食：片儿川、虾爆鳝面

地址：杭州市解放路 124 号（近中河高架）

★ Kuiyuanguan Noodles Restaurant

Kuiyuanguan Noodles Restaurant is a well-known time-honored noodle restaurant in Hangzhou, which was founded in 1867. There are as many as 100 kinds of noodles, but the most famous are Pian'er Chuan Noodles and Noodles with Quick-Fried Eel Shreds and Shelled Shrimps.

The noodles at Kuiyuanguan have their own characteristics. Made of high-quality flour, the noodles are made by professionals. Noodles should not be paste after being boiled in water. Instead, it should be tough, slippery and nicely chewy. The ingredients should also be very particular. Soup is boiled out of meat bones, and by adding a little green onion in it, you can feel its fragrance and freshness, which makes you happy and comfortable.

In 1996, Mr. Jin Yong, a famous martial arts novelist, left a good story of "pay visits to Kuiyuanguan noodles Restaurant three times" within half a year during his stay in Hangzhou. Mr. Jin Yong wrote the impromptu inscription "Hangzhou Kuiyuanguan Noodles Restaurant has the best pastry in the world" on the guest book immediately after he tasted the noodle.

Signature dishes: Pian'er Chuan Noodles, Noodles with Quick-Fried Eel Shreds and Shelled Shrimps

Address: No.124, Jiefang Road, Hangzhou City (near Zhonghe Elevated Road)

★ 天香楼

天香楼，创办于 1927 年秋，由苏州陆冷年出资。陆冷年的祖父陆川江清末任苏州知府，民国初迁居杭州。他以唐代诗人宋之问的名句"桂子月中落，天香云外飘"为该店命名。

天香楼开业之初，生意不是特别好，陆冷年受到来西湖游玩的客人喜欢寻购杭州土特产的启示，就决定以杭州风味为特色。陆冷年聘请杭州名厨能师，广搜杭州传统风味于一家。1929 年，杭州举办西湖博览会，国内外宾客纷纷进入天香楼，天香楼的杭帮菜颇受赞誉。1931 年，陆冷年聘请杭州饮食业行家孟永泰经营，数年后，孟永泰积聚财力，从陆冷年手中盘过天香楼。天香楼供应的杭帮菜，口味纯正，特色鲜明。

招牌菜：东坡肉、西湖醋鱼、龙井虾仁、叫花童鸡、干炸响铃、油焖春笋、鲜栗炒子鸡、春笋炒步鱼、火踵神仙鸭

地址：杭州市延安路 447 号

★ Tianxianglou Restaurant

Tianxianglou Restaurant was founded in the autumn of 1927. It was funded by Lu Lengnian from Suzhou whose grandfather Chuanjiang was the governor of Suzhou in the late Qing Dynasty and moved to Hangzhou in the early Republic of China. He named the shop after the famous sentence of Song Zhiwen, a poet of the Tang Dynasty, "On the Mid-Autumn Festival, osmanthus flowers often fall into the temple, and the fragrance of Buddha can float up to the heavens."

At the beginning of its opening, the business was not very good. Enlightened by the visitors' preference to Hangzhou local products when they travelled to the West Lake, Lu Lengnian decided to make the restaurant feature Hangzhou flavor. He employed some famous chefs in Hangzhou, and searched for traditional Hangzhou dishes to make them available in his restaurant. In 1929, when the West Lake Exposition was held in Hangzhou, the guests from home and abroad came to Tianxianglou Restaurant, and Hangzhou dishes there were highly praised. In 1931, Lu Lengnian employed Meng Yongtai, an expert in catering industry, to manage it. Years later, Meng Yongtai accumulated financial resources, and bought the restaurant from Lu Lengnian. Hangzhou dishes in Tianxianglou Restaurant has authentic taste and distinctive characteristics.

Signature dishes: Dongpo Pork, West Lake Fish in Vinegar Sauce, Shelled Shrimps with Longjing Tea, Beggar's Chicken (Baked Chicken), Fried Ring Bell (Stir-fried Beancurd Rolls Stuffed with Minced Tenderloin), Braised Spring Bamboo Shoots, Fried Chicken with Fresh Chestnut, Spring Bamboo Shoots Fried with Odontobutis Obscura, Pig Knuckle Stewed with Duck

Address: No.447, Yan'an Road, Hangzhou City

★ 张生记

张生记创办于 1988 年，是一家新型超大型纯餐饮酒店，以其优质的食材和精湛的制作工艺而著称。张生记所代表的餐饮文化是地地道道的江南特色美食，其中，又以杭帮菜为主打菜色。在众多著名特色杭帮菜中，张生记又以其"笋干老鸭煲"闻名。此道菜鸭汤味道鲜美，有嫩鸭肉、笋干、火腿和芦苇叶，为张生记的美名立下了汗马功劳。

招牌菜：笋干老鸭煲、龙井虾仁、铁板牛仔骨、蟹粉豆腐、小鲍鱼炖鹅掌、红烧肉目鱼头、上汤娃娃菜

地址：杭州市拱墅区双菱路 77 号

★ Zhangshengji Restaurant

Founded in 1988, Zhangshengji Restaurant is a new-type super large pure catering restaurant, famous for its high-quality ingredients and exquisite production technology. The food and beverage culture represented by Zhangshengji is the authentic cuisine with Jiangnan characteristic, among which Hangzhou cuisine is the main dish, as Hangzhou is the birthplace of Zhangshengji. Among so many famous specialties of Hangzhou cuisine in Zhangshengji, the most famous one is Old Duck Soup with Dried Bamboo Shoots. The soup is so delicious with tender duck meat, dried bamboo shoots, ham and reed leaves cooked together. This dish has helped to gain a good reputation for Zhangshengji Restaurant.

Signature dishes: Old Duck Soup with Dried Bamboo Shoots, Shelled Shrimps with Longjing Tea, Sizzling Calf Ribs, Bean Curd with Crab Powder, Stewed Goose Feet with Small Abalone, Braised Squid Head with Pork in Soy Sauce, Braised Baby Cabbage in Broth

Address: No. 77, Shuangling Road, Gongshu District, Hangzhou City

★ 杭州酒家

杭州酒家始建于 1921 年，原名为高长兴酒菜馆，以兼营绍兴陈年黄酒闻名，1951 年更名为杭州酒家，是传统杭帮菜的知名品牌店。

杭州酒家深谙中华饮食之道，主张"饮食多元，顺应四时"，遵循二十四节气变化规律，精选当季食材、时令蔬果，融汇地道杭帮菜烹制技艺，最大限度地保留食材的营养价值，以期得到原汁原味的特色菜品，倡导健康饮食新概念。

招牌菜：龙井虾仁、东坡肉、焖烧南瓜、杭州熏鱼、果木泥烤叫花鸡、文思豆腐

地址：杭州市延安路 205 号 1—3 楼

★ Hangzhou Restaurant

Hangzhou Restaurant was founded in 1921, formerly named Gao Changxing Restaurant, and famous for selling the Old Shaoxing Wine on the side. In 1951, it was named Hangzhou Restaurant. It is a famous restaurant serving traditional Hangzhou dishes.

Hangzhou Restaurant has a deep understanding of Chinese diet, advocating "Diversified diet to comply with the four seasons". Seasonal ingredients, fruits and vegetables should be selected to follow the changing law of twenty-four solar terms. Besides, to keep the original taste of the special dishes of Hangzhou and advocate the new concept of healthy diet, authentic cooking skills are used so as to retain the nutritional value of the ingredients to the greatest extent.

Signature dishes: Shelled shrimps with Longjing Tea, Dongpo pork, Smoldered Pumpkin, Hangzhou Smoked Fish, Roasted Beggar's Chicken Wrapped in the Mud Made of Fruit Wood, Sliced Tofu Soup

Address: 1—3 F, No.205, Yan'an Road, Hangzhou City

★ 皇饭儿

杭城百年老店皇饭儿，又名王润兴，始创于 19 世纪 60 年代，至今已有近 150 年历史，为杭帮菜的龙头菜馆。民间传说乾隆皇帝品尝鱼头豆腐的故事，就发生在这家菜馆里。乾隆皇帝为报答店小二的一餐之赠，亲笔给他题了"皇饭儿" 3 个字。从此，"乾隆鱼头"名扬四海，成为当家名菜。皇饭儿之所以名气震耳，一是其佳肴制作精细、味道鲜美；二是常有名人光顾。

招牌菜：龙井虾仁、杭州酱鸭、乾隆鱼头、宁式鳝丝、八宝酱丁、西湖醋鱼、火腿甜豆、虾爆鳝片

地址：杭州市高银街 53—57 号

★ Emperor's Meal

Emperor's Meal, also known as Wang Runxing, is a time-honored restaurant in Hangzhou. Founded in 1860s, it has a history nearly 150 years up to now. Emperor's Meal is a leading restaurant of Hangzhou dishes. It is where the story of the folklore, Emperor Qianlong tasted Fish Head and Bean Curd Soup, took place. In return for the meal by the shopkeeper, Qianlong personally inscribed three characters "皇饭儿" (Huang Fan Er/Emperor's Meal). From then on, "Qianlong Fish Head" became the specialty dish of the restaurant, which was famous all over the world. Emperor's Meal is so famous not only because foods are delicately cooked and taste delicious but also because it is a favourite haunt of celebrities.

Signature dishes: Shelled shrimps with Longjing Tea, Hangzhou Seasoned Duck in Soy Sauce, Qianlong Fish Head, Shredded Eel with Ningbo Style, Stir-fried Eight Ingredients with Sauce, West Lake Fish in Vinegar Sauce, Fried Sweet Bean with Ham, Quick-Fried Eel Shreds with Shelled Shrimps

Address：No. 53—57, Gaoyin Street, Hangzhou City

★ 龙井菜馆

龙井菜馆，全称杭州龙井菜馆，位于著名的龙井茶文化村，曾荣获首届中国浙江餐饮博览会百佳名店及浙江省餐饮行业服务质量优胜企业。餐馆环抱青山绿水，拥有700多平方米室内营业面积及300多平方米户外休闲区。菜品以农家菜为主，口味清淡。

招牌菜：龙井虾仁、土鸡煲、麻婆鱼、私房香酥骨

地址：杭州市西湖区龙井路1号

★ Longjing Restaurant

Longjing Restaurant, with the full name Hangzhou Longjing Restaurant, is located in the famous Longjing Tea Culture Village. It was awarded among the batch of 100 Famous Restaurants in the first Zhejiang Catering Expo, and the Excellent Enterprise in Service Quality in Catering Industry of Zhejiang Province. The restaurant is surrounded wonderful landscape, with more than 700-square-meter indoor business area and more than 300-square-meter outdoor leisure area. Most of the dishes are farmhouse foods with bland tastes.

Signature dishes: Shelled shrimps with Longjing Tea, Free-range Chicken Pot, Mapo Fish (Stir-fried Fish in Hot Sauce), Home-made Crisp Fried Spareribs

Address: No.1, Longjing Road, Xihu District, Hangzhou City

★ 外婆家

外婆家餐饮集团成立于 1998 年，从最初的马塍路"外婆家"餐厅发展至今，已成为在全国拥有 200 余家门店 10000 多名员工的大型餐饮连锁机构。外婆家以亲民的价格、精心制作的菜肴和优质的服务缔造了 10 多年外婆家吃饭排队的餐饮业神话。不到 100 元就可以品尝到当地最好的食物！外婆红烧肉和剁椒鱼头是菜单上最常点的 2 道菜。龙井鸡是餐厅里最贵的菜。这道菜的独家配方是 2 道杭州传统菜肴——叫花鸡和龙井虾仁的现代结合。在外婆家用餐，会让人有家的感觉。

招牌菜：外婆红烧肉、剁椒鱼头、龙井鸡

杭州部分分店：

杭州大厦 B 座店：拱墅区杭州大厦 B 座 8 楼

杭报店：拱墅区体育场路 218 号（杭州日报大楼裙楼）

湖滨店：上城区湖滨国际美食街湖滨路 3 号 2 楼

万象城店：上城区富春路 701 号杭州万象城 4 楼

萧山店：萧山区北干街道金城路 333 号 3 楼

西溪印象城店：余杭区五常大道 1 号西溪印象城 3 楼

西溪天堂店：西湖区紫荆港路 21 号西溪天堂旅游综合体 20 号楼

★ Grandma's Home (Wai Po Jia)

Grandma's Home (Wai Po Jia) was founded in 1998. Starting from the "Grandma's Home" on Macheng Road, it has developed into a large catering chain with more than 200 stores and more than 10,000 employees across the country. It has 20 branches in Hangzhou City, which is the best place for people to have business banquets and get together with friends. Grandma's Home has created a myth of queuing for dining which has lasted over 10 years, with its affordable prices, elaborately prepared dishes and high-quality services. You can taste the best local food for less than 100 yuan! Grandma's Braised Pork in Soy Sauce and Fish Head with Chopped Peppers are the two dishes ordered most often. Chicken Cooked with Longjing Tea is the most expensive dish in the restaurant. The dish's exclusive recipe is a modern combination of two traditional Hangzhou dishes—Beggar's Chicken and Shelled Shrimp with Longjing Tea. Dining in Grandma's Home makes people feel at home.

Signature dishes: Grandma's Braised Pork in Soy Sauce, Fish Head with Chopped Peppers, Chicken Cooked with Longjing Tea

Some branches in Hangzhou City:

Hangzhou Tower Building B Branch: 8th Floor, Hangzhou Tower Building B, Gongshu District

Hangzhou Daily Branch: No. 218 Stadium Road, Gongshu District (podium building of Hangzhou Daily Building)

Hubin Branch: 2nd Floor, No. 3 Hubin Road, Hubin International Food Street, Shangcheng District

THE MIXC Branch: 4th Floor, Hangzhou MIXC, No. 701 Fuchun Road, Shangcheng District

Xiaoshan Branch: 3rd Floor, No. 333 Jincheng Road, Beigan Street, Xiaoshan District

Xixi Incity Plaza Branch: 3rd Floor, Xixi Impression City, No.1 Wuchang Avenue, Yuhang District

Xixi Paradise Branch: Building 20, Xixi Paradise Tourism Complex, No. 21 Zijinggang Road, Xihu District

★ 新丰小吃

新丰小吃创办于 1958 年，几十年来只做江南小吃，始终坚持传统手工制作。 自杭州新丰小吃股份有限公司成立以来，门店区域持续拓展，已经覆盖全杭城，成为杭城家喻户晓的江南经典小吃品牌。虾肉小笼、虾肉馄饨、牛肉粉丝并称为"新丰小吃明星三大件"，尤以虾肉小笼为特色招牌，其皮薄馅多、汤汁鲜醇，受到众多美食家的极力推荐。特味大包、香菇菜包、虾肉小笼、虾肉馄饨、麻球、牛肉粉丝、喉口馒头入选"中国杭帮菜十大名点"，其中特味大包、虾肉馄饨、喉口馒头被杭帮菜博物馆永久收藏。

新丰小吃获得浙江省工商行政管理局（现为浙江省市场监督管理局）首批颁发的"浙江省知名商号"，先后获得杭州市政府颁发的"新丰小吃大众名品"，行业协会颁发的"中国十佳小吃名店"等荣誉称号。

招牌点心：特味大包、香菇菜包、虾肉小笼、虾肉馄饨、麻球、牛肉粉丝、喉口馒头

杭州部分分店：

保俶路分店：西湖区保俶路 161-1 号商铺

城站分店：上城区环城东路 2-1 号

河坊街分店：上城区中河中路 35 号

丰潭路分店：拱墅区丰潭路 403-4 号

滨盛路分店：滨江区浦沿街道滨盛路 4313 号杭州彩虹农贸市场 1 楼 7 号摊位

★ Xinfeng Snack

Xinfeng Snack originated in 1958. For decades, it only makes Jiangnan snacks and always adheres to traditional craftsmanship. Since the establishment of Hangzhou Xinfeng Snack Co., Ltd., the store area has continued to expand, covering the whole city of Hangzhou, and has become a well-known Jiangnan classic snack brand in Hangzhou. Shrimp Steamed Bun, Shrimp Wonton, and Beef and Vermicelli Made from Bean Starch are known as "3 Star Snacks". Special-flavour Big Bun, Mushroom and Greens Bun, Steamed Shrimp Bun, Shrimp Wonton, Fried Sesame Ball, Beef and Vermicelli Made from Bean Starch, and Houkou Steamed Bun was successively selected "10 Famous Snacks of Hangzhou Cuisine", out of which 3 snacks—Special-flavour Big Bun, Shrimp Wonton, and Hangzhou Steamed Bun have become permanent collections of Hangzhou Cuisine Museum.

Xinfeng Snack is one of the first batch of "Zhejiang Well-known Firm" issued by Zhejiang Administration Bureau of Industry and Commerce (now Zhejiang Administration Bureau of Market Surveillance), and has successively won the honorary titles of "Xinfeng Snack, Famous Brand" issued by Hangzhou Municipal Government and "Top Ten Snack Bars in China" issued by the Industry Association.

Signature snacks: Special-flavour Big Bun, Mushroom and Greens Bun, Steamed Shrimp Bun, Shrimp Wonton, Fried Sesame Ball, Beef and Vermicelli Made from Bean Starch, Houkou Steamed Bun

Some branches in Hangzhou City:

Baochu Road Branch: Shop 161-1, Baochu Road, Xihu District

Chengzhan Branch: No. 2-1 Huancheng East Road, Shangcheng District

Hefang Street Branch: No. 35 Zhonghe Middle Road, Shangcheng District

Fengtan Road Branch: No. 403-4 Fengtan Road, Gongshu District

Binsheng Road Branch: Booth No. 7, 1st Floor, Hangzhou Rainbow Farmers' Market, No. 4313 Binsheng Road, Puyan Street, Binjiang District

第四节　美食街

在杭州这座美丽的城市，想要真正地融入，那就要去逛逛这 10 条最地道的美食街。虽然大多数美食街都非常拥挤和喧闹，但它们是品尝当地美食，了解当地人生活方式的最佳去处。

Ⅳ Famous Food Streets

If you want to really integrate into the beautiful city of Hangzhou, you should visit the 10 most authentic food streets. Although most of them are very crowded and noisy, they are the best places for you to taste local cuisines and get a chance to know how local people lead their life.

★ 中山南路美食街

中山南路美食街又叫南宋御街中华美食夜市，据称全国最长，总共 1400 米，位于河坊街的尽头。

这里汇集了全国各地的美食，街上有装修高档的大酒店，也有价廉物美的大排档，还有小吃摊、烧烤摊，是吃夜宵、喝夜老酒的好地方。如果有喜欢吃羊肉的朋友，必然不能错过这里的羊汤饭店。这是家杭州百年老店，老底子味道，羊肉肉质鲜嫩。尤其是他家的羊肉烧卖，羊肉味浓郁，一口下去吃到嘴里满腔都是羊油香。小吃摊位中，有日本、泰国等国家和地区最具特色的小吃。烧烤摊位中，有韩国、澳大利亚、巴西、俄罗斯、土耳其、牙买加等国家和地区的风味。

地址：杭州市上城区南宋御街（吴山广场，高银街旁）

★ South Zhongshan Road Food Street

South Zhongshan Road Food Street, also known as the Southern Song Imperial Street Chinese Food Night Market, is said to be the longest in China, with a total length of 1,400 meters, located at the end of Hefang Street.

Here is a collection of delicious foods from all over the country. There are luxuriously decorated restaurants, cheap but excellent food stalls, snack stalls and barbecue stalls on the street. It is a good place to eat snack and drink at night. If you like mutton, you must not miss the Mutton Soup Restaurant, a time-honored restaurant in Hangzhou, with the old taste and fresh meat.

Especially its mutton Shaomai (steamed dumpling with the dough gathered at the top) has a strong mutton flavor, which is fragrant with mutton oil once bitten into the mouth. In the snack stalls, there are snacks with the most local characteristics from Japan, Thailand, and other countries and regions. In the barbecue stalls, you can enjoy the flavor of Korea, Australia, Brazil, Russia, Turkey, Jamaica and other countries and regions.

Address: Southern Song Imperial Street, Shangcheng District, Hangzhou City (Wushan Square, next to Gaoyin Street)

★ 胜利河美食街

胜利河美食街亦称古水街，是位于杭州市拱墅区的一条街巷，于 2009 年 12 月底开街。它长 460 米，宽 13 米，东连上塘路，西接德胜巷，沿胜利河北岸而建。古色古香的大运河畔，满街的红灯笼亮起来，既市井又不失文艺。这里有 30 余家知名餐馆入驻，如许府牛杂、老头儿油爆虾、小绍欣、鑫隆鸡爪王、南翔馆、胖哥肉蟹煲等。这里的美食包括上海南翔小笼包、牛肉面、臭豆腐等。沿街还有很多工艺品出售，可以买一些作为旅行的纪念品，或者作为礼物送给家人和朋友。

地址：杭州市霞湾路南侧（上塘路万安桥）

★ Shenglihe Food Street

Shenglihe Food Street, also known as Gushui street, is a street in Gongshu District of Hangzhou, opened at the end of December, 2009. It is 460 meters long and 13 meters wide, connecting Shangtang Road in the east and Desheng Lane in the west. It is built along the north bank of the Shengli River. Along the ancient Beijing-Hangzhou Grand Canal, the street is full of lighted red lanterns, which is not only civic but also literary and artistic. There are more than 30 well-known restaurants in the street, such as Xu's Beef Offal, Old Chap Sauteed Shrimps, Xiao Shaoxin, Xinlong Chicken Claw King, Nanxiang Restaurant, Fat Brother Meat Crab Pot, etc. Cuisines here include Shanghai Nanxiang small steamed buns, beef noodles, and stinky tofu, etc. There are also many artware for sale along the street. You can buy some as souvenirs of your trip or as gifts for your family and friends.

Address: South of Xiawan Road, Hangzhou City (Shangtang Road—Wan'an Bridge)

★ 河坊街

杭州夜市美食街里，名声最大的自然是河坊街、高银街一带。作为南宋皇城根下第一街，繁华热闹的河坊街经改造以后现在是一条明清仿古步行街。河坊街全长 1800 多米，吴山广场至中山中路段为步行街。河坊街里藏着无数的传统美食，如定肺糕、葱包桧、臭豆腐、酥油饼、酱鸭、酱肉、咸肉蒸河虾、咸肉蒸湖蟹药膳、龙须糖等，还有羊肉串、牛肉串、竹筒饭、冰糖葫芦、棉花糖、炸鱿鱼、烤猪脚、酸辣粉等，更有撕下一块就香气四溢的叫花鸡。

河坊街还有另一令人咋舌的美食——昆虫宴！有蚕蛹、蜈蚣、蝎子、知了、蜘蛛等。大多昆虫都采用了油炸的方法，入口非常酥香。

地址：杭州市吴山广场附近

★ Hefang Street

Among all the night food streets in Hangzhou, the most famous is undoubtedly in the area of Hefang Street and Gaoyin Street. As the first street in the Southern Song Dynasty Imperial City, the bustling and lively Hefang Street is now a pedestrian street with the style of Ming and Qing Dynasties after reconstruction. Hefang Street has a total length of more than 1,800 meters. The section from Wushan Square to Zhongshan Middle Road is a pedestrian street. There are numerous traditional foods in Hefang Street, such as Dingsheng cake, Shallot Stuffed Pancake, Stinky tofu, Crispy Cake, Duck Seasoned in Soy Sauce, Pork Seasoned in Soy Sauce, Bacon Steamed with Shrimps, Medicated Diet of Bacon Steamed with Lake Crab, Candy with Silky Skin. Besides, there are Mutton String, Beef String, Bamboo Rice, Bingtanghulu (Candied Haws on a Stick), Spun Sugar, Fried Squid, Roasted Pork Knuckle, Hot and Sour Rice

Noodles, etc. What's more, there is extremely fragrant Beggar's Chicken.

There is another kind of breathtaking food—insect feast! They are silkworm pupa, centipede, scorpion, cicada, spider and so on. Most insects are fried so that they taste extremely crispy and fragrant.

Address: near Wushan Square, Hangzhou City

★ 近江海鲜城大排档

近江海鲜城大排档于 2006 年 6 月在一块空地上开张，以新鲜的舟山直运海鲜、地道的口味和超高的性价比，逐渐赢得了杭州人民的喜爱，成为杭城最早的"不夜城"。后来逐渐改造，搭起了 2 层小楼，也有了包厢和独立卫生间，直到 2018 年 12 月，由于拆迁规划，近江海鲜城在望江地区完成了最后一天营业。

1 年后，近江海鲜城大排档在紧挨着西湖和湖滨繁华商业区的涌金广场重新开业，营业面积达 7000 多平方米，是原来规模的 2 倍。搬迁后的海鲜城继续使用"近江海鲜城大排档"的名字，有原来的老品牌经营户，也有新的品牌入驻，成了杭州西湖边另一道亮丽的风景线。

地址：杭州市延安路 135 号涌金广场 1 楼

★ Jinjiang Seafood Stall

Jinjiang Seafood Stall was open in June, 2006 on a vacant lot. With fresh seafood directly shipped form Zhoushan, authentic taste and great value, it gradually won its popularity with people in Hangzhou, and became the first "City Without Night" in Hangzhou. Later, a two-story building was built on the site with several rooms and a toilet. In December 2018, due to the demolition plan, Jinjiang Seafood City finished its last day of business in Wangjiang area.

After a year, Jinjiang Seafood Stall was reopened in Yongjin Plaza, next to the West Lake and Hubin downtown, with a business area of more than 7,000 square meters, twice the original size. After the relocation, the original name "Jinjiang Seafood Stall" is still in use. Beside the former operators, some new operators located there. Jinjiang Seafood Stall has become another beautiful scenic spot by the West Lake in Hangzhou.

Address: 1F, Yongjin Plaza, No.135, Yan'an Road, Hangzhou City

★ 惠兴路吴山夜市

吴山夜市位于杭州仁和路的东段（到东方金座止）和惠兴路上。总长度不超过 200 米，在 200 米的街道上挤进了大大小小 400 个摊位，是杭州城里最早、最出名的一个夜市。从最开始吴山路上卖古董、丝绸，做外国人和游客的生意，到后来发展到仁和路、惠兴路一带，卖舶来品和潮品，做女生和潮人们的生意。再后来，在这里吃吃喝喝轧马路买东西，可以打发一个晚上。吴山夜市早已成为杭州的一个传奇。在这里几乎可以找到所有的小吃，比较典型的有章鱼小丸子和热干面。这里的美食味道好，价格也十分实惠。

地址：杭州市仁和路、惠兴路（工人文化宫前）

★ Wushan Night Market on Huixing Road

Wushan Night Market is located in the eastern section of Hangzhou Renhe Road (to the Oriental Golden Plaza) and Huixing Road, with a total length of less than 200 meters. There are 400 stalls of different sizes on the 200-meter-long street. It is the earliest and most famous night market in Hangzhou. At the very beginning, antique and silk were sold there and the customers were mainly foreigners and tourists. Then, Wushan night market moved and extended to Renhe road and Huixing Road, with imported and fashionable goods for sale, and its target customers are girls and fashion lovers. Later, you can spend the whole night eating, drinking and shopping here. Nowadays it has become a legend in Hangzhou. You can find almost all kinds of snacks here, such as Small Octopus Balls and Hot and Dry Noodles. Foods here are delicious and affordable.

Address: Renhe Road and Huixing Road, Hangzhou City (in front of Workers' Cultural Palace)

★ 百井坊巷美食街

百井坊巷美食街在杭城最繁华的武林广场附近，靠近银泰百货，是唯一一条地处杭城黄金地段的美食街，一边是个性潮流服饰的天堂，另一边是小吃美食的聚集地。在逛街逛到筋疲力尽的时候，可以去百井坊巷寻找美食，休息一下。

这条街的店面都比较小，但是有大家喜欢吃的商户入驻，比如精武面馆、骨头饭、老诚一锅羊蝎子等。三五好友逛街之余小聚，选择这样的店真心不错。

地址：杭州市拱墅区百井坊巷和延安路交叉口

★ Baijingfang Lane Food Street

Baijingfang Lane Food Street is located near the most prosperous Wulin Square in Hangzhou, close to Intime Department Store. It is the only food street in the golden area of Hangzhou. On one side, it is a paradise for personalized and fashionable clothing; and on the other side, it is a gathering place for snacks and food. When you are exhausted after shopping, you can go to Baijingfang Lane to find delicious food and have a rest.

The restaurants in this street are relatively small, but there are some popular restaurants such as Jingwu Noodle Restaurant, Bone Rice, Laocheng Lamb Spine Hot Pot, etc. It's really good for a handful of friends to get together to eat there after shopping.

Address: Intersection of Baijingfang Lane and Yan'an Road, Gongshu District, Hangzhou City

★ 竞舟路美食街

竞舟路美食街位于杭州城西，街道两边饭馆的装修很有特点，味道也各具特色。随着竞舟路美食口碑相传，加上城西一带居住人口比较多，竞舟路美食街坐稳"城西第一美食街"的宝座，连不少留学生都会慕名而来。这条街的特色在于各地风味的馆子都有，省内省外的，甚至还有不少异国的。

从街头走到街尾，好像随时都能进入一个不同的时空，菜色多得让味蕾都来不及反应。

地址：杭州市西湖区竞舟路

★ Jingzhou Road Food Street

Jingzhou Road Food Street is located in the west of Hangzhou City. The restaurants on both sides of the road are furnished with their own characteristics and provided distinctive flavor. As the food in Jingzhou road is passed from mouth to mouth, coupled with the increasing population in the west of the city, Jingzhou Road Food Street has become "the first food street in the west of the city". Many international students are attracted to come. This street features all kinds of local restaurants inside and outside Zhejiang Province, and there are even a few restaurants with exotic flavor.

Walking down the street, you will feel like entering another time and space, and your taste buds will have no time to react to so many dishes.

Address: Jingzhou Road, Xihu District, Hangzhou City

★ 河东路美食街

在杭州，有一条路被誉为杭州人的食堂，它就是河东路。河东路上最多的就是小吃店、面馆，还有海鲜馆子。口味基本上囊括整个浙江的美食，你想吃的应有尽有，尤其是一些温州的海鲜。来这里可以尝尝排长队的梁大妈妈菜馆、知名老字号老昌盛面馆等等。这里夜宵的香气和味道，好像勾走了吃货们的魂魄，也勾起了老杭州人的怀旧思绪。这条街的建筑和装饰是复古的，但是环境非常嘈杂，体现了中国人的市井生活。

地址：杭州市拱墅区河东路（近朝晖路）

★ Hedong Road Food Street

In Hangzhou, there is a road known as the canteen of Hangzhou locals, which is "Hedong Road". Hedong Road is dominated by snack bars, noodle restaurants, and seafood restaurants. You can taste almost all types of Zhejiang cuisine, especially some seafood from Wenzhou, which are extremely delious.

You can try Liang Da Mama Restaurant for which you have to wait in long queue, the time-honored Laochangsheng Noodles Restaurant and so on. The aroma and taste of the night snack here seem to hook the soul of the foodies and also remind the natives of Hangzhou of their nostalgic thoughts. The buildings and decorations are vintage, but the environment is very noisy. That's just the civic life of Chinese people.

Address: Hedong Road, Gongshu District, Hangzhou City (near Zhaohui Road)

★ 大兜路美食街

大兜路美食街位于大兜路历史街区，从运河大关桥至江涨桥段东岸，街区全长约 780 米，于 2010 年 9 月底开街。全新修复的大兜路历史街区西面是运河，东面是商铺。整条街既开阔又整齐，风格统一的仿古建筑，让这里的每一家店都具有了一种与众不同的气质。

除了绿茶餐厅和江南驿这些比较实惠的大众餐饮品牌，还有一些颇具品质的餐饮会所，如禧堂·私宴。最重要的是，在这儿吃饭，绝对不用遭遇人挤人的烦恼。即使你选的是要排队的绿茶餐厅，也同样可以先领号，然后悠闲地到运河边看着风景等叫号。

地址：杭州市拱墅区大兜路（运河大关桥至江涨桥段东岸）

★ Dadou Road Food Street

Dadou Road Food Street is located in the Dadou Road Historical and Cultural District, the east bank of the section of the Grand Canal from Daguan Bridge to Jiangzhang Bridge, with a total length of about 780 meters. It was open at the end of September, 2010. The newly renovated Dadou Road Historical and Cultural District has the Grand Canal in the west and some shops in the east. The whole street is wide and tidy, and the antique buildings with unified style give every shop here a kind of distinctive temperament.

In addition to popular and affordable restaurants like Green Tea and Jiangnan Post, there are also some restaurants with a sense of quality, such as

Xitang (Private Banquet). The most important thing is that you don't need to feel annoyed by so many people around when you eat here. Even if you choose Green Tea for which you need to queue up, you can get the number first, and then go to the Grand Canal to enjoy the scenery and wait for your turn at the same time.

Address: Dadou Road, Gongshu District, Hangzhou City (the east bank of the section of the Grand Canal from Daguan Bridge to Jiangzhang Bridge)

★ 高银街美食街

杭州有一条遍布美食的街，从南宋火到现在，它就是高银街。说起高银街的来历，还真和"吃"脱不了关系。最早的时候，这里叫肉市巷，又称灌肺岭，以出售糯米灌猪肺出名。南宋时，一个姓高的人捡到了银子，做了拾金不昧的好事，这里就改名为高银街。

在这条美食街上，散布着川、鲁、闽、粤、浙等菜系，涵盖素菜、海鲜、快餐等20多家风味餐馆。来高银街落户的不仅有老字号皇饭儿、知味观，而且有后起之秀木杨城、东伊顺等酒楼，更有数家小吃店。由于背靠河坊街，又离火车站特别近，到这里吃饭的游客总是络绎不绝。

地址：杭州市上城区清河坊历史街区

★ Gaoyin Street Food Street

In Hangzhou, there is a street full of delicious food and popular from the Southern Song Dynasty to this very day, which is Gaoyin street. Speaking of the history of Gaoyin street, it really has something to do with "eating". In the early days, it was called Roushi Lane, also known as Guanfeiling. It was famous for selling pig lungs filled with glutinous rice. In the Southern Song Dynasty, a man surnamed Gao picked up silver and returned it to the owner, so it was changed to name Gaoyin Street.

In this food street, there are more than 20 restaurants and you can taste various kinds of cuisines such as Sichuan, Shandong, Fujian, Guangdong, and Zhejiang cuisine with varieties of dishes like vegetable, seafood, fast food and so on. There are not only time-honored restaurants such as Emperor's Meal and Zhiweiguan Restaurant, but also up-rising start restaurants such as Muyangcheng and Dongyishun, as well as some snack bars. As it is behind Hefang Street and near to the railway station, there is always a constant stream of tourists dining here.

Address: Qinghefang Historical and Cultural District, Shangcheng District, Hangzhou City

第五章　购物之城

　　杭州传统的百货商场主要集中在商业中心延安路沿线，武林、湖滨和吴山这三大商圈聚集了杭州大厦、银泰百货、国大城市广场、利星名品广场、解百新元华、解放路百货大楼等商场商厦。近些年，随着杭州城市的不断扩展，不少传统百货公司纷纷在城市不同区域开出了新的分部，并紧跟时代步伐，在保留传统商场的同时，逐步演变为大型购物中心。

Chapter Five
Paradise for Shopping

The traditional department stores in Hangzhou, such as Hangzhou Tower, Intime Department Store, Guoda Plaza, Lixing Plaza, Jiebai Xinyuanhua, Jiefang Road Department Store and so on, are mainly concentrated in the three major shopping areas of Wulin, Hubin, and Wushan in the downtown along Yan'an Road. In recent years, with the continuous urbanization, most of these traditional department stores have opened new branches in different areas of the city; while retaining their traditional business, they have evolved into super shopping malls to keep pace with the times.

第一节 传统百货

Ⅰ Traditional Department Stores

★ **杭州解百**

　　杭州解放路百货商场（简称"解百"），位于上城区，紧邻西湖。解百前身为诞生于1918年的"浙江省商品陈列馆"，1928年更名为"国货陈列馆"。中华人民共和国成立后更名为"百货公司"，是杭州市最早建立的国营零售商店。1958年正式更名为"杭州解放路百货商店"，1992年改制为股份有限公司。近些年来，结合杭州"生活品质之城"的城市品牌、消费需求的变化和所处的地理位置贴近西湖等优势，公司确立了"精致生活、休闲人生"的经营定位，以具有一定消费能力、追求生活品质的中青年白领为主力消费群，实施品牌经营战略，创新营销服务，全力打造品牌经营氛围浓郁、市场活力强劲的现代百货商场，一大批国内外知名品牌进驻，成为一个传递现代生活理念、引领时尚的窗口。公司先后荣获"中国服务业500强企业""中华老字号百强企业""中国商业服务名牌""全国商业顾客满意企业"等荣誉称号，并被商务部评定为"金鼎百货店"。

★ **Jiefang Road Department Store (Jiebai)**

　　Jiefang Road Department Store, short for Jiebai, is situated in Shangcheng District and close to the West Lake. Jiebai was known as "Zhejiang Commodity Exhibition Hall" founded in 1918. In 1928, it was renamed as "Domestic Goods Exhibition Hall". After the founding of the People's Republic of China in 1949, it was given a new name "Department Store", being the earliest state-owned retail store in Hangzhou. In 1958, it was officially and finally named "Jiefang

Road Department Store". In 1992, it was restructured as a limited-liability company. In recent years, taking into account the changes of the consumers' demands, and the city's proposal of "building a city of high quality life", the company has established the "refined and leisure life" orientation, targeting at those young and middle-aged white-collar workers pursuing a quality life, by means of implementing brand strategy and innovating marketing. A large number of well-known brands at home and abroad have entered Jiebai, making it a window to demonstrate the concept of modern life and fashion trend. The company has been one of "China's Top 500 Service Enterprises", "China's Top 100 Time-honored Enterprises", "China's Famous-brand Commercial Enterprises", "China's Famous Brands for Commercial Service", "National Customer Satisfaction Enterprises", etc., and won the prize of "Jinding (Gold Tripod) Department Store" (the highest rank for department store in China) awarded by the Ministry of Commerce.

★ 杭州大厦

杭州大厦地处杭州商贸中心武林广场，紧邻京杭大运河和西湖两大世界文化遗产，是一家以零售百货业为主体，集多项经营功能为一体的大型零售服务企业。自1988年开业以来，逐步发展成全国高端精品百货业的领军力量，成功缔造了"高端百货＋奢侈品"的精品百货模式，树立起了行业风向标，网罗了LV（路易威登）、Chanel（香奈儿）、Hermes（爱马仕）、Cartier（卡地亚）、Gucci（古驰）、Bottega Veneta（葆蝶家）等国际顶级奢侈品品牌及国内众多知名品牌，成为高端商务人士杭州购物的理想之地。杭州大厦曾连续8年蝉联全国大型百货商场单店销售第一名。2018年，杭州大厦购物城以销售额656884万元位列中国零售百强名单第81位。[①]

★ Hangzhou Tower

Hangzhou Tower, situated in the commercial center of Wulin Square and

---

[①]CGCC, CNCIC. 2018年度中国零售百强［EB/OL］.（2019-09-07）［2023-04-06］. https://www.cncic.org/?p=2116.

close to the two World Cultural Heritage sites, the Beijing-Hangzhou Grand Canal and the West Lake, is a large retail enterprise integrated with department store as the main body and a number of other businesses. It was opened in 1988, and since then it has gradually taken the lead in the national high-end department store industry, successfully creating the boutique department store model of "high-end department store plus luxury goods" and setting an example for the industry in China. It has gathered a great number of international top luxury brands such as LV, Chanel, Hermes, Cartier, Gucci, Bottega Veneta, as well as many well-known domestic brands, having long been an ideal place for high-end business people to shop in Hangzhou. Hangzhou Tower has been ranked first in single store sales of large department stores in China for eight consecutive years. In 2018, Hangzhou Tower ranked the 81st in China's top 100 retail enterprises with a sales volume of over RMB 656 million yuan.

★ 银泰百货

1998 年 11 月，银泰百货（简称"银泰"）首家门店及旗舰店杭州武林银泰百货商场开业，营业面积 35 万平方米。银泰百货以"传递新的生活美学"为理念，以年轻人和新型家庭为主要客户群，树立"年轻活力、时尚品位"的百货形象。经过 20 多年的发展，武林银泰百货历久弥新，店内多个品牌业绩创下全国最高销售纪录。以销售额计算，银泰百货已成为浙江省内最大的百货连锁企业。作为独具银泰商业文化特色的知名百货连锁品牌，银泰百货被认为是中国零售百货业的标杆，以独具魅力的流行、时尚元素改变了人们的生活，推动了中国城市新时尚文化建设。目前全国各地共分布了 58 家银泰百货商场，[①] 营业面积、经营业绩和业务创新能力皆居中国零售业前茅。近些年来，百货整合优化供应链，银泰创新新零售，推出多个"互联网＋"产品，着力打造智能化新商场，开创了线上线下融合的购物场景和运营模式。

---

① 银泰.银泰服务全门店导览［EB/OL］.［2023-04-06］. https://www.intime.com.cn/store.

★ Intime Department Store

Intime Department Store (generally short for "Intime") opened its first and flag store in Wulin shopping area in November 1998, with a business area of 350,000 square meters. It holds the concept of "spreading new life aesthetics", taking the young people and new families as the mainstream of customers, and building an image of "young and vital, stylish and tasteful". Intime Department Store has achieved substantial growth ever since its opening; and especially, some brands in this flag store have set the sales record in China. To adjust to the demands of the market, Intime has evolved into the mode of chain operation. In terms of sales, it has become the largest department store chain enterprise in Zhejiang Province. As a well-known brand with unique commercial and cultural characteristics, Intime is said to have become the benchmark of the department store industry in China, and it's no exaggeration that Intime has changed the Chinese people's life to some degree, promoted the fashion in Chinese cities with its unique fashion concept and elements. At present, 58 stores are distributed all over the country, with the business area, performance and innovation among the best in China's retail industry. In recent years, Intime has optimized the supply chain, launched new retail and introduced a number of "Internet plus" products, attempting to build new intelligent shopping centers and create an "online plus offline" shopping experience.

★ 豫丰祥

百年杂货店豫丰祥位于中山中路繁华商业区，因其冬令商品质优价廉，一直深受杭州市民欢迎，尤其受中老年人的青睐。

在护肤品中，国产品牌孔凤春是畅销品，几十年不变的是面霜称重售卖。顾客既可以购买包装产品也可以携带空瓶零买。除孔凤春外，豫丰祥也出售其他品牌的面霜，尤其是雅霜、百雀羚和友谊等老牌产品。

★ **Yu Fengxiang**

A century-old grocery located in a prosperous commercial block on Middle Zhongshan Road, thanks to its winter goods with satisfactory quality and favorable prices, the shop has been popular among the locals for several decades, especially among those above middle-age.

Among all the skin care products that the shop supplies, the home-made face-cream brand Kong Fengchun is the best seller. Part of its rarity may lie in the fact that the face-cream is sold by weight, as was done decades ago. Customers would either bring their own containers to the store for a refill or buy packed ones. Besides Kong Fengchun, Yu Fengxiang offers other types of face cream, especially some time-honored brands, such as Yashuang, Pechoin and Youyi, etc.

第二节　购物中心

进入 21 世纪后，特别是近些年来，随着社会、经济的发展，以及人们生活、消费需求和理念的不断变化，集购物、餐饮、休闲、娱乐和观光旅游等为一体的"一站式"消费购物中心在杭州不断涌现。杭州传统的百货业如杭州大厦、银泰百货等在保留传统百货业的同时，也在不断拓宽业务，相继开发了多家购物中心。在杭州各城区落地开业的购物中心有银泰城、国大广场、工联 CC、万象城、印象城、来福士、龙湖天街、宝龙城、大悦城、嘉里中心、万达广场、港龙城、乐堤港、西田城、天阳 D32、亲橙里等，还有大批在建设或规划落地中。位于这些购物中心或独立成为市场的大型超市有世纪联华、华润万家、沃尔玛、山姆会员店、永辉、大润发、欧尚、物美等，除此之外，还有全球知名的商业巨头，如家具和家居零售商宜家等。

在这些购物中心，除了购物和休闲娱乐，还可以品尝杭州及全国各地乃至国外的著名美食，以及观看文化演出等。这些购物中心成为人们节假日聚会放松的理想之地。

Ⅱ Shopping Malls

In the 21st century, especially in recent years, with the development of the society, the booming of economy, and the changes of people's living standards, and consumer needs and ideas, one-stop shopping malls integrating shopping, catering, recreation, entertainment and sightseeing have sprung up all over Hangzhou. The traditional department stores, such as Hangzhou Tower and Intime Department Store, have opened many shopping centers and malls in succession while maintaining their traditional department store business. There are dozens of shopping centers and malls in Hangzhou, such as Intime City, Guoda Plaza, Gonglian CC, The Mixc, Incity, Raffles, Paradise Walk, Power Long City, Joy City, Kelly Center, Wanda Plaza, Parc Mall, Grand Canal Place, Citymall, Tianyang D32, Qinchengli, etc., with many more still under construction or in planning.Large supermarkets in these malls or those as independent markets elsewhere include Century Mart, Vanguard Mart, Wal-Mart, Sam's Club, Yonghui, RT-Mart, Auchan, Wumart, as well as the well-known Swedish furniture and home furnishing giant retailer IKEA.

In these shopping centers and malls, besides shopping, people can taste Hangzhou cuisine and other famous cuisines from all over the country even abroad, as well as watch performances and visit various exhibitions, making the malls preferable places for holiday.

第三节 特色购物街

杭州自古商业发达，特别是改革开放以来，逐步形成了一批独具特色的市场和购物街，如杭州中国丝绸城、四季青服装特色街区、武林路时尚女装街区等。

Ⅲ Specialty Commercial Streets

Hangzhou has long been prosperous in commerce, especially since the reform and opening up, and it has gradually bred a number of characteristic markets, shopping streets and blocks, such as Hangzhou • China Silk Town, Sijiqing Clothing Market Block, and Wulin Road Women's Fashion Block, etc.

★ 杭州中国丝绸城

杭州被誉为"丝绸之府"。杭州中国丝绸城建于 1987 年，是杭州起步最早的商业特色街，位于凤起路以北，体育场路以南的西健康路、健康路及新华路一带，占地面积约 2.5 万平方米，400 多家丝绸商户进驻营业，包括知名厂商凯喜雅、都锦生等。[①]

古朴典雅的建筑风格、底蕴浓厚的文化气息、绚丽多彩的商品展示等特点，使丝绸特色街成为一条充满江南婉约之风和丝绸柔性之美的"丝绸

---

① 马赛洁，王逸群，金焕英，等. 杭州丝绸城步行街焕新升级今晚开街 有啥亮点看过来［EB/OL］.（2020-11-19）［2023-04-06］. https://appm.hangzhou.com.cn/article_pc.php?id= 351797.

之路"，海内外游客络绎不绝。丝绸城经营的各种真丝面料、丝绸服装、丝织工艺品、围巾、领带、丝绸原料及各类纺织品，辐射全国城乡，远销欧美及东南亚地区，广受欢迎。

近来，经过不断提升改造，丝绸城推出线上线下融合展销模式。丝绸城精品馆展出了来自柬埔寨、老挝、意大利、巴西、孟加拉国等多个国家的丝绸产品。

杭州中国丝绸城正逐步成为全国丝绸的购物中心、丝绸新产品信息中心、丝绸服饰演示中心和丝绸文化展示中心。

★ Hangzhou • China Silk Town

Hangzhou has long been known as the "Capital of Silk". Hangzhou • China Silk Town, founded in 1987, is the earliest specialty commercial block in Hangzhou. It is located in the area between the north of Fengqi Road and the south of Tiyuchang Road, including West Jiankang Road, Jiankang Road and Xinhua Road along with the adjacent areas, covering an area of about 25,000 square meters with over 400 commercial tenants, including top labels such as Cathaya and Du Jinsheng.

With its classical and elegant architectural style and colorful silk commodity display, this modern "silk road" combines the graceful, restrained style of Jiangnan with the soft, gentle beauty of silk, attracting large number of tourists from home and abroad. Various kinds of silk fabrics, silk garments, silk handicrafts, scarves, neckties, silk raw materials and textiles are sold to Europe, the United States, Southeast Asia, enjoying great popularity.

Upgraded and retrofitted in recent years, the silk town has introduced the technology of "Internet plus" to promote its business and culture. In the Boutique Museum of China Silk Town, silk products from Cambodia, Laos, Italy, Brazil and Bangladesh, etc. are exhibited.

China Silk Town has developed into a national center for silk shopping, an information center for new silk products, and a demonstration center for Chinese silk clothing and silk culture.

★ 四季青服装特色街区

杭州四季青服装特色街区位于杭海路西，全长约 1100 米。从 20 世纪 80 年代末开设第一家服装市场开始，逐步发展为全国规模最大的服装集散地之一，汇集了四季青服装市场、杭派精品服装市场等 15 家专业服装市场，云集了众多国内外知名品牌，拥有注册商标近 1000 个，形成了一批较有影响的自主品牌及一大批国内外著名品牌的特约总经销、总代理。① 街区内的杭派女装和四季青服装辐射全国主要大中城市，遍及全国的加盟店、连锁店、专柜等，已形成一个覆盖全国的立体销售网络。

街区依托当地雄厚的产业基础和华东第一大服装市场的先发优势、集聚优势，以整体的品牌战略形成一个互动的产业价值链，有效地拉动了相关产业的蓬勃发展。四季青服装特色街区多次获得国家级及省市级荣誉称号，如"中国特色商业街"等，"四季青"商标也被认定为浙江省著名商标。

杭州四季青服装特色街区正致力于打造中国服装新品的交易中心、展示中心、信息中心，以及杭州女装产业面向全国、面向国际市场的形象展示窗口，成为融旅游、购物、休闲、展示于一体的时尚街区。

★ Sijiqing Clothing Block

Hangzhou Sijiqing Clothing Block is located in the west of Hanghai Road and its adjacent area, with a 1,100-meter-long main street. Since the late 1980s when its first clothing bazaar was opened, it has gradually grown into one of China's largest apparel distribution center, hatched 15 clothing markets, such as Sijiqing Clothing Market, Hangzhou-Style Boutique Market. There are many famous foreign and domestic brands in the block and it holds nearly 1,000 registered trademarks, having hatched a group of independent influential brands and gathered a large number of master franchises, general agents of famous brands at home and abroad. The trademarks of Hangzhou-style Women's

① 佚名. 四季青服装特色街区［EB/OL］.（2022-06-04）［2023-04-06］. https://baike.baidu.com/item/%E5%9B%9B%E5%AD%A3%E9%9D%92%E6%9C%8D%E8%A3%85%E7%89%B9%E8%89%B2%E8%A1%97%E5%8C%BA/16244276?fr=aladdin.

Apparel and Sijiqing Clothing have spread to the major cities, with franchise stores, chain stores, etc., distributed nationwide.

Relying on the solid industrial foundation in the district and industry agglomeration of East China's largest garment market, the block has formed an interactive industrial value chain based on the overall brand strategy, and promoted related industries. Sijiqing Clothing Block has won many municipal, provincial and national honorary titles, such as "China Characteristic Commercial Street", and the trademark "Sijiqing" has been identified as a famous trademark of Zhejiang Province.

Nowadays, Sijiqing Clothing Block is committed to building a trading, display and information center for Chinese fashion, as well as a window to display the image of Hangzhou-style women's clothing industry to the national and international market, and forming a fashion block integrating tourism, shopping, entertainment and exhibition.

★ 武林路时尚女装街区

2001年底，杭州市提出了打造"中国女装之都"，打响"中国女装看杭州"的目标。个性女装店尤其是杭州女装品牌集聚的武林路，成为展示杭州女装风采、女装品牌的载体和窗口。经过两次提升改造，武林路逐步发展成一片以展示销售时尚女装及女性用品为主，集旅游、购物、休闲于一体的商业特色街区。武林路时尚女装街区包括全长1880米的主干道武林路，以及狮虎桥路、龙游路等多条支路。东与杭州商贸中心延安路相连接，西经龙游路与西湖贯通，南端衔接历史保护地段石库门里弄林氏家宅。街区内共有以服装为主的各类商家七八百家，总营业面积4万多平方米，[①]先后被评为"浙江省十大商业特色街""中国最具升值前景商业街"等。

★ Wulin Road Women's Fashion Block

At the end of 2001, Hangzhou put forward a goal to build "the Capital

---

① 佚名. 武林路［EB/OL］.（2022-03-06）［2023-04-06］. https://baike.baidu.com/item/
%E6%AD%A6%E6%9E%97%E8%B7%AF%E6%97.

of Women's Dress in China" and launched a campaign of "Making Hangzhou Lead in Women's Dress in China". Wulin Road, as a base to many personalized women's clothing stores and shops, with various Hangzhou-style women's apparel brands concentrated, has become the window to show the styles and brands of Hangzhou women's apparel. After two retrofits and upgrades, Wulin Road, along with the neighboring areas, has gradually developed into a commercial block which mainly displays and sells fashionable women's clothing and feminine products, and integrates tourism, shopping and recreation. Wulin Road Women's Fashion Block includes Wulin Road, a main road with a total length of about 1,880 meters, as well as several branches such as Shihuqiao Road and Longyou Road. It connects Yan'an Road in the east, the business center of Hangzhou, and the West Lake through Longyou Road in the west. In the south, it neighbors Lin family residence at the Shikumen Lane, a preserved historic site. There are seven to eight hundred clothing businesses in the block, with a total business area of more than 40,000 square meters. Wulin Road Women's Fashion Block has been rated as "Ten Commercially Characteristic Streets in Zhejiang Province", "Commercial Streets with the Most Appreciation Prospect in China", etc.

★ 河坊街

　　河坊街位于上城区吴山脚下，毗邻西湖。在旧城改造过程中抢救性保护下来的这条街曾是古代都城临安（今杭州）的皇城根儿，更是南宋的文化中心和经贸中心。作为杭州市区保持古城历史风貌的老街，河坊街凝聚了杭州最具代表性的历史文化、商业文化、市井文化和建筑文化。街上众多"老字号"药铺、绸庄、茶庄、名人故居、传统小吃摊、传统工艺品店和非物质文化遗产展示体验点鳞次栉比。修复和改造后的河坊街，再现了杭城历史文脉，为人们留下了一份宝贵的历史文化遗产，是海内外游客了解杭州历史、体验杭州文化的理想目的地。

★ Hefang Street

Hefang Street, located at the foot of Wushan Hill and adjacent to the West Lake, was once the "core of the imperial city" and the cultural and economic center of Lin'an (now known as Hangzhou), the capital of the Southern Song Dynasty. It was saved and protected in the retrofit and reconstruction of the old and dilapidated quarters of the city. Being the only ancient street in the downtown area of Hangzhou, it retains the historical style of ancient Hangzhou, and embodies the most representative culture of Hangzhou in history, commerce, market and architecture. In the street, there are "time-honored" medicine shops, silk shops, tea houses, residences of former celebrities, traditional food stalls, handicraft shops and spots for displaying and experiencing intangible cultural heritages. After restoration and retrofit, Hefang Street reproduces the historical context of Hangzhou while retaining its historical and cultural value, making it an ideal destination for tourists to learn about the history of Hangzhou and experience its culture.

第六章 运动休闲之城

在过去的 10 多年，杭州承办了一些大型的体育赛事，如 2007 年女足世界杯、2011 年第 8 届全国残疾人运动会、2016 年第 10 届全国大学生运动会、2017 年第 13 届全国学生运动会、2018 年第 14 届 FINA 世界游泳锦标赛（25 米）和第 5 届世界水上运动大会等。再加上万众期待的第 19 届亚运会和世界杯杭州赛区比赛，杭州承办了多场国际 A 类体育赛事，举办各类特色品牌赛事活动，每年开展全民健身培训服务和组织全民健身活动等。杭州，这座几千年来以美闻名的城市正在逐渐烙上鲜明的体育印记。

Chapter Six
City of Sports and Leisure

Over the past decade, Hangzhou has hosted some large-scale sporting events. Hangzhou is the hosting city for FIFA Women's World Cup in 2007. Since then, several large-scale sports events were held in Hangzhou, including the 8th National Games of Disabled Persons in 2011, The 10th National University Games of the People's Republic of China in 2016, the 13th National Student Sports Games in 2017, the 14th FINA World Swimming Championship (25m) and the 5th FINA World Aquatics Convention in 2018. Including the much-anticipated 19th Asian Games and the Hangzhou Site of FIFA, There are A-level international events and sports of characteristic brands held in Hangzhou. Training and service is provided annually for those engaged in national extensive mass fitness programs. Known for its beautiful scenery for thousands of years, the city Hangzhou is now vividly branded with its sports events.

第一节　体育盛会

Ⅰ Large-scale Sports Events

★ 第 19 届亚洲运动会

第 19 届亚洲运动会原定于 2022 年 9 月 10 日至 25 日在杭州举行，后因新冠疫情推迟。2022 年 7 月 19 日，亚洲奥林匹克理事会宣布：第 19 届亚运会将于 2023 年 9 月 23 日至 10 月 8 日举办，赛事名称和标识保持不变。协办城市为绍兴、湖州和宁波，比赛项目分别在六大赛区——杭州赛区、宁波赛区、温州赛区、金华赛区、绍兴赛区和湖州赛区进行。杭州是中国第三个取得夏季亚运会主办权的城市，另外 2 个城市为北京和广州，分别于 1990 年和 2010 年举办了第 11 届和第 16 届夏季亚运会。杭州亚运会拟设比赛项目 40 项，其中包括 31 个奥运项目和 9 个非奥运项目，同时，电子竞技（竞技电子游戏或专业电子游戏）和霹雳舞 2 个竞赛项目将纳为正式比赛项目。[①] 亚运会后，杭州将举办第四届亚洲残疾人运动会。

★ The 19th Asian Games

The 19th Asian Games is planned to be held in Hangzhou in 2022 at the beginning, from September 10 to September 25, lasting for 15 days. The Games was delayed due to the COVID-19 pandemic. On 19 July 2022, the Olympic Council of Asia announced that the 19th Asian Games would be held from 23 September to 8 October 2023, with the name and logo remaining the same. Besides Hangzhou, there are three other co-host cities: Shaoxing, Huzhou and Ningbo in

① 肖拓. 杭州亚运会定于 2023 年 9 月 23 日至 10 月 8 日举行［EB/OL］.（2022−07−19）［2023−04−06］. https://sports.rednet.cn/content/2022/07/19/11539988.html.

Zhejiang Province. The events will be held in six competition divisions, namely Hangzhou, Ningbo, Wenzhou, Jinhua, Shaoxing and Huzhou. Hangzhou is the third city in China succeeding in bidding to host the Summer Asian Games, the other two cities are Beijing and Guangzhou, Beijing hosted the 11th Summer Asian Games in 1990 and Guangzhou the 16th in 2010. There will be 40 sports events in the 19th Asian Games, including 31 Olympic Sports and 9 non-Olympic Sports. For the first time, E-sports (electronic competitive sports such as competitive video gaming or professional video gaming) and break dancing would be included as official events at the Asian Games. Following the closing of the 19th Asian Games, the 4th Asian Para Games would also be held in Hangzhou.

▶ 场馆建设

第 19 届亚运会建设的相关基础设施包括 14 条道路、7 座桥和 6 个立体交通网，已于 2021 年完工。2016 年杭州国际博览中心投入使用，2017 年主体育场投入使用，2018 年网球中心建成，2019 年体育游泳馆基本建成，2020 年综合训练馆投入使用。[①]2022 年"杭州之门"双塔建成。

杭州亚运会、亚残运会共有 56 个竞赛场馆，以"杭州为主，全省共享"的原则，分布在杭州、宁波、温州、湖州、绍兴、金华各地，充分整合绍兴、嘉兴、湖州、淳安等杭州都市经济圈范围内以及宁波等滨海城市现有的场馆资源。新建场馆 12 个，改造场馆 26 个，续建场馆 9 个，临建场馆 9 个。另有 31 个训练场馆、1 个亚运村和 4 个亚运分村（运动员分村）。2022 年 3 月 31 日，绍兴棒（垒）球体育文化中心、绍兴柯桥羊山攀岩基地先后通过赛事功能验收。至此，历时近 5 年建设，杭州 2022 年亚运会、亚残运会 56 个竞赛场馆全面竣工并通过赛事功能综合验收。[②]

场馆建设秉承"绿色、智能、节俭、文明"办赛理念，确保满足赛事要求，助推城市建设，展现城市形象，服务市民群众。围绕"互联网＋体育"

---

① 杭州亚运倒计时一周年：欢迎全亚细亚相聚西子湖畔［N］.中国青年报，2021-09-10.
② ArchiDogs.杭州亚运会，虽迟但到！56 个竞赛场馆，哪个最能代表你心目中的杭州？［EB/OL］.（2022-06-21）［2023-04-06］.https://mp.weixin.qq.com/s?__biz=MzIwNjg0MDIzMg==&mid=2247522447&idx=1&sn=acf6878bf3c6d1394021101028c03819&chksm=97195048a06ed95efe6c610a9984e85a061320b8f4761200aaabb36068597ad264e09cd4835e&scene=27.

这个概念，"智能亚运"可望得到广泛应用，包括实现赛事报名、服务的智能化等，如通过互联网的"一键通"，运动员在出征前就能准确了解组委会提供的宾馆、交通、接站、志愿服务、赛事编排等信息。

▶ **Construction of Venues**

As the 19th Asian Games is drawing near, construction of corresponding infrastructure facilities, including 14 roads, 7 bridges and 6 three-dimensional traffic networks, were completed in 2021. In the past few years, we saw venues completed: Hangzhou International Expo Center was put into use in 2016, the Main Stadium was put into service in 2017, Tennis Center was completed in 2018, Natatorium was completed in 2019 and Composite Gymnasium was in operation in 2020, and "Gate of Hangzhou" was in service in 2022.

56 competition venues are jointly built for Hangzhou Asian Games and Asian Para Games. Under the principle of "Hangzhou as the main city, share the whole province", they are distributed in Hangzhou, Ningbo, Wenzhou, Huzhou, Shaoxing and Jinhua. The construction fully integrated the existing venue resources in Shaoxing, Jiaxing, Huzhou, Chun'an and other Hangzhou urban economic circle as well as Ningbo and other coastal cities.There are 12 newly built stadiums, 26 renovated stadiums, 9 continued construction stadiums and 9 temporary stadiums. There are also 31 training venues, 1 Asian Games village and 4 Asian Games sub-villages (athletes sub-villages). On March 31, 2022, Shaoxing Baseball (Softball) Sports Culture Center, Shaoxing Keqiao Yangshan Rock Climbing Base passed the event function acceptance. So far, after nearly five years of construction, the 56 venues of Hangzhou 2022 Asian Games and Asian Para Games have been completed and passed the comprehensive acceptance of their functions.

The venue construction adheres to the concept of "green, intelligent, frugal and civilized" to ensure meeting the requirements of the event, boosting the city construction, showing the city image and serving the public. Centre on the concept of "Internet + sports", "smart Asian games" can be used widely, including the realization of intelligent competition registration and service, etc. For example, by "one key" via the Internet, provided by the Organizing Committee online ahead of time, information about hotels, traffic, docking station, voluntary services and event scheduling, etc. is available to athletes any time.

▶ 亚运村建设

亚运三村（运动员村、技术官员村、媒体村）共 108 幢楼，于 2020 年 12 月 24 日实现主体结顶。亚运村为 10000 余名运动员和随队官员、近 4000 名技术官员和约 5000 名媒体人员提供住宿、餐饮、医疗等保障服务。2021 年 12 月 29 日，亚运村全部竣工。[①]

▶ Construction of Asian Games Village

The main parts of all 108 buildings in the three Villages of Asian Games (Athletes Village, Technical Officials Village and Media Village) were topped on December 24, 2020. The Villages will provide accommodation, catering and medical services for more than 10,000 athletes and team officials, nearly 4,000 technical officials and 5,000 media personnel. The Asian Games Village was completed on December 29, 2021.

▶ 杭州之门

"杭州之门"是杭州亚运会重点配套项目，坐落于钱江世纪城奥体板块核心位置，2019 年动工建设，于 2022 年 10 月完成。"杭州之门"双塔超高层区由 2 栋 302.6 米高的塔楼组成，中间以钢结构桥相连，形似展翅的造型，源自杭州城市拼音的第一个字母"H"。该项目落成后，将集企业总部、综合商务、超五星级宾馆、精品商场等功能为一体，成为钱塘江南岸地标性建筑。建成的"杭州之门"成为杭州第一高楼，不仅是杭州城市未来新地标，更代表着杭州的城市形象。

Gate of Hangzhou

As a supporting project for the 19th Asian Games, located at Qianjiang

① 李佳.杭州 2022 年第 19 届亚运会亚运村今天竣工［EB/OL］.（2021-12-29）［2023-04-06］. https://baijiahao.baidu.com/s?id=1720473044075326552&wfr=spider&for=pc.

Century CBD, Gate of Hangzhou started ground construction in 2019 and was completed in October, 2022. The twin-tower and super high-rise area of Gate of Hangzhou is composed of 302.6-meter-high towers which are connected by steel bridge in the middle in a sculpt like spreading wings and are originated from the first letter—"H" from the Chinese pinyin of the city Hangzhou. It is served as headquarters for the enterprise, integrated business, super five-star hotel and boutique shopping mall. Gate of Hangzhou is the first high-rise building in Hangzhou, it is not only the future new landmark of the city, but an icon for Hangzhou.

▶ **杭州奥体中心主体育场（大莲花）**

杭州奥林匹克体育中心（奥体中心）主体育场也称"大莲花"，位于钱塘江南岸，于 2016 年完工。"大莲花"是亚运会主场馆，也是杭州的城市地标。容纳 80800 人的"大莲花"是国内第三大体育馆，仅次于国家体育馆鸟巢和广东奥林匹克中心。奥体中心主体育场由 28 片大花瓣和 27 片小花瓣组成，看起来动感飘逸，远看状如一朵大莲花，实际上这些花瓣由钢结构制成。主体育场观景平台后面不远处是开阔的钱塘江，从平台处进去能看到主体育场内场全貌，四周尽是色彩斑斓的座椅，令人心生赞叹。2021 年，"大莲花"荣获中国建筑工程鲁班奖（国家优质工程）。

▶ **Hangzhou Olympic Sports Center (Big Lotus)**

The main stadium of Hangzhou Olympic Sports Center, also known as "Big Lotus" is located in the south bank of the Qiantang River. Completed in 2016, it is the main stadium of the 19th Asian Games and the landmark of Hangzhou. With the capacity of 80,800 people, "Big Lotus" has become the third-largest stadium in China, following the National Stadium Bird's Nest and the Guangdong Olympic Sports Center. "Big Lotus" is composed of 28 big petals and 27 small petals, shaping like a big lotus, which looks dynamic and elegant from far away, but actually these petals are made up of steels. Standing on the viewing platform in the stadium, you can see the broad Qiantang River, while walking inside, you may have the whole view of the stadium, with so many colorful seats in it. "Big Lotus" was awarded the Luban Prize for Construction Project of China (National Prime-quality Project) in 2021.

▶ 主题口号

杭州亚运会主题口号为"心心相融，@未来"，2019 年 12 月 15 日在杭州 2022 年第 19 届亚运会倒计时 1000 天时发布。

▶ Slogan

"Heart to Heart，@ Future", the slogan of the 19th Asian Games Hangzhou 2022 was unveiled on Dec. 15, 2019, the mark of the 1,000-day countdown to the 19th Asian Games in Hangzhou.

▶ 吉祥物

杭州亚运会吉祥物是一组名为"江南忆"的机器人，出自唐朝诗人白居易的名句"江南忆，最忆是杭州"。3 个吉祥物分别取名"琮琮""莲莲"和"宸宸"。"琮琮"以机器人的造型代表世界遗产良渚古城遗址，名字源于良渚古城遗址出土的代表性文物玉琮，象征坚强刚毅、敦厚善良、体魄强健和热情奔放。"莲莲"以机器人的造型代表世界遗产西湖，名字源于西湖中无穷碧色的接天莲叶，象征纯洁善良、活泼可爱、热情好客、美丽动人，传递着共建人类命运共同体的期许。"宸宸"以机器人的造型代表世界遗产京杭大运河，名字源于京杭大运河杭州段的标志性建筑拱宸桥，象征机智勇敢、聪慧灵动、乐观向上、积极进取。

杭州亚运会吉祥物穿越时空，怀揣梦想，抒体育之欢畅，亮文化之灿烂，树经济之标杆，和杭州这座城市的特质相契合，与杭州亚运会会徽、主题口号相呼应。"江南忆"融合了杭州的历史人文、自然生态和创新基因，承载着深厚底蕴，充满时代活力。"琮琮""莲莲"和"宸宸"，3 个亲密无间的好伙伴，将作为传播奥林匹克精神，传递和平与友谊的使者，向亚洲和世界发出"2022，相聚杭州亚运会"的盛情邀约。

亚运会吉祥物由位于杭州的中国美术学院的 2 位教师设计，从国内外提交的 4600 多件参赛作品中选出，结合了中国的文化、杭州的城市特色、亚运精神和亚洲大陆，希望他们给亚洲和世界带来快乐与健康。

▶ Mascots

The mascots of the 19th Asian Games are a group of robots proclaiming the host city's profound heritage and contemporary vibrancy. The combination—Memories of Jiangnan—derives its name from a poem by Bai Juyi. This great poet of the Tang Dynasty wrote, "When I recall Jiangnan, Hangzhou brings back the most of my memories." The three mascots—named Congcong, Lianlian and Chenchen—represent the Liangzhu Archaeological Ruins, the West Lake and the Grand Canal in Hangzhou respectively, all of which have been inscribed on the UNESCO World Heritage List. Congcong was named after the renowned jade cong artifacts that were excavated from the Liangzhu Archaeological Site, which symbolize indomitable courage and self-transcendence. The green-colored Lianlian is inspired by lotus leaves, which are symbolic of Hangzhou's West Lake, representing purity, hospitality and opening-up. Lianlian also conveys the wish of building a shared future for mankind. Chenchen, derived from the Gongchen Bridge over the Hangzhou section of the Grand Canal, is colored blue to represent science and technology. This mascot embodies courage, optimism and inclusiveness.

The three mascots, transcending time and space, inspire everyone to reach for their dreams. They stand for not only the joy of sports but the culmination of cultural and economic development, so much so that they agree with the character of Hangzhou and proudly join the ranks of the emblem and slogan of the 19th Asian Games Hangzhou 2022. The name itself speaks volumes about Hangzhou's heritage, scenic splendor and drive for innovation. Congcong, Lianlian and Chenchen, this trio of robots will act as the envoys of the Olympic spirit, conveying peace and friendship. Together, they are calling out to Asia and the world, inviting everyone to meet in Hangzhou for the Asian Games 2022.

The mascots, designed by two teachers at the Hangzhou-based China Academy of Art, were selected from over 4,600 submissions from home and abroad since April 2019. The mascots integrate Chinese culture, characteristics of the city of Hangzhou, the spirit of the Asian Games and the Asian continent, and they are expected to bring joy and health to Asia and the world.

▶ 志愿者招募

杭州亚组委计划面向全球招募约 5.2 万名赛会志愿者。2021 年 5 月 22 日，杭州亚运会赛会志愿者全球招募启动。经注册报名、初始培训、在线测试等环节，截至 2021 年 10 月 31 日报名通道关闭，注册总人数约 32.1 万。他们来自各个年龄段，分布在各行各业：有小语种、医疗、财务、竞赛、救援等领域的专业人士，有残疾人代表性群体，有服务过北京奥运会、东京奥运会、雅加达亚运会的志愿者，有企业白领、知名演员，也不乏在杭州的国际友人。他们怀着满腔热情，希望能为亚运做出自己的贡献。

志愿者将在杭州及 5 个协办城市宁波、温州、湖州、绍兴、金华工作，均在浙江省内。他们为开幕式、闭幕式、各项竞赛及活动提供竞赛运行服务、礼宾语言服务、观众服务、媒体运行服务、后勤保障服务、交通出行服务等 13 类志愿服务。根据分配的职责和履行的服务，志愿者主要分为三大类：普通志愿者、专业志愿者和领导。志愿者选拔将优先考虑那些有体育赛事志愿者经历，能在整个亚运会期间提供服务的候选人。

亚奥理事会主席艾哈迈德亲王发来贺信。他表示，志愿者是杭州亚运会举办的重要支持，志愿者们的微笑和服务，将成为赛会交流的纽带。他衷心欢迎和鼓励青年朋友参与亚运会志愿服务，共同分享亚运盛会带来的喜悦。

▶ Volunteer Recruitment

Hangzhou Asian Games Organizing Committee (HAGOC) aims to recruit about 52,000 Asian Games volunteers from around the world. Global volunteer recruitment for the 19th Asian Games began on May 22, 2021. After registration, initial training, online testing and other links, the registration channel was closed by October 31, 2021, with a total number of about 321,000 people registered. They come from all walks of life and of all ages; Among them are professionals in the fields of minor languages, medical care, finance, competition and rescue, representative groups of the disabled, volunteers who served for the Beijing Olympics, Tokyo Olympics and Jakarta Asian Games, white-collar workers from enterprises, famous actors and international friends in Hangzhou. They are full of enthusiasm, hoping to make their own contribution to the Asian Games.

Volunteers may work in any venue of play across Hangzhou and the co-host cities, namely Ningbo, Wenzhou, Huzhou, Shaoxing and Jinhua, all of which are located in Zhejiang Province. Volunteers are also needed in one or more of the following 13 types of supportive works for the Games: Competition Operations, Accreditation, Protocol, Language Service, Arrivals & Departures, Ceremonies and Events, Spectator Services, Media Operations, Games Services, Transport, Official Conference Services, the Asian Games Village and Official Hotels or Information Technology. According to the assigned duties and services performed, volunteers will be grouped, among which the three major groups are the general group, professional group, and organizing group. Priority will be given to those candidates who have volunteer experiences in sports events and can provide services throughout the Asian Games.

Prince Ahmed, President of the Olympic Council of Asia (OCA), sent a congratulatory message. He said that volunteers are an important support for the Asian Games in Hangzhou. Their smiles and services will become a bond of communication between the Games. He welcomed and encouraged young people to participate in voluntary work of the Asian Games and share the joy of the Games together.

★ **第 14 届 FINA 世界游泳锦标赛（25 米）和第 5 届世界水上运动大会**

2018 年 12 月，第 14 届 FINA 世界游泳锦标赛（25 米）在杭州奥体中心的"小莲花"举行，这是杭州有史以来举办的较大规模和规格的国际体育赛事，向世界展示了杭州的综合实力和办赛能力。国际泳联主席胡里奥·马格利奥尼称赞杭州：我们在杭州这座充满活力的城市度过了非常难忘的时光。比赛前，国际泳联举办了为期 3 天的第 5 届世界水上运动大会。自 2014 年起，世界水上运动大会与世界游泳锦标赛（25 米）联合举行。

世界短池游泳锦标赛共设置 46 个项目，来自世界 178 个国家和地区代表队参加了短池世游赛，运动员人数近 1000 人，包括南非的勒克罗斯、俄罗斯的莫佐洛夫、匈牙利游泳名将霍斯祖等在内的世界名将。孙杨、傅园慧等杭州籍游泳运动员在家门口参赛。据统计，2018 年第 14 届 FINA 世界游泳锦标赛（25 米）及第 5 届水上运动大会共有来自世界各地 185 个国家和地区的 3179 名代表来杭参赛参会，其中外宾 2503 名。赛事共打破了 9 项世界纪录和 22 项赛会纪录。中国队以 3 金 5 银 5 铜的成绩位列奖牌榜第三、金牌榜第五，是近 4 届以来中国队取得奖牌最多的一次。[①]

★ **The 14th FINA World Swimming Championship (25m) 2018 and The 5th FINA World Aquatics Convention 2018**

The 14th FINA World Swimming Championship (25m) was held in "Small Lotus" of Hangzhou Olympic Sports Center in 2018. It's the first time that Hangzhou has hosted the international sports events of comparatively large scale, demonstrating comprehensive strength and the ability to organize competitions. Julio Maglione, President of FINA gave Hangzhou a thumb-up, saying that they had an unforgettable memory of this dynamic city. Before World Swimming Championship (25m), the 5th FINA World Aquatics Convention was held by FINA, which lasted for 3 days. Since the year 2014, FINA World Swimming Championship and FINA World Aquatics Convention were held at the same time.

178 delegates, more than 1,000 athletes from the world and regions entered for the competition, including world famous athletes like Chad le Clos from South Africa, Mozorov from Russia, famous swimmer Hosszu from Hungary, etc. Sun Yang and Fu Yuanhui participated in it in their home city. According to statistics, there are 3,179 athletes and representatives from 185

---

① 汪浩. 杭州　为你点赞! [EB/OL]. (2018-12-17) [2023-04-06]. https://z.hangzhou.com.cn/2018/ydhz/content/content_7116582.htm.

countries and regions either entered the competition or attended the convention, among them, there were 2,503 people from foreign countries. Nine world records and 22 competition records were broken. With three gold medals, five silver and five bronze, China National Team ranked the third on the medal tally and the fifth on the gold medal standing, gaining the most medals since the last four competitions.

★ 第 13 届全国学生运动会

第 13 届全国学生运动会于 2017 年 9 月在杭州举行，这是杭州承办的当时规格与级别最高的一次综合型运动会，也是首次将全国大学生和中学生运动会合并举办，共设置 10 个大项和 326 个小项。在 13 天的比赛中，来自全国各省、自治区、直辖市、新疆生产建设兵团和香港、澳门特别行政区 36 个代表团的 5966 名运动员同场竞技，共产生奖牌 987 枚，其中金牌 333 枚，银牌 322 枚，铜牌 332 枚，有 30 人 49 次破 35 项赛会纪录。①

★ The 13th National Student Sports Games of the People's Republic of China

The 13th National Student Sports Games were held in Hangzhou in September, 2017. This is the first time that Hangzhou has hosted the nationwide comprehensive games in terms of scale and level at the time, combining sports games of both university and high school students. Totally, there are 10 major sports events and 326 minor events. In the competition lasting for 13 days, 5,966 athletes from 36 delegates competed in the same field, they are from all provinces, autonomous regions, municipalities directly under the Central Government, Xinjiang Production and Construction Corps, Hongkong Special Administration Region and Macao Special Administration Region. A total of 987 medals were produced, of which 333 gold medals, 322 silver medals and 332 bronze medals,

---

① 刘潇翰. 第十三届全国学生运动会闭幕 [EB/OL]. （2017-09-16）[2021-04-13]. http://www.moe.gov.cn/jyb_xwfb/moe_2082/s6236/s6358/dssjxsydh/201710/t20171027_317643.html.

35 records were broken by 30 athletes in the 49 competition events.

★ 第 10 届全国大学生运动会

第 10 届全国大学生运动会于 2016 年 9 月在杭州举办，这是全国高校体育竞技级别最高、规模最大、项目最多、水平最高的体育盛会，每 4 年举办一次。近万名来自全国各省、自治区、直辖市、新疆生产建设兵团和香港、澳门特别行政区的运动员、教练员和裁判员来杭州参与赛事。

★ The Tenth National University Games

The Tenth National University Games were held in Hangzhou in September, 2016. It's the sports events in terms of scale and level, with the features of most events and highly competitive. The Games were held every four years. Nearly ten thousand athletes, coaches and referees involved in the competition in Hangzhou, they are from all provinces, autonomous regions, and municipalities, Xinjiang Production and Construction Corps, Hongkong Special Administration Region and Macao Special Administration Region.

★ 第 8 届全国残疾人运动会

全国残疾人运动会始自 1984 年，每 4 年举办一次，由中国残联和国家体育总局主办。2011 年 10 月，第 8 届残疾人运动会由浙江省人民政府承办，主会场设在杭州。本次残运会是继 2008 年北京残奥会之后举行的一次全国综合性残疾人体育赛事，共设 18 个比赛大项。36 个代表团来自全国各省、自治区、直辖市、新疆生产建设兵团和香港、澳门特别行政区，参赛运动员 5000 名左右，还有来自社会各界的领导、来宾、代表团、工作团、观摩团、裁判员、技术官员、媒体记者、工作人员及志愿者等，总人数超过 16000 人。[①]

★ The 8th National Games of Disabled Persons

Initiated from 1984, sponsored by China Disabled Persons' Federation and General Administration of Sport of China, National Games of Disabled Persons are held every four years in different cities. People's Government of Zhejiang

---

① 佚名. 生命阳光 情满浙江：第八届全国残疾人运动会综述［EB/OL］.（2012-02-12）［2022-11-26］. http://www.bdpf.org.cn/n1544/n1689/n1766/n1804/c56248/content.html.

Province hosted the 8th National Games of Disabled Persons in October, 2011. The main venue was in the city of Hangzhou. It's the first nationwide comprehensive games of the disabled persons since the Paralympic Games held in Beijing in 2008. Totally, there are 18 major sports events. 36 sports delegations come from all provinces, autonomous regions, municipalities, Xinjiang Production and Construction Corps, Hongkong Special Administration Region and Macao Special Administration Region. About 5,000 athletes participated in the games. A total of 16,000 people were involved, including leaders, guests and delegations of all walks of life, work groups, observation groups, referees, technical officials, media reporters, staff and volunteers.

★ 第 5 届女足世界杯

2007 年 9 月，第 5 届女足世界杯在上海虹口足球场落下帷幕。这届世界杯分别在中国的 5 个城市举办，它们是成都、武汉、上海、天津和杭州。共有 16 支球队参与了角逐，最终德国队获得女足世界杯冠军，中国队名列第五。在杭州赛区，从 9 月 12 日到 9 月 27 日，先后有挪威、澳大利亚、加纳、加拿大、德国、日本、丹麦、新西兰、美国等 9 个国家的足球队参加了在黄龙体育中心主体育场举行的 7 场小组赛和 1 场半决赛，观众人数平均每场达到 4 万余人。①

★ The 5th FIFA Women's World Cup 2007

The 5th FIFA Women's World Cup came to a close at Hongkou Football Stadium, Shanghai in September, 2007. Shanghai is one of the five cities in China which hosted the World Cup, the other four cities are Chendu, Wuhan, Tianjin and Hangzhou. A total of 16 football teams competed in the game. Germany won the championship and China finished fifth. At the main stadium in Huanglong Sports Center, Hangzhou Division, teams from nine countries (Norway, Australia, Ghana, Canada, Germany, Japan, Denmark, New Zealand

---

① 佚名.历史回顾［EB/OL］.（2018-11-19）［2022-12-21］. http://www.hlsports.net/lishihuigu/.

and America) competed in the seven group matches and one semi-finals. Each match drew an average of 40,000 spectators.

第二节　城市体育休闲活动

Ⅱ Sports and Leisure Activities

★ 杭州国际马拉松

杭州国际马拉松历史悠久，最早始于 1987 年，是在原西湖桂花国际马拉松赛和杭州国际友好西湖马拉松赛两大赛事的基础上合并而成的。1987 年，2 场比赛的报名人数分别为 640 人和 650 人。从 1987 年到 2020 年 34 年的时间，杭州国际马拉松从一场 640 人的环湖赛升级成一场 3.6 万人的城市狂欢。2019 年，世界田径协会授予其金牌赛事，成为中国最具品牌的马拉松赛。马拉松赛分全程马拉松、半程马拉松、小马拉松、夫妻马拉松和家庭马拉松等。2020 年 11 月 22 日，第 34 届杭州马拉松开跑，万名跑者从杭州中心地标武林广场出发，从环城西路进入精致浪漫的北山街，跑过大半个西湖，最后跑向杭州市奥林匹克体育中心（2022 年亚运会主会场）。这是一条被赞为最美的赛道，西湖的残荷分外迷人。

34 年来，杭州马拉松线路大大小小共调整过 20 余次，素有国内最美赛道之称。2020 年，杭州马拉松线路特别调整起点和终点，沿着西湖和钱塘江（杭州的母亲河），经过杭州最美的景点。起点武林广场代表着杭州之心，终点杭州市奥林匹克体育中心连接着杭州的未来之心，寓意"心心相融"，也寄寓着对 2022 年杭州亚运会的期待。

★ Hangzhou International Marathon

Marathon in Hangzhou has a history of more than 30 years. First launched in 1987 as West Lake Osmanthus International Marathon and Hangzhou International Friendship West Lake Marathon, 640 and 650 people entered for the two marathons respectively. In the span of 34 years from 1987 to 2020, Hangzhou International Marathon, upgraded from the race of 640 participants running around the West Lake to the city carnival of 36,000 people. Awarded the Gold Label Race by World Athletics in 2019, it is one of the most time-honored marathons in China. The event mainly includes a full marathon, half marathon, mini-marathon, couple marathon and family marathon. On November 22, 2020, in the 34th Hangzhou Marathon, ten thousand runners started from Wulin Square, landmark of Hangzhou, along West Huancheng Road to the exquisite and romantic Beishan Street, running around the West Lake, the destination was Hangzhou Olympic Sports Center, the main venue of the 2022 Asian Games. This is called the most beautiful track, the withering lotus leaves in the lake are so charming.

In the past 34 years, the course has been adjusted about 20 times, winning the title of the most beautiful course in China. The course was set along the West Lake and the Qiantang River (the mother river of the city), covering the most beautiful scenic places in Hangzhou. The starting point Wulin Square represented the "Heart of Hangzhou", and the terminal point Olympic Sports Center is connected to "the Future Heart of Hangzhou", which means "Heart to Heart" and the expectation for the 2022 Hangzhou Asian Games.

★ 西湖国际博览会

西湖国际博览会历史悠久，首届西湖国际博览会于 1929 年成功举办，开创了中国会展业之先河。停办 70 年后，从 2000 年开始，杭州恢复举办西湖国际博览会。第二届西湖博览会定名为"中国杭州—2000 西湖国际博览会"（简称"中国杭州西湖国际博览会"或"西湖国际博览会"），每年举办一届，已成为杭州的金名片。博览会包括展览和各种活动，有来自世界各地的商品、食品、家居装饰和旅游推介，如端午文化节、西湖国际音乐节和国际汽车工艺展等，市民可以在展会上逛遍世界。

每届博览会紧扣发展趋势，吸引世界各地友好城市、国内主要城市及企业参与。数万名专业观众以及近10万的杭州市民参加，贸易额、意向成交额逐年提升。鉴于杭州已经具有成功举办西湖国际博览会的经验，2002年8月10日，世界休闲组织理事会通过投票表决，同意杭州为2006世界休闲博览会的举办城市。作为每年的大型会展，西湖国际博览会是杭州走向世界、世界了解杭州的重要窗口，也为21世纪拓展商务旅游、发展会展经济、传播先进文化奠定新的基础。

★ West Lake International Exposition

West Lake International Exposition has a long history, began in 1929, it's the first exposition in China. Suspended for 70 years, it was restarted in 2000 and was renamed as "Hangzhou China—2000 West Lake International Exposition" (short for "West Lake International Exposition, Hangzhou China" or "West Lake International Exposition"). Held once each year, it has become the gold card of Hangzhou. The Exposition includes exhibitions and activities about shopping, food, housing and tourism from all over the world, such as Dragon Boat Cultural Festival, West Lake International Music Festival and International Automobile Craft Exhibition, providing citizens the possibility for "Traveling the World".

By following the development trend, the annual West Lake International Exposition not only attracts sister cities all over the world, but also main cities and enterprises in China with tens of thousands specialized participants. There is a steady rise of volume of trade and intended turnover. In view of the experiences gained in holding West Lake International Exposition, on August 10, 2002, the Council of World Leisure Organization voted by ballot to approve that Hangzhou would be the host city of 2006 World Leisure Exposition. As a large scale exposition held annually, West Lake International Exposition is an important window for Hangzhou to go out to the world and for the world to learn about Hangzhou. In the 21st century, it lays a new foundation for the expanding business travel, promoting exhibition economy and spreading advanced culture.

★ 杭州文化创意产业博览会

一年一度的杭州文化创意产业博览会始于 2007 年。2020 年，第 14 届杭州文化创意产业博览会在杭州白马湖国际会展中心开幕，汇集六大展区，总面积 7 万平方米。来自 27 个国家和地区的 1700 多家文化企业参展，英国、法国、意大利和瑞士等国参与了盛会。[①] 杭州本土有西泠印社、良渚文化博物馆、浙江大学、中国美术学院等展示了他们的创新文化产品。

杭州文化创意产业博览会为游客提供了体验的机会——当地杭州人的一天。乘坐仿古船游览西湖，在中国茶叶博物馆沏一杯茶，购买体现江南元素的文化创意产品。因为新冠疫情，主办方为不能到场亲历的海外客人举办网上展览，吸引了来自 41 个国家和地区的 3100 多家公司和个人。

★ Hangzhou Cultural and Creative Industry Exposition

Started in 2007, Cultural and Creative Industry Exposition is held annually in Hangzhou. In 2020, The 14th Hangzhou Cultural & Creative Industry Exposition opened at the Whitehorse Lake International Exhibition Center featuring six exhibition areas with a total area of 70,000 square meters. Over 1,700 cultural enterprises from 27 countries and regions such as the United Kingdom, France, Italy and Switzerland attended the gala. Local Hangzhou organizations such as the Xiling Seal Art Society, Liangzhu Culture Museum, Zhejiang University, and China Academy of Art also showcased their creative cultural products.

The event offers visitors the opportunity to experience a day in the life of local Hangzhou residents—taking them on a tour of the West Lake on a

---

① 贾亭沂. 第十四届（2020）杭州文化创意产业博览会开幕［EB/OL］.（2020-10-30）［2022-05-20］. https://baijiahao.baidu.com/s?id=1681955337265222492&wfr=spider&for=pc.

pseudo-classical boat, brewing a cup of tea at the China National Tea Museum, and buying creative cultural products featuring cultural elements of Jiangnan (referring to regions south of the Yangtze River). An online exposition was launched simultaneously for overseas exhibitors who couldn't attend in person due to COVID-19 pandemic. It has attracted 3,100 companies and individuals from 41 countries and regions.

★ 中国国际茶叶博览会

2021年5月21日，在第二个国际茶日到来之际，由农业农村部和浙江省人民政府共同主办的第4届中国国际茶叶博览会在浙江杭州开幕，共有1500多家企业、4000多家采购商参展，现场交易额2.238亿元。尽管受疫情影响，但茶博会仍吸引了来自肯尼亚、摩洛哥、荷兰、俄罗斯、智利、越南、斯里兰卡等20国驻华大使、使节以及联合国驻华协调员等外宾。第二届茶博会以"茶和世界·共享发展"为主题，以全面推进乡村振兴为主线，以塑强茶品牌和促进茶消费为核心，全面展示我国茶产业发展成就及新品种、新技术、新业态。茶博会期间举办了中华茶诗品鉴交流会、"西湖论茶"中国茶业国际高峰论坛暨2021年"国际茶日"中国主场活动、第4届中国当代茶文化发展论坛、2021茶乡旅游发展大会等活动。

茶不仅是日常生活的上佳饮品，也是中华文化的重要载体，更成为世界各国人民交流合作的桥梁纽带。未来，随着人们更加关注健康和生活品质，对茶叶等健康饮品和茶旅游、茶文化的需求会越来越旺盛，茶产业发展潜力巨大。

★ China International Tea Exposition

On May 21, 2021, the 4th China International Tea Exposition, co-sponsored by Ministry of Agriculture and Rural Affairs and the People's Government of Zhejiang Province, opened in Hangzhou, Zhejiang Province on the occasion of the arrival of the second International Tea Day. More than 1,500 enterprises and over 4,000 purchasers participated in the exhibition, with a turnover of 223.8 million yuan. Despite the impact of the epidemic, the Tea Exposition attracted the ambassadors and envoys from 20 countries including Kenya, Morocco, the Netherlands, Russia, Chile, Vietnam and Sri Lanka, as well as the United Nations coordinator in China and other foreign guests. With the theme of "Tea and the World, Shared Development", the Tea Exposition takes comprehensively promoting rural revitalization as the main line, building strong tea brands and promoting tea consumption as the core, and comprehensively displays the development achievements of China's tea industry, new varieties, new technologies and new forms of business. During the Tea Exposition, the Chinese Tea Poetry Appreciation Exchange Symposium, "West Lake Tea" China Tea Industry International Summit Forum and 2021 "International Tea Day" China Main Event, the 4th China Contemporary Tea Culture Development Forum, 2021 Tea Township Tourism Development Conference and other activities were held.

Tea is not only a good drink for our daily life, but also an important carrier of Chinese culture. It has become a bridge for exchanges and cooperation among people around the world. In the future, as people pay more attention to health and quality of life, the demand for tea and other health drinks, tea tourism and tea culture will be more and more vigorous, and the development potential of the tea industry will be huge.

★ 中国国际动漫节

自 2005 年在杭州成功举办以来，中国国际动漫节作为我国首个国家级国际性动漫节展，每年春夏在杭州白马湖动漫广场举办。连续 16 届共吸引全球五大洲 80 多个国家和地区参与。动漫节内容包括会展、论坛、大赛、活动四大板块 20 多个品牌项目，每年都评选出中国动漫最高奖项"金猴奖"，颁发给世界各地的漫画家和动画节目制作者及其爱好者。作为国际动漫工业和动漫爱好者的大型聚会，国际动漫节深受关注和热爱。疫情期间，人们通过线上线下方式参与互动。除动漫游戏企业参展、国内外优秀动漫作品参赛和动漫产业高峰论坛外，动漫节还推出国际动画电影周、抗疫主题漫画展等丰富多彩的项目载体，彰显动漫带给生活、带给城市的美好。

★ China International Cartoon and Animation Festival (CICAF)

Initiated in 2005, being the first of its kind in China, International Cartoon and Animation Festival has been held annually for 16 consecutive years. Held in Baima Lake Animation Plaza in spring and summer every year, it attracts people from more than 80 countries and regions in the world. The Festival possesses a variety of rich activities, including over 20 brand events, such as exhibitions, forums, competitions and activities. The best works are selected and awarded "Golden Monkey King" every year, which stands for a contest prestigious to all cartoonists and animated program makers and their enthusiasts worldwide. As a big party for the international animation industry and animation lovers, it has been deeply noticed and loved. During the epidemic period in 2020, people participated and interacted in the activities either online or offline. Participants included enterprises of animation games, excellent animation works of both at home and abroad, summit forum of animation industry. Besides, there are international animation film week, cartoon display featuring in anti-epidemic, which brings better life to the city.

★ 国际（杭州）毅行大会

国际（杭州）毅行大会由杭州市体育局主办，旨在通过活动，为杭州地区乃至全国的户外运动爱好者提供一个交流、体验、运动的大众参与平台。毅行大会以"健康生活、休闲运动"为核心，倾力打造属于老百姓自己的户外休闲运动盛典。活动自 2011 年在杭州举办以来就被赋予了全新的概念，成为杭州全民参与的休闲群众体育运动。

活动每年举办，设 5 千米、15 千米、30 千米、50 千米 4 个组别。从 2011 年首届的 2000 余人参与，逐步发展为杭州最具影响力的群众体育休闲运动，形成"杭州毅行"特有的运动品牌，成为备受广大徒步爱好者推崇的运动项目。[①]

★ International (Hangzhou) Trailwalk Conference

International (Hangzhou) Trailwalk Conference was initiated by Hangzhou Sports Bureau in 2011, aiming to provide a platform for outdoor enthusiasts from Hangzhou and the whole country where they can communicate, experience and doing sports. The core of the conference centers on "Healthy Lifestyle, Leisure Sports", building outdoor leisure activities suitable for ordinary people. Since it was first held in 2011, new concepts have been given and has become mass leisure sports activities participated by all citizens.

Trailwalk is held annually. There are four groups of different distance, that is, 5 km, 15 km, 30 km and 50 km. About 2,000 citizens participated in the Trailwalk in 2011. Since then, it has developed into the most influential mass leisure sports activities in Hangzhou and the unique sports brand "Hangzhou Trailwalk", which now is the highly regarded sports event by most hiking enthusiasts.

★ 全民健身日

后奥运时期，大众体育越来越受到关注。为满足人民群众日益增长的健身需求，也为了纪念2008年北京奥运会的成功举办，从2009年起，国务院把每年的8月8日定为"全民健身日"，以此传达健康体育精神，传播公众健康的生活理念。这一天，杭州的游泳馆、健身房、球场等场地免费开放。市民走出家门，在体育场馆、健身点、公园、西湖边、钱塘江边、城市河道边、山上、水上、广场上、市属高校、中小学等地进行体育锻炼。

全民健身日的成立，对满足人民群众的体育需求，促进全民健身运动有着重要的影响，让人们真正享受到体育带来的健康和快乐，让体育在构建和谐社会中发挥更积极的作用。全民健身日也是纪念北京奥运会的最好

---

① 佚名.国际（杭州）毅行大会［EB/OL］.（2023-04-04）［2023-04-18］. https://baike. baidu.com/item/%E5%9B%BD%E9%99%85%EF%BC%88%E6%9D%AD%E5%B7%9E%EF%BC%89%E6%AF%85%E8%A1%8C%E5%A4%A7%E4%BC%9A/16637257?fr=aladdin.

方式。

★ National Fitness Day

In the post-Olympic era, more and more attention is paid to mass sports. In order to satisfy people's growing demand for physical fitness and to commemorate the success of the Beijing Olympic Games in 2008, the State Council designated the day, August 8, as "National Fitness Day" in 2009 to convey healthy sporting spirit to the public and spread the concept of healthy living. On the day of August 8 each year, swimming pools, gyms and courts are open to the public for free. Citizens are out for doing different kinds of sports not only in stadiums, fitness centers, parks, places around the West Lake, the Qiantang River and city rivers, but also on top of hills, waterside, squares, universities and colleges, primary and secondary schools and other places, etc.

The establishment of National Fitness Day plays a positive role in satisfying people's sport needs and promoting the national fitness campaign. By doing sports, people can enjoy the benefits of being healthy and happy. Sports will play a more active role in the construction of harmonious society. The most important is that National Fitness Day is the best way to commemorate the Beijing Olympic Games.

第七章　创新活力之城

　　2016年，国家主席习近平在杭州G20峰会上致辞时向世界介绍"杭州是创新活力之城"。这不仅是因为杭州有阿里巴巴、海康威视等享誉国内外的知名公司和成千上万充满活力的小微企业，而且是因为杭州基于国内领先的"互联网＋"平台服务所形成的创新创业土壤和生态。早在杭州作为古代吴越国的都城时，就以积极的方式发展贸易和商业，这种风格延续至今，使其成为中国的创业创新中心，拥有巨大的电子商务市场。一座城市的创造力，取决于它的创新程度。杭州，这座拥有多年人文历史的文化名城，如今正以浓厚的创业氛围、独一无二的创业精神跑在全国创业创新的最前列。这座富有传奇浪漫艺术气息的城市，在"大众创业、万众创新"的今天，已经成为创业者和实干家的乐园。

Chapter Seven
City of Innovation and Vitality

In 2016, Chinese President Xi Jinping introduced to the world "Hangzhou is a city of innovation and vitality", when addressing at the G20 Summit in Hangzhou. This is not only because Hangzhou has Alibaba, Hikvision and other well-known companies at home and abroad as well as tens of thousands of dynamic small and micro enterprises, but also because Hangzhou is based on the leading domestic "Internet +" platform services formed by the soil and ecology of innovation and entrepreneurship. Hangzhou has long taken a progressive approach to trade and commerce, which can be traced back to when the city was the capital of the ancient Kingdom of Wu and Yue. This development path continues to this day and Hangzhou is an enterprise and innovation hub and huge ecommerce market. The creativity of a city depends on how innovative it is. Hangzhou, a famous cultural city with many years of cultural history, is now leading in the forefront of entrepreneurship and innovation in China with its strong entrepreneurial atmosphere and unique entrepreneurial spirit. This legendary, romantic and artistic city has become a paradise for entrepreneurs and doers in the era of "mass entrepreneurship and innovation".

第一节 G20 峰会

G20（二十国集团）峰会是 20 个重要的工业化国家组成的国际经济合作论坛。2016 年 9 月 4 日至 9 月 5 日，世界的目光聚焦东海之滨、钱塘江畔，二十国集团领导人第 11 次峰会在杭州圆满举行。二十国集团领导人聚集杭州国际博览中心，就气候变化、难民、反恐融资及其他问题展开讨论，最后达成广泛的共识，也称"杭州共识"。国家主席习近平主持会议并致开幕辞，强调二十国集团要与时俱进，推动世界经济强劲、可持续、平衡、包容增长，这是杭州首次向世界展示自己。

在杭州 G20 峰会上，习近平主席指出：杭州是一座历史名城，也是一座创新之城，既充满浓郁的中华文化韵味，也拥有面向世界的宽广视野。我相信，大家共同努力，杭州 2016 年峰会将呈现给世界一份别样的精彩。

Ⅰ G20 Summit

The G20 Summit (or G-20 or Group of Twenty) is an international forum for the governments and central bank governors from 20 major economies. From September 4 to 5, 2016, the world's view focused on the shore of China's East Sea and the bank of the Qiantang River as the 11th G20 Summit was successfully held in Hangzhou. G20 leaders gathered at the Hangzhou International Exposition Center discussing climate change, refugees, antiterrorist, financing and other issues, and finally reached broad consensus, namely Hangzhou Consensus. President Xi Jinping presided over the forum and delivered an opening speech, emphasizing G20 to keep pace with the times and to foster "an innovative, invigorated, interconnected and inclusive world economy". It is the first time for Hangzhou to show itself to the world.

In Hangzhou G20 Summit, President Xi pointed out that Hangzhou, renowned for its rich history, is also a city of innovation. It is a cosmopolitan city with a distinctive Chinese cultural appeal. He said he was sure that, through joint efforts, Hangzhou will deliver a uniquely impressive summit to the world this time.

第二节　创新型企业

杭州引人注目的科技遗产使它成为创业中心。2020 年 9 月 28 日，中国企业联合会和中国企业家协会发布了中国企业 500 强名单，其中杭州企业表现突出，共有 20 家在杭企业上榜。排名靠前的 3 家分别是阿里巴巴（34 位）、物产中大集团（56 位）和吉利汽车（65 位）。[①]杭州上榜企业涵盖互联网、汽车、贸易、石化、房地产、金融、高端制造业、信息技术、物流等多个领域，彰显了杭州经济发力数字经济与新制造业两大引擎，在国内乃至国际产业细分领域打响杭州品牌。

---

① 贾晓芸. 20 家在杭企业上榜中国企业 500 强［EB/OL］.（2020-09-30）［2022-12-15］. http://www.hangzhou.gov.cn/art/2020/9/30/art_812266_58870838.html.

Ⅱ Innovative Enterprises

The city's impressive tech heritage has made Hangzhou a center for entrepreneurship. Twenty companies headquartered in Hangzhou made onto the 2020 list of the top 500 Chinese companies, which was unveiled by the China Enterprise Confederation and China Enterprise Directors Association on September 28, 2020. The top three companies are all headquartered in Hangzhou, and they are Alibaba (34), WZ Group (56) and Geely (65). These 20 companies specialize in such areas of internet, automobiles, trade, petrochemical, real estate, finance, high-end manufacturing, information technology and modern logistics. The development of the economy of Hangzhou benefits from digital economy and new manufacturing which lead to Hangzhou brand known both home and abroad.

★ 阿里巴巴集团

全球领先的电子商务集团阿里巴巴，成立于 1999 年，总部位于杭州。最初只有 18 名员工，包括马云。今天，阿里巴巴已成为世界最大的零售商之一，旗下有淘宝、天猫、支付宝和菜鸟驿站等，给中国和世界带来创新的购物便利。阿里巴巴的手机支付应用程序——支付宝，改变了中国人的消费方式。有了支付宝，用手机简单一扫就可付款，即使在最小的街头餐馆和蔬菜摊贩那儿也不例外，人们可以不带钱包，轻松出门。每年 11 月 11 日，天猫一年一度的全球购物节深受购物者喜欢，这一天被年轻的网民们戏称为单身日。2009 年，阿里巴巴集团年轻的经理们将这一天设为网上购物日，以"双 11 购物节"闻名。这一天，网上商品以低价出售，至今已连续了 10 多年。创立 20 多年来，作为互联网巨头，阿里巴巴已经发展为世界上最大的网络商业公司，涉及电子商务、物流、云计算和数字媒体服务、在线健康和娱乐软件。可以毫不低调地说，阿里巴巴改变了中国人的生活。根据

2020 年 11 月《福布斯》（中国版）杂志的排名，在互联网行业和互联网服务方面，阿里巴巴位居全球第 4。

作为以科技创新为驱动的世界级科技企业，阿里巴巴积极参加国家科技创新体系建设，将企业战略与国家战略高度耦合，形成同频共振，在操作系统、云计算、数据库等颠覆性领域深度布局，在研发领域始终保持高水平投入。截止到 2020 年 3 月底，阿里巴巴集团累计获得中国专利授权近 8000 件，公开专利申请约 1.4 万件，累计申请外国专利授权近 4000 件，公开专利申请约 1.2 万件。[①]

★ Alibaba Group Holding Ltd.

Alibaba, the world's leading e-commerce group, is headquartered in Hangzhou. Founded in 1999 by 18 people, including Jack Ma. Today, it is one of the world's largest retailers, with brands such as Taobao, Tmall, Alipay and Cainiao Yizhan, bringing innovative shopping convenience to China and the whole world. Alipay—Alibaba's mobile payment application—has changed the way Chinese people do shopping. People can easily get by without a wallet as the App allows them to pay bills with a simple swipe of their smart phones—even at the smallest street restaurants and vegetable vendors. On November 11 every year, annual global shopping festival is very popular with shoppers. It was unofficially teased among young internet users as the day for the singles for how the number "11·11" looks like. In 2009, the young managers in the Alibaba Group made it into an online shopping day, known as the "Single's Day Shopping Festival" (Double Eleven Sales) on which almost everything was sold at low price. It has been celebrated for over 10 consecutive years. Over 20 years, regarded as the internet giant, Alibaba has grown to become the world's biggest online commerce company. It offers ecommerce, logistics, cloud and digital media services, as well as online health and entertainment subscription software. It's no understatement to say that Alibaba has reshaped Chinese life.

---

① 智汇百川. 献礼祖国：阿里巴巴技术创新之路［EB/OL］.（2020-10-01）［2022-12-23］. http://www.360doc.com/content/20/1001/13/36536556_938417114.shtml.

The Hangzhou-based Alibaba Group ranked fourth for engaging in the industry of internet and internet service according to a ranking by *Fortune* (China edition) on November 3, 2020.

As a world-class science and technology enterprise driven by scientific and technological innovation, Alibaba actively participates in the construction of the national scientific and technological innovation system, highly coupling corporate strategy with national strategy, forming common frequency resonance. Alibaba has a deep layout in operating system, cloud computing, database and other disruptive fields, and always maintains a high level of investment in research and development. By the end of March 2020, Alibaba Group has accumulated nearly 8,000 patent licenses in China, about 14,000 patent applications have been published, nearly 4,000 foreign patent licenses have been applied, and about 12,000 patent applications have been published.

▶ 云计算

云计算是中国唯一一个自主研发的计算引擎。2017 年，云计算获得中国电子协会颁发的科技进步特等奖。这也是奖项设立 15 年来第一次颁发的特等奖。阿里巴巴研制了飞天云操作系统，提出了"以数据为中心的云计算"体系结构原则，首次实现将百万服务器连成一台超级计算机，同时，孵化培育了城市大脑、工业大脑、农业大脑等创新应用，构建了一批行业解决方案。

▶ Cloud Computing

Cloud computing is China's only self-developed computing engine. In 2017, cloud computing won the Special Prize for Progress in Science and Technology of China Electronics Association. It is also the first time in the 15 years since the awards were launched that a grand prize has been awarded. Alibaba developed the Feitian Cloud operating system, put forward the architectural principle of "data-centered cloud computing", and realized the connection of millions of servers into a supercomputer for the first time. At the same time, with the incubation and cultivation of urban brain, industrial brain, agricultural brain and other innovative applications, a number of industrial solutions have been built.

▶ **数据库**

阿里巴巴投入六七百人力，耗时近 10 年，打造了一系列先进的数据库产品，服务着整个阿里巴巴的经济体并跻身世界领先阵营。走过"商业—开源—自研"的演进路线，阿里巴巴不断突破数据库技术和应用生态，实现了数据库领域的自主可控，为上千万中小企业的在线商业数据提供实时数据服务，并为政务、制造、金融、通信、海关、交通等重点行业提供稳定可靠的数据存储与分析服务。

▶ **Database**

Alibaba invests 600 to 700 people, and takes nearly ten years to make achievements, creating a series of advanced database products, which serve the whole economy of Alibaba and it is the among the world's leading camp. Through the evolution of "business—open source—self research", Alibaba has constantly broken through database technology and application of ecology, realized autonomous control in the field of database, providing online business data for tens of millions of small and medium-sized enterprises with real-time data services, and providing government affairs, manufacturing, financial, telecommunications, customs, transportation and other key industries with stable and reliable data storage and analysis services.

▶ **达摩院**

达摩院是致力于探索未知科技的技术型研究院，主要研究未来 5—20 年的问题，如量子计算、人工智能、数据库和基础的视觉计算等。达摩院设立了机器智能、数据计算、机器人、金融科技和 X 等研究方向，以及"4＋X"研究领域，成立了 14 个实验室。达摩院与全球顶级的高校科研机构开展多学科、多领域的学术合作，取得多项学术成果。在未来能惠及所有用户和客户，能让他们加快商业创新，用技术更好地做商业。

▶ **The Damo Institute**

A technology-oriented research institute has dedicated to exploring the scientific and technological unknown, focusing on the next five to twenty years of problems such as quantum computing, artificial intelligence, database and basic visual computing. The institute has set up 14 laboratories in the fields of machine intelligence, data computing, robotics, fintech and X, as well as the "4+X" research field. With the world's top universities and research institutions to carry out multi-disciplinary, multi-field academic cooperation, it has achieved a number of academic achievements. In the future, it can help the whole users and customers, so that they can speed up business innovation and use technology to do business better.

★ 浙江吉利控股集团

浙江吉利控股集团（简称"吉利控股"）始建于 1986 年，从生产电冰箱零件起步，发展到生产电冰箱、电冰柜、建筑装潢材料和摩托车，1997年进入汽车行业，一直专注实业，专注技术创新和人才培养，不断打基础、练内功，坚定不移地推动企业转型升级和可持续发展。现资产总值超过3900 亿元，员工总数超过 12 万人，连续 9 年进入《财富》公布的"世界500 强"名单。[①]

吉利控股现已发展为一家集汽车整车、动力总成和关键零部件设计、研发、生产、销售和服务于一体，并涵盖出行服务、数字科技、金融服务、教育等业务的全球创新型科技企业集团。集团总部设在杭州，旗下拥有吉利、领克、几何、沃尔沃、极星、宝腾、路特斯、英伦汽车、远程新能源商用车、太力飞行汽车、曹操出行、钱江摩托、盛宝银行、铭泰等品牌，在新能源科技、共享出行、车联网、智能驾驶、车载芯片、低轨卫星、激光通信等前沿技术领域不断提升能力，积极布局未来智慧立体出行生态。

2019 年 4 月，吉利控股成为第 19 届杭州亚运会官方合作伙伴。以此为契机，吉利汽车启动主题为"科技吉利，悦行亚运"的亚运战略，通过绿色科技、智能科技、人文责任等举措，实现区域范围内完全自动驾驶，全

---

① 佚名.吉利位列世界 500 强第 243 位　连续 9 年进入［EB/OL］.（2020-08-18）［2022-12-23］. https://www.sohu.com/a/413628053_114798.

方位赋能杭州亚运会。

★ **Zhejiang Geely Holding Group**

Zhejiang Geely Holding Group (Geely) was founded in 1986 and went from manufacturing refrigerator parts to refrigerators, construction and decorative materials and motorcycles. In 1997, the group entered the automotive industry and has continued to grow with a dedication towards technological innovation, talent cultivation, focusing on core strengths and staying committed developing sustainably. Today, Geely Holding Group total assets are valued over 390 billion yuan with more than 120,000 employees, and has been listed on the Global 500 issued by *Fortune* for nine consecutive years.

Zhejiang Geely Holding Group has developed into a global enterprise engaged in the design, R&D, production, sales, and service of vehicles, powertrains, and key components. The Group is in the midst of transforming into a global innovative technology enterprise engaged in the fields of mobility services, digital technology, financial services, education, and other business. Headquartered in Hangzhou, the Group owns several brands including Geely Auto, Lynk & Co, Geometry, Volvo Cars, Polestar, PROTON, Lotus, London Electric Vehicle Company, Farizon Auto, Terrafugia, CAOCAO, Qianjiang Motorcycle, Joma, Saxo Bank, Mitime Group, etc. Geely is constantly advancing through the development of cutting edge technologies in new energy, shared mobility, vehicle networks, autonomous drive, vehicle microchips, low orbit satellites, and laser communication as it lays the foundation for a future three-dimensional mobility ecology.

In April 2019, Geely Holding Group became the official prestige partner of the 19th Asian Games in Hangzhou. Under the slogan "Enjoy E-mobility @ the Asian Games with Geely", the Group empowers the games with green, intelligent, and humanistic technologies. Geely develops a series of full autonomous mobility solutions to serve the 19th Asian Games.

★ 杭州海康威视数字技术股份有限公司

总部在杭州的杭州海康威视数字技术股份有限公司（简称"海康威视"）创建于 2001 年，是安全产品和解决方案的重要提供商。公司提供以视频为核心的智能物联网解决方案和大数据服务，业务聚焦于综合安防、大数据服务和智慧业务，构建开放合作生态，为公共服务领域用户、企事业用户和中小企业用户提供服务，致力于构筑云边融合、物信融合、数智融合的智慧城市和数字化企业。公司全球员工超过 5.2 万人（截止到 2021 年 12 月 31 日），其中研发人员和技术服务人员超过 2.5 万人。[①]

海康威视产品和解决方案应用于 150 多个国家和地区，在 G20 杭州峰会、北京奥运会、上海世博会、APEC 会议、英国伦敦邱园、德国科隆乐业艺术博物馆、北京大兴机场、港珠澳大桥等重大项目中发挥了重要作用。

★ Hangzhou Hikvision Digital Technology Co. Ltd.

Founded in 2001, the Hangzhou-based Hikvision Digital Technology (Hikvision) is a leading provider of security products and solutions. As the provider of intelligent internet of things solutions and big data service with video as the core, the business of the company focuses on the integrated security system, big data service and smart business, building an open and cooperative ecosystem, providing service for public service users, enterprise and public institution users, small and medium-sized enterprise users, etc. striving for building digital enterprises and smart cities featuring in cloud edge fusion, integration of things and information and digital intelligence integration. The company has over 52,000 employees globally (by December 31, 2021), among them 25,000 are engaged in research and development and technical service.

Products and solutions are applied in more than 150 countries and regions, playing a vital part in the following key projects as the G20 Summit in Hangzhou, the Olympic Games in Beijing, the World Exposition of Shanghai,

---

① 佚名. 公司简介［EB/OL］.［2022-12-23］. https://www.hikvision.com/cn/aboutus/CompanyProfile/.

APEC Conference, Kew Gardens in London (The Royal Botanic Gardens at Kew), East Asian Art Museum of Cologne, Germany, Beijing Daxing International Airport and Hong Kong-Zhuhai-Macao Bridge, etc.

★ 网易（杭州）网络有限公司

网易（杭州）网络有限公司（简称"网易"）是中国领先的互联网公司之一，1997年在广州创立。创始人丁磊自1999年7月起担任网易的董事长，2005年11月起担任首席执行官。网易在开发互联网应用、服务等方面始终保持中国业界领先地位。本着"网聚人的力量，用科技创新缔造美好生活"的愿景，网易利用最先进的互联网技术，加强人与人之间信息的交流和共享，始终坚持"以优质的内容和服务，为用户创造惊喜"，提供网络游戏、电子邮件、新闻、博客、搜索引擎、论坛、虚拟社区等服务。

多年来，网易致力于在创新和多样化内容、社区、交流与商业方面提供优质的服务，研发和运营中国最受欢迎的手机和电脑游戏并在全球手机游戏市场获得重大成功。近年来，网易拓展了包括日本和南美的市场。网易还研发出了一系列出色的创新业务，包括智能学习服务平台"有道"、中国领先的媒体音乐平台"网易云音乐"以及自有电商品牌"严选"等。

★ NetEase. Inc.

NetEase. Inc. (NetEase), was founded in 1997 in Guangzhou by Ding Lei (William Lei Ding), Director and Chief Executive Officer, who served as the director since July 1999 and as the Chief Executive Officer since November 2005. NetEase is a leading internet technology company in internet application and service based in China. With the purpose to deliver "Power to the people, Create a better life with scientific and technological innovation" by using the latest Internet technologies to enhance meaningful information sharing and exchange, the company strives to bring surprise to clients through high quality service and provides services such as online games, e-mail, news, blogs, search engine, forum and virtual community, etc.

For years, NetEase has been dedicated to providing premium online services centered on innovative and diverse content, community, communication and commerce. NetEase develops and operates some of China's most popular mobile and PC-client games and also achieved marked success in the global mobile games market. In more recent years, NetEase has expanded into international markets including Japan and North America. NetEase's other innovative service offerings include the intelligent learning services of its majority-controlled subsidiary — Youdao, music streaming through its leading NetEase Cloud Music business, and its private label e-commerce platform Yanxuan.

第三节　创意产业园

　　文化创意园区不仅是以文化为主题的生产集聚空间，也是文化休闲与消费活动的空间，更是革新与创意的空间。近些年来，杭州文创产业蓬勃发展，涌现出了一批具有代表性和影响力的创意产业园，吸纳了大量从业人员，并创造了巨大的社会经济效益。

Ⅲ Cultural and Creative Industry Parks

Cultural and creative industry park is not only the soil for culture-themed production, but also a place for cultural recreation and consumption, as well as a realm for innovation and creativity. In recent years, the cultural and creative industry in Hangzhou has been developing vigorously, and a lot of representative and influential creative industry parks have emerged, offering a large number of jobs and creating huge social and economic benefits.

★ 运河天地文化创意园

运河天地文化创意园位于京杭大运河最南端的杭州市拱墅区，是杭州文化创意产业的发祥地。以工业遗产保护与利用为特色的文化创意产业基地如雨后春笋般汇聚拱墅运河畔。运河天地文化创意园沿京杭大运河古文化遗存与杭州老工业遗存规划园区，穿珠成链，通过将老厂房改造成文创基地，进行文创企业孵化、产业集群化、创意商业的建设与布局。昔日的"夕阳厂房"注入"朝阳产业"，改变了工业老厂房在城市化进程中因大面积旧城改造而终将消失的命运，使之萌发出新的生机和活力。在模式上，沿河而生，缘文化而发展，不局限于一园一区，一地一楼，而是围绕京杭大运河两岸选取合适的历史文化遗存和老工业厂房进行改造，形成独具特色的"一园多点"的园区模式。运河天地文化创意园在运河沿线不断开发、挖掘文化创意的种子，打造出了大批文创园区和特色楼宇。近年来，园区发展迅速，文创主导产业特色日益鲜明，形成了以设计服务业、现代传媒业、动漫游戏业为主导的产业布局，美誉度日益凸显，先后被评为"杭州市高新技术产业园""浙江省文化产业示范基地"等。其中，乐富智汇园被评为国家级科技孵化器、国家文化产业示范基地。

★ Grand Canal Horizon Cultural and Creative Park

The Grand Canal Horizon Cultural and Creative Park, located by the Beijing-Hangzhou Grand Canal, a world heritage site, is the matrix of Hangzhou's cultural and creative industry, with cultural and creative industry bases built on the industrial legacies along the Grand Canal. The park strings the ancient cultural relics of the Grand Canal and the old industrial relics of Hangzhou, having the old factories converted into cultural and creative bases, and aiming to incubate enterprises, industrial clusters, and promote creative business. Preserved rather than demolished in urbanization and city reconstruction, those former "sunset" factories have been vitalized by the "sunrise" industries. The park takes shape along the Grand Canal and grows on culture, and it is not confined to any individual site, building, or region; instead, it selects appropriate historical and cultural relics and old industrial plants on both sides of the Grand Canal and has them renovated, restored and retrofitted, making a unique mode of "one park with multiple sites". The park keeps developing and tapping the historical and cultural heritage, and has created a lot of cultural and creative complexes and buildings. It has evolved into an industrial layout with distinctive features of culture and creativity, dominated by design service, modern media, animation and game. The Grand Canal Horizon Cultural and Creative Park has built a reputation, and won various titles, such as "Hangzhou High-tech Industrial Park", "Zhejiang Cultural Industry Demonstration Park", etc. And especially, Loft Power, one of the complexes in the park, has been rated as a national science incubator and a national cultural industry demonstration base.

★ 之江文化创意园

　　杭州之江文化创意园是杭州市首批命名的十大文化创意园之一，总规划面积约 1.57 平方千米，围绕"创意、产业、居住"三位一体的功能定位，集产业孵化与发展、展览展示、艺术休闲、特色配套于一体。2010 年 11 月，被教育部、科技部联合命名为"中国美术学院国家大学科技（创意）园"，成为全国第一个以艺术创意为特色的国家大学科技园。

　　园区分为核心示范区、产业拓展区、综合配套区 3 个区块，共 7 个项目。这些项目功能清晰，各具特色。如项目一"凤凰·创意国际"为研发孵化基地，位于西湖区转塘街道创意路 1 号，由双流水泥厂改造而成，别具一格，总占地面积约 0.22 平方千米，规划建筑面积约 0.1 平方千米，初步形成了现代设计、动漫、艺术品、新媒体 4 个特色产业，先后吸引了一大批文创名人入驻。园区是中国国际动漫节和杭州文化创意产业博览会的分会场，曾举办一系列国内国际文创交流活动，并成为新车发布、时装展示和影视广告等的拍摄基地。

★ Zhijiang Cultural and Creative Park

Zhijiang Cultural and Creative Park is one of the first ten authorized cultural and creative parks in Hangzhou. With a total planning area of about 1.57 square kilometers, it aims to build a park comprising industrial incubation and development, exhibition, cultural recreation, and characteristic supporting facilities, focusing on the functions of creativity, industry and residence. In November 2010, it was entitled "China Academy of Art National University Science (Creative) Park" jointly by the Ministry of Education and the Ministry of Science and Technology, turning into the first national university science park featuring art and creativity.

The park is divided into three areas: the main demonstration area, industrial development area, and comprehensive support area, with a total of seven projects. These projects have distinct functions and distinctive features. Take Project One, "Phenix Creative", as an example, it functions as an incubation base for creative research and development. Located in No.1 Zhuantang Street, Xihu District, it's converted from the Shuangliu Cement Plant, with a very impressive and unique style. Having a total area of over 0.22 square kilometers and a floorage of about 0.1square kilometers, Phenix Creative is cultivating four characteristic industries of modern design, animation, artwork and new media, attracting a large number of artistic practitioners and masters. The park is a branch venue of China International Animation Festival, Hangzhou Cultural and Creative Industry Exposition, and a shooting base for new car launches, fashion shows, commercials, having hosted a series of domestic and international cultural and creative activities.

★ 西湖数字娱乐产业园

西湖数字娱乐产业园位于西湖区古荡街道，2006 年 8 月成为文化部首个国家数字娱乐产业示范基地，是长三角最大的数字娱乐产业集聚地，主要从事数字娱乐开发、运营和增值服务、影视动画制作及衍生产品开发等，形成了较为完备的数字娱乐动漫游戏产业链。产业园主要为数字娱乐产业链上的企业提供发展空间、技术支持、政策扶持和公共服务。产业园内产业齐全，有专业从事网络游戏开发的公司，也有能提供手机业务增值的配套服务，如手机游戏、手机桌面等制作单位，还有从事动漫真人秀服装制作的企业，这在国内属于比较新颖的一个产业。

★ **West Lake Digital Entertainment Industrial Park**

Located in Gudang Street, Xihu District, the West Lake Digital Entertainment Industrial Park was authorized by the Ministry of Culture as the first "National Digital Entertainment Industry Demonstration Base" in August 2006. It is the largest cluster of digital entertainment industry in the Yangtze River Delta, mainly engaged in industrial operation, value-added services, development of digital entertainment products, animations and their derivatives, etc. The industrial park has formed a relatively complete industry chain for digital entertainment, animation and game, providing enterprises with development space, technical support, policy support and public services. In the industrial park, there are professional companies engaged in developing online games and providing value-added mobile phone business, like mobile phone games, desktop design and production, as well as enterprises engaged in COSPLAY (animation reality show) clothing production, a relatively new industry in China.

★ **西溪创意产业园**

西溪创意产业园位于西溪国家湿地公园桑梓漾区域，占地面积约 0.9 平方千米。园区依托不同时期遗存的建筑，按照"生态化、功能化、差异化"的标准进行修缮、新建，是一个具有西溪特色的原生态的创意设计艺术庄园。创意园分两大功能区块、三大主力业态。两大功能区块分别是：西区艺术村落区，主要由各类创意工作室、艺术创作和展示、艺术经营机构和配套商业组成；东区创意产业区，主要由创意产业企业总部、大型创意产业机构和研发中心等组成。三大主力业态即艺术创作及艺术经营类、创意设计类、总部基地类业态。园区努力打造以艺术创作为主体，集艺术展示、艺术交易及文化、休闲、旅游为一体的艺术综合体。

目前有大批海内外著名的画家、音乐家、作家、剧作家、导演、漫画家、策划家、创意大师等入驻，如徐沛东、余华、麦家、赖声川、朱德庸、潘公凯、吴山明、约翰·霍金斯、皮托夫等；还有部分来自国内及日本和法国的艺术大师也已达成初步进驻意向。

★ Xixi Creative Industry Park

Xixi Creative Industry Park lies in the Sangziyang area of Xixi National Wetland Park, covering an area of 0.9 square kilometers. Relying on the preserved buildings of different periods of time, the creative park was renovated and built according to the standards of "ecology, function and differentiation". It is a creative design realm with Xixi wetland characteristics of original ecology, divided into two functional blocks and three main business forms. The two functional blocks are: the art village in the west, which is mainly composed of various creative studios, art creation and exhibition enterprises, art management institutions and business services; the creative industry block in the east, including headquarters, large creative industry institutions, research and development centers. The three main forms of business are art creation and management, creative design, and headquarter base. The creative park aims to be an art complex with artistic creation as the main bushiness, integrating art exhibition, art trading, culture, leisure and tourism.

At present, in the park there are studios of many famous artists, painter, musicians, writers, playwrights, directors, cartoonists, planners and creative masters from home and abroad, such as Xu Peidong, Yu Hua, Mai Jia, Stan Lai, Zhu Deyong, Pan Gongkai, Wu Shanming, John Hawkins (Father of creative industry from Britain), Pitof from Hollywood, etc., and many more masters from China, Japan and France have intended to open studios or branches in the park.

★ 西湖创意谷

2007 年，杭州市上城区和中国美术学院联手打造西湖创意谷文化创意产业园区。园区建设以高端创意为起点，具有浓重的探索性、原创性和时尚性，迈开了"环美院创意产业带"建设的第一步，开创了浙江创意经济的先河，该项目被列为杭州市十大创意产业项目之一。创意谷由创意产业孵化基地、创意产业生活区、创意体验区等组成，以中国美术学院的人才、技术和成果为依托，以"原创、高端、精品、时尚"为主题，突出创意、创新、创造的功能定位，结合钱江新城建设和城市改造，大力发展环境规划设计、园林设计、城市色彩设计等新兴产业，构建完整的设计产业链。同时园区注重国内外招商引资，为创意企业的集群化、规模化发展提供空间。园区在发展产业孵化区的同时发展展示交易区，启用全息流量商业生态运行模式，人文景观与自然生态景观有机融合，积极推动中国古文化、艺术产业经济圈的崛起。

★ West Lake Creative Valley

West Lake Creative Valley was founded jointly by the government of Shangcheng District and China Academy of Art in 2007. The construction of the creative valley was exploratory, original and fashionable, aiming to build a high-end creative industry. It is the first step of the construction of the "Creative Industry Belt Encircling the China Academy of Art", and a pioneer of a creative economy in Zhejiang Province, listed as one of the top ten creative industry projects in Hangzhou. It consists of creative industry incubators, living quarters, experience areas, etc. Relying on the talents, technology and achievements of the China Academy of Art, and with the theme of "being original, high-end, premium, and fashionable", it highlights creativity, innovation and creation. Combined with the construction of Qianjiang New City and urban retrofitting, the valley aims to foster industries of environmental planning and design, landscape design, urban color design, etc., to build a complete design industry chain. At the same time, the valley tries to attract relevant enterprises and capital from home and abroad, so as to provide space for a cluster and scale development for creative enterprises. It attempts to develop areas for incubation, exhibition and trade, and applies the commercial ecological operation mode of holographic flow, integrates cultural, natural and ecological landscape, intending to helps with the rise of China's ancient culture and art industry.

★ 白马湖生态创意城

白马湖生态创意城位于杭州滨江高新区南部，总面积约 15 平方千米，核心区域为白马湖区域，该区域依山傍水，自然景观优美、人文积淀深厚。创意城的总体布局包括一核——冠山城市核，二业——文化创意业和生态旅游业，三带——紧缩城市带、田园城市带、山水城市带，四种生活区——生态示范特色居住区、家居改造特色居住区、高端生态特色居住区、新建特色居住区，五园——设计公园、文化创意公园、动漫公园、白马湖生态旅游度假公园、大地生态产业公园。滨江白马湖地区力争打造成杭州经济社会发展的增长极，建设成具有时代特点、杭州特色、钱塘江特征，宜业、宜居、宜旅、宜文的生态新城，形成创业发展与生活品质、文化价值与经济运行、个人创业与整体发展、政府与民间、对外开放与内生创新有机结合的良好局面。

目前，白马湖生态创意城是杭州乃至全国规模最大、产业基础最优越的文化创意产业集聚区，聚集大批文化创意企业，先后获评"2009 中国创意产业最佳园区""2010 当代城市化项目杰出蓝本""浙江省现代服务业集聚示范区""浙江省文化创意产业示范园区"等荣誉，获得"亚洲都市景观奖"，并于 2020 年 12 月 25 日入选"国家级文化产业示范园区"。中国国际动漫节、海峡两岸文化创意产业高校研究联盟论坛已永久落户。

★ White Horse Lake Ecological Creative Town

The White Horse Lake Ecological Creative Town sits in the south of Binjiang High-tech Zone, with an area of about 15 square kilometers. The core is the area of the White Horse Lake, which is dotted with hills and lakes, with picturesque landscape and profound cultural accumulation.The creative town comprises: one centre—Guanshan residential quarter; two industries—cultural and creative industry, eco-tourism industry; three belts—restricted urban belt, idyllic urban belt, picturesque urban belt; four modes of residential areas— ecological demonstration residential area, renovated residential area, high-end ecological residential area and newly built residential area; five parks—design park, cultural and creative park, animation park, White Horse Lake ecological tourism resort park, Dadi ecological industry park. The creative town aims to be a growth pole of the economic and social development for Hangzhou, an new ecological town embodying the characteristics of the times, Hangzhou City and the Qiantang River, livable and suitable for cultural creation, career development, and travel; a paradise in which entrepreneurship and quality life, cultural value and economic operation, individual development and the collective progress, government and the public, opening up and endogenous innovation are balanced and in harmony.

The White Horse Lake Ecological Creative Town is said to be the largest creative industry cluster with the best foundation in Hangzhou and even in China, holding lots of cultural and creative enterprises. It has been rated "China Best Creative Industry Park 2009", "Outstanding Contemporary Urbanization Project Blueprint 2010", "Zhejiang Demonstration Area of Modern Service Industry Cluster", "Zhejiang Demonstration Park for Culture Creative Industry", etc., and won the "Asian City Landscape Prize". On December 25, 2020, it was entitled "National Cultural Industry Demonstration Park". The China International Cartoon and Animation Festival and the Forum of University Research Alliance of Cross-Taiwan Strait Cultural and Creative Industry have taken it as the permanent venue.

★ 下沙大学科技园

下沙大学科技园位于全国唯一集工业园区、高教园区、出口加工区于一体的国家级开发区——杭州下沙经济技术开发区，地理位置优越，交通方便，坐拥 14 所高等院校丰富的人力资源。科技园总规划面积约 88 万平方米，是由杭州经济技术开发区管理委员会在秉承"共建、共享、共发展"理念，以"依托高校、政府引导、工学结合、市场运作"为原则的基础上，采取"以校为主、校区共建"发展模式所创立的大学科创园，以"一园多点"的格局分布在各大高校。已建成中国计量大学国家大学科技园、浙江理工大学创业孵化园、杭州电子科技大学创业园、高职科技（学生）创业园、安防科技产业园、浙江传媒学院传媒文化创意产业园、第五时尚设计产业中心、开发区 IT 服务外包园等 10 多个特色园区，主要发展工业设计、平面设计、软件设计、影视制作、文艺创作、时尚设计、传媒文化、旅游及城市规划等产业。

★ Xiasha University Science Park

With a total planning area of about 880,000 square meters, the Xiasha University Science Park is located in Hangzhou Economic and Technological Development Zone, which is the only national development zone integrating industrial park, higher education zone and export processing zone. It owns convenient transport and abundant human resources from 14 colleges and universities in the biggest higher education zone of Zhejiang Province. Constructed by the Administrative Committee of Hangzhou Economic and Technological Development Zone, the science and technology park embodies the concept of "joint construction, sharing and development". It is based on principles of "relying on the colleges and universities, government leading, learning integrated with working, market operation", with a development model of "colleges and universities playing the dominant role, with assistance from the local government". With a layout of "one park plus multi-site", distributed on or off the campuses of those colleges and universities are over ten distinctive cultural and creative industry incubators, blocks, complexes, such as China Jiliang University National Science Park, Zhejiang Sci-tech University Innovation Incubator, Hangzhou Dianzi University Enterprise Incubator, Higher Vocational and Technical Technology College Students' Enterprise Incubator,

Security Technology Industrial Park, Communication University of Zhejiang Media Culture and Creative Industry Park, the 5th Fashion Design Industry Center, IT Service Outsourcing Park and so on. The main industries in Xiasha University Science Park are mainly about industrial design, graphic design, software design, film and television production, literary and artistic creation, fashion design, media culture, tourism and urban planning, etc.

★ 湘湖文化创意产业园

湘湖文化创意产业园成立于 2007 年，是杭州市十大文化创意产业园区之一，也是浙江省唯一的省级文化创意产业实验区，地处杭州市萧山区风情大道以东休博园区域，距西湖和萧山国际机场约 15 分钟车程，地铁 1 号线湘湖站毗邻园区入口。园区规划建筑面积约 15.1 万平方米，已建成用于发展文创产业的建筑面积约 8.1 万平方米。园区由杭州宋城集团投资建设，杭州世界休闲博览园有限公司负责日常运营，重点引进信息服务业、动漫游戏业、设计服务业、现代传媒业、艺术品业、教育培训业、文化旅游休闲业、文化会展业等文创行业，并特别注重与演艺、旅游等相关行业的紧密结合。目前湘湖文化创意产业园已经形成了一批以市场为导向，颇具规模和实力、具有良好发展前景和影响力的文化企业和文化品牌，比如阿优文化、希蒙文化等。

★ Xianghu Cultural and Creative Industry Park

Founded in 2007, the Xianghu Cultural and Creative Industry Park is one of the top ten cultural and creative industry parks of Hangzhou, and the only experimental park on cultural and creative industry at the provincial level. It lies in the Leisure Exposition Park at the east of Fengqing Avenue, Xiaoshan District, and is about 15 minutes' drive from the West Lake and Hangzhou Xiaoshan International Airport, with Xianghu Station of Metro Line 1 next to the entrance of the park. The planned building area of the park is 151,000 square meters, of which 81,000 square meters have been in service to house cultural and creative industry enterprises. The park was invested by Hangzhou

Worldland Group, and is operated by Hangzhou World Leisure Exposition Park Co., Ltd. It introduces industries of information service, animation and game, design service, modern media, art, education and training, cultural tourism and leisure, cultural exhibition, etc., and makes these industries integrated with entertainment, tourism and other related industries. The Xianghu Cultural and Creative Industry Park has created a number of market-oriented, influential, competitive and promising cultural enterprises and brands, such as A-U Culture, Ximeng Culture, and so on.

第四节　特色小镇

　　特色小镇是在块状经济和县域经济基础上发展而来的创新经济模式，是供给侧改革的浙江实践。该名称于 2014 年在杭州云栖小镇被正式提及。2016 年起，建设和培育特色小镇的实践在全国各省区市纷纷展开。特色小镇的特色主要表现为：产业上坚持特色产业、旅游产业两大发展架构；功能上实现"生产＋生活＋生态"，形成产、城、乡一体化功能聚集区；形态上具备独特的风格、风貌、风尚与风情；机制上实行以政府为主导，以企业为主体，社会共同参与的创新模式。目前杭州市已建成或正在培育中的各类特色小镇达几十个。

Ⅳ Characteristic Towns

　　Characteristic Towns, as an innovative economic model developing on the basis of block economy and county economy, is the practice of supply side reform of Zhejiang Province. This term was formally mentioned in the Cloud Town of Hangzhou in 2014. Since 2016, the practice of incubating and building Characteristic Towns has been carried out across the country. The characteristics of the so-call Characteristic Towns are as follows: in terms of the industrial framework, it adheres to the characteristic industry and the tourism industry; functionally, it aims to realize the combination of "production＋life ＋ecology" and to form a concentration area integrating industries, town and the countryside; morphologically, it owns a unique style, townscape, fashion and local customs; as for its mechanism, it is an innovation model with the government taking the lead, enterprises as the main body and the society as the participants. At present, dozens of towns with various characteristics have been built or are in incubation in Hangzhou.

★ 云栖小镇

云栖小镇地处杭州之江国家旅游度假区，核心区面积约 3.5 平方千米，规划总面积约 13.8 平方千米。小镇的前身是 2002 年成立的传统工业园区。2011 年 10 月，杭州云计算产业园在这里开园，成为全省首个云计算产业园区，奠定了云计算和大数据的产业发展方向。2013 年，在原来传统工业园区的基础上，建设了基于云计算、大数据和智能硬件产业的特色小镇，孵化出"飞天 5K"云操作系统、互联网汽车、"城市大脑"等科技成果。云栖小镇是浙江省特色小镇的发源地，是促进转型发展，探索以产业为先导的新型城镇化之路的成功实践，成为浙江省数字经济发展的缩影和高质量发展的代表。云栖小镇是浙江重点数字经济产业平台，是国家 3A 级景区和杭州"数字经济旅游"景区。

★ Cloud Town

The Cloud Town is located in Zhijiang National Tourism Resort, Xihu District, with a core area of about 3.5 square kilometers and a planned area of 13.8 square kilometers. The town has been an old-fashioned industrial park established in 2002. In October 2011, the Hangzhou Cloud Computing Industrial Park was founded here, making it the first cloud computing industrial park in Zhejiang Province, and laying the foundation for the industrial development with cloud computing and big data as the orientation. In 2013, a characteristic town on cloud computing, big data and intelligent hardware industry was built on the basis of the original industrial park. It has incubated the "Flying 5K" cloud operating system, internet of vehicles, "Smart City Brain" and other scientific and technological achievements. As the birthplace of Characteristic Towns in Zhejiang Province, the Cloud Town is a successful attempt on industrial transformation and development and an exploration of urbanization led by industry. It is the epitome of the development of digital economy and the representative of high-quality development in Zhejiang Province. The town is a key digital economy industry platform at the provincial level, a national 3A level scenic spot and a "digital economy tourism" scenic spot of Hangzhou City.

★ 玉皇山南基金小镇

玉皇山南基金小镇创建于 2015 年 5 月，占地面积约 5 平方千米。它背靠玉皇山，面对钱塘江，坐落于上城区南宋遗址核心区，是一个类似于美国对冲基金天堂格林尼治的基金小镇。2013 年，小镇获得由联合国颁发的"杰出环境治理工程奖"，2018 年被批为国家 4A 级旅游景区，并入选全国最美特色小镇 50 强。截至 2020 年 9 月，已累计入驻金融机构 2430 家，总资产管理规模约 11660 亿元，累计税收收入位列浙江省已命名特色小镇首位。[①]未来，玉皇山南基金小镇将努力打造世界级基金小镇经典样板。

★ Fund Town at the South of Yuhuang Hill

Yuhuang Shannan Fund Town was founded in May 2015, covering an area of about 5 square kilometers. The town sits in the heart of the Southern

---

① 祝婷兰. 玉皇山南基金小镇五周年 [EB/OL]. (2020-10-30) [2023-04-06]. http://www.hangzhou.gov.cn/art/2020/10/30/art_812262_59015569.html.

Song Dynasty ruins between Yuhuang Hill (the Jade Emperor Hill) and the Qiantang River in Shangcheng District. It is a fund town similar to Greenwich, the hedge fund paradise of the United States. In 2013, the town won the "Award for Outstanding Environmental Management Project" by the United Nations. In 2018, it was approved as a national 4A level tourist attraction and listed in the Top 50 Most Beautiful Characteristic Towns in China. As of September 2020, it has accumulated 2,430 financial institutions and a total asset management scale of about 1,166 billion yuan. The cumulative tax revenue ranks first among all the accredited Characteristic Towns in Zhejiang Province. The Fund Town is aiming to make a world-class fund town

★ 梦想小镇

梦想小镇位于余杭区仓前街道，于 2014 年 9 月正式启动建设，占地面积约 3 平方千米。小镇包括"互联网创业小镇"和"天使小镇"两大内容。"互联网创业小镇"重点支持"泛大学生"群体创办电子商务、软件设计、网络安全、信息服务、集成电路、动漫设计等互联网相关领域产品的研发、生产和经营；"天使小镇"则重点培育和发展科技金融及互联网金融。梦想小镇为"泛大学生"群体的创新创业提供优惠贷款、租房补助等一系列优惠支持政策。梦想小镇是国家 3A 级景区，并于 2018 年入选全国最美特色小镇 50 强。

★ Dream Town

Dream Town lies in Cangqian Street, Yuhang District, with an area of 3 square kilometers. The town was officially started in September 2014. It comprises two parts, the "Internet Entrepreneurship Town" and the "Angel Town". The "Internet Entrepreneurship Town" focuses on supporting college students or graduates to engage in e-commerce, software design, network security, information services, integrated circuits, animation design and the development, production and operation of other internet-related products; and the "Angel Town" on the cultivation and development of sci-tech finance and internet finance. The Dream Town provides a series of preferential support policies, such as preferential loans and rental subsidies, encouraging the innovation and entrepreneurship of college students and graduates. The town is a national 3A level tourist attraction, and it was selected as one of the Top 50 Most Beautiful Characteristic Towns in China in 2018.

★ 滨江物联网小镇

物联网小镇位于滨江区，总规划面积 3.66 平方千米。小镇交通便利，除了城市公路网，地铁 1 号线、6 号线可达，距萧山国际机场约 15 分钟车程。物联网小镇被评为国家物联网产业示范基地、国家数字服务出口基地、国家 3A 级旅游景区。经过多年发展，小镇逐步成为"特色产业鲜明、人才高度集聚、配套功能完善、创新文化深厚"特色小镇标杆，形成了一批以物联网、云计算、大数据、信息安全、先进传感设备及 5G 为主导的高、精、尖数字经济产业，吸引了一批数字经济产业领域创业创新团队和领军型人才在小镇生根发展，汇集了海康威视、大华技术、宇视科技、安恒信息、矽力杰等一批具有国际竞争力和行业领导力的企业，形成了较为成熟的数字经济产业链及产业生态，成为具有较大影响力的中国物联网产业示范区。

★ IoT Town in Binjiang District

The IoT town is situated in Binjiang District, with a planned area of 3.66 square kilometers. The town is accessible by Metro Line 1 and 6, and the city road network. It is about 15 minutes' drive from Hangzhou Xiaoshan International Airport. Being a national 3A level tourist attraction, the town is a national demonstration base of IoT industry and a national export base of digital service. It has gradually evolved into a model Characteristic Town featuring "distinctive industries, talents aggregation, complete ancillary facilities, and profound innovation". The town has generated a batch of high-grade, precision and advanced digital economy enterprises in the fields of the Internet of Things, cloud computing, big data, information security, advanced sensing equipment and 5G technology, attracting a number of entrepreneurial and innovative teams and leading talents. It has gathered a cluster of internationally competitive and leading enterprises such as Hikvision, Dahua Technology, Uniview Technology, DBAPP Security, and Silergy Semi-conductor, forming a relatively mature industrial chain and ecology for digital economy. The IoT Town in Binjiang District has turned into an influential demonstration area for the IoT industry in China.

★ 建德航空小镇

　　航空小镇位于杭州市下辖县级市建德市西南部，距建德市区约 18 千米，规划面积约 3.57 平方千米，实际控制面积约 10 平方千米。小镇在 2016 年 1 月被列入浙江省特色小镇创建名单，是目前省内唯一打造通航全产业链的特色小镇。小镇基建配套完善，区位交通发达，产业逐步聚集，品牌影响凸显。毗邻小镇的千岛湖通用机场是华东地区乃至全国飞行最自由、配套最完善、业务最繁忙的通航机场之一，也是浙江省首家取得 A 类民用机场许可证的通用机场，机场跑道 800 米 ×30 米（并正在延伸跑道至 1200 米），飞行等级为 1B；拥有高度 1200 米以下，覆盖整个千岛湖湖面多达 4500 平方千米的报告空域，为全国通用机场中最大的。[①]

　　航空小镇相继获得首批国家级青年信用小镇、国家第一批低空旅游示范区、国家第一批航空飞行营地示范工程、第二批国家级特色小镇及浙江省军民融合产业示范基地等多项荣誉。

★ Aviation Town in Jiande City

Aviation Town lies in the southwest of Jiande City, a county-level city under the jurisdiction of Hangzhou. It is about 18 kilometers away from the urban area of Jiande, covering a planned area of about 3.57 square kilometers and an actual controlled area of about 10 square kilometers. In January 2016, the town was included in the list of Characteristic Towns in Zhejiang Province. As the only characteristic town in the province to build a whole industry chain

---

① 佚名. 浙江建德航空小镇项目案例［EB/OL］.（2019-06-04）［2023-04-07］. https://baijiahao.baidu.com/s?id=1635417762586026058&wfr=spider&for=pc.

of navigation, it has perfect infrastructure and supporting facilities, convenient transportation, industrial aggregation and brand influence. The Thousand-islet Lake General Airport adjacent to the town is one of the most popular general airports with most flying freedom and optimal ancillary service in East China and even the whole country. It is the first general airport in Zhejiang Province to obtain the license of Class A. The airport has a runway of 800×30 meters (which is being extended to 1200 meters long), with a flight grade of 1B. It has a flight airspace covering 4,500 square kilometers of the entire Thousand-islet Lake at a height of under 1,200 meters, the largest of the general airports in China.

The aviation town has been listed in the first batch of the National Youth Credit Town, National Low-altitude Tourism Demonstration Zone, and National Aviation Camp Demonstration Project, the second batch of the National Characteristic Town and Zhejiang Demonstration Base of Military-civilian Integration Industry, etc.

★ 艺尚小镇

　　艺尚小镇于2015年6月入选浙江省首批特色小镇，位于临平区临平新城，地处长三角城市群发展的核心，总规划面积约3平方千米，是杭州连接上海的桥头堡。这里交通便利，杭州地铁1号线和沪杭高铁在此零换乘。小镇空间格局划分为主体项目艺尚中心——东湖文化艺术中心，以及时尚文化街区、时尚历史街区、时尚艺术街区和瑞丽轻奢街区等4个街区。小镇依托电商、产业互联网等，主攻以服装为主的时尚产业，集聚全国高端时尚设计人才，融现代时尚与古典艺术于一体，致力打造"东方米兰"。同时，当地政府与中国纺织工业联合会、中国服装协会、中国服装设计师协会签署了合作协议，合力将艺尚小镇建设成文化创意推动、科技创新聚集、可持续发展导向的数字时尚高地，打造成"中国时尚风向地、中国奢侈品海淘地、中国网红直播引领地、中国潮流文化集聚地、中国数字时尚融合地"，并促进"布局国际化、内容数字化、活动多样化"等。

艺尚小镇是中国服装杭州峰会和亚洲时尚联合会中国大会永久会址、中国服装创新示范基地、浙江省标杆小镇和国家 3A 级景区。

★ The E-fashion Town

The E-fashion Town, situated in Linping New Town, entered the first batch of Characteristic Towns in Zhejiang Province in June 2015. With an planned area of about 3 square kilometers, the town is a bridgehead connecting Hangzhou with Shanghai, making the best of the development of the Yangtze River Delta urban agglomeration. The transportation in the town is convenient, with Metro Line 1 and Shanghai-Hangzhou high-speed railway zero-distance transfer. The town is divided into a main project—the Donghu (East Lake) Culture and Art Center, and four blocks- the blocks of fashion culture, history, fashion art, and light luxury. Relying on e-commerce and industrial internet, the town concentrates on the garment industry. It gathers high-end talents of fashion design from all over the country and integrates modern fashion with classical art, committed to creating the "Oriental Milan". The local government has signed agreements with China National Textile and Apparel Council, China National Garment Association, and China Fashion Association to jointly build the town into a digital fashion height driven by cultural creativity, scientific and technological innovation and sustainable development, aiming to make it a mirror of "fashion trend, overseas online shopping of luxuries, live streaming of internet celebrities, pop culture, digital fashion" in China, and to achieve a style of internationalization, digitization, and diversification.

The E-fashion Town is the permanent venue for China Fashion Hangzhou Summit and Asia Fashion Federation China Conference, entitled China Fashion Innovation Demonstration Base, Zhejiang Benchmark Town and National 3A Level Scenic Spot, etc.

★ 西湖艺创小镇

艺创小镇位于杭州之江文化产业带核心区域，规划面积约3.5平方千米，是西湖区携手中国美术学院、浙江音乐学院，以政校合作模式携手打造的艺术、产业、社区高度融合的生态、生产、生活小镇。小镇定位"艺术＋产业"，以产业集聚为重点，坚持招优引强和产业孵化培育，形成了以设计服务业为主，现代传媒、信息服务、动漫游戏等产业特色鲜明、错位发展的格局。小镇引进的九月九号设计、北斗星等承担了多项国家级项目的设计和制作，如2010上海世博会中国馆"中国红"色彩设计、G20杭州峰会会标设计、世界互联网大会会徽设计、2022杭州亚运会会徽及亚运会体育图标设计等。

★ Artinno Town

The Artinno Town, an art creation town covering a planned area of about 3.5 square kilometers, sits at the core area of Zhijiang Cultural Industry Belt in Hangzhou. As an ecological and livable town fully integrated with art, industry and community, it is jointly created by Xihu District, China Academy of Art and Zhejiang Conservatory of Music. The town is "art-industry-oriented", focusing on industrial concentration, high-quality investment and industry incubation to form a pattern with distinctive features and complementary development of design industry, modern media, information service, animation and game. Studios like September 9, Beidouxing, etc. in the town have undertaken the design and production for a number of national projects, such as the color design of "China red" for the China Pavilion of Shanghai Expo 2010, and the design of the logos for G20 Summit Hangzhou 2016 and World Internet Conference. The logo for the 19th Asian Games Hangzhou 2022, and the sports icons of the Games are their noticeable new works, which have won them a national and worldwide fame.

★ 萧山信息港小镇

信息港小镇位于国家级经济技术开发区萧山经济技术开发区，规划面积约3.04平方千米，距萧山国际机场、杭州东站、城站、杭州南站均在半小时车程以内，与地铁1号线、2号线毗邻，7号机场专线穿镇而过，交通便利。小镇于 2019 年入选浙江省特色小镇。小镇依托杭州湾信息港为主要载体，以新一代信息技术为主导，以"互联网＋""人工智能＋"为特色，聚焦发展数字经济，围绕"信息改变生活"这一主题，打造科技创新驱动的新引擎、互联网经济的新硅谷、大众创业的新空间、跨境电商的先行区。

目前，信息港小镇已经形成了"一港多谷"的产业架构。"一港"就是杭州湾信息港，它是小镇的智汇港。还有多个"互联网＋"智慧谷，包括以互联网医疗独角兽企业微医集团为龙头的"中国智慧健康谷"，以中国大陆第一个 SATA 固态硬盘控制器芯片"设计者"华澜微为龙头的"中国集成电路设计谷"，以 5G 自动驾驶领军企业博信智联为龙头的"中国智慧交通谷"，以人工智能领军企业科大讯飞为龙头的"中国人工智能谷"，以及"中国场景科技谷""中国智慧移动谷""中国智慧化纤谷""中国智慧包装谷""中国智慧家居谷"等。信息港小镇聚集了一批有影响力的企业和高端人才，强有力地带动了小镇人工智能、生命健康、集成电路产业生态圈的集聚发展。

萧山信息港小镇已获得"国家级科技企业孵化器""国家小微企业双创示范基地""国家级众创空间"和"国家级中小企业公共服务示范平台"等称号，是国家 3A 级旅游景区。

★ HiPark

The HiPark, an infoport town, situated in the state-level Xiaoshan Economic and Technological Development Zone, covers a planned area of about 3.04 square kilometers. It is easily accessible, within half an hour's drive from Hangzhou Xiaoshan International Airport, Hangzhou East Railway Station, Hangzhou Railway Station and Hangzhou South Railway Station; and close to Metro Line 1, Line 2, and the Airport Line. In 2019, it was officially labeled as "Zhejiang Characteristic Town". The town featuring "Internet +" and "artificial intelligence +" is based on the Hangzhou Bay Infoport, and makes the new generation of IT the dominant role. It concentrates on digital economy, with the notion of "information changing the life", to bring a boom to scientific and technological innovation, internet economy, public entrepreneurship, and cross-border e-commerce.

The infoport town has formed an industrial structure of "one port plus multi-valley". The "one port" is the Hangzhou Bay Infoport, a hub of intelligence and wisdom of the town. The multi-valley comprises a number of "Internet +" intelligent valleys, including "China Smart Health Valley" led by the internet medical unicorn Wedoctor, "China Integrated Circuit Design Valley" led by Sage Microelectronics, the first designer of SATA solid-state drive controller chip in Chinese mainland, "China Smart Traffic Valley" led by the 5G automated driving enterprise BroadXT, "China Artificial Intelligence Valley" led by the artificial intelligence leader Iflytek, as well as "China Scene Sci-tech Valley", "China Smart Mobile Valley", "China Smart Chemical Fiber Valley", "China Smart Packaging Valley", "China Smart Home Valley", and so on. The town gathers a batch of influential high-end enterprises with many a high-end talent, which greatly promotes the ecosystem and concentration of industries in terms of artificial intelligence, life and health, and integrated circuit in the town.

The HiPark has won the titles of "National Science and Technology Enterprise Incubator", "National Demonstration Base for Double-creation (Mass Entrepreneurship and Innovation) of Small and Micro Enterprises", "National Mass Entrepreneurship Space" and "National Demonstration Platform of Public Service for Small and Medium-sized Enterprises". Moreover, it is a national 3A-level tourist attraction.

第五节　杭州城市大脑

　　杭州城市大脑总部位于云栖小镇，是为城市生活打造的一个数字化界面，是杭州的城市操作系统。通过大数据、云计算、人工智能等手段推进城市治理现代化，是智慧城市建设的重大实践。它起步于2016年4月，以治理交通拥堵为突破口，开启了利用大数据改善城市交通的探索之路，现已迈出了从"治堵"向"治城"跨越的步伐，应用场景不断丰富，形成了警务、交通、文旅、健康等11大系统、48个场景同步推进的良好局面。杭州城市大脑建设以"五位一体"为顶层架构，即覆盖经济、政治、文化、社会、生态五大领域，成为城市数字化的核心引擎。在五大领域之下，细分为各子板块，各子板块以信息化系统做支撑。同时，充分发挥全市各部门信息化建设成效，通过补齐短板、融合计算，形成一体化的城市大脑体系。市民凭借它可以感知城市、享受城市服务，城市管理者通过它配置公共资源、做出科学决策、提高治理效能。到2020年下半年，日均协同数据达2亿余次。

　　杭州城市大脑建设提出了"531"的逻辑体系架构。"5"即5个"一"："一张网"，一张确保数据无障碍流动的网，通过统一标准，支撑城市大脑的数据资源需求；"一朵云"，一朵将各类云资源联结在一起的"逻辑云"；"一个库"，形成城市级数据仓库，同时做好数据治理，确保数据鲜活、在线；"一个中枢"，作为数据、各系统互通互联的核心层，实施系统接入、数据融合、反馈执行；"一个大脑"，在全市实施统一架构、一体化实施，彻底打破各自为政的传统建设模式，实现市、区两级协同联动，防止重复建设。"3"即"三个通"，市、区、部门间互联互通，中枢、系统、平台、场景互联互通，政府与市场互联互通。"1"即"一个新的城市基础设施"。城市大脑通过全面打通各类数据，接入各业务系统，实施融合计算，力争为城市建设打造一个会思考、能迭代进化的数字化基础设施。未来，城市大脑将会随时为杭州市民、来杭游客提供服务，如同道路、水电一样，成为必不可少的基础设施。

　　杭州城市大脑给市民游客带来了实实在在的便利体验。如"最多付一次"服务把原来的诊室、自助机多次付费减少到一次就诊就付一次费；"便捷泊车·先离场后付费"服务让"先离场后付费"的车主无须任何行为即可快速离开停车场，为车主节省离场时间；同时，车主一次绑定，全城通停，停车系统为市民提供了"全市一个停车场"的便民体验；"一键护航"服务使救护车在不闯红灯、不影响社会车辆的前提下，安全、快速、顺利地通过每一个路口，打通全自动绿色通道；"杭州健康码"于 2020 年 2 月 11 日在全国率先上线，后在全国推广，为疫情防控和复工复产提供了有力保障；"亲清在线"新型政商关系数字平台实现了"企业诉求在线直达""政府政策在线兑付""政府服务在线落地""服务绩效在线评价""审批许可在线实现"等。

杭州城市大脑建成以来，接待了一批又一批的国内外领导人和城市管理者，赢得了广泛赞誉。城市大脑的成功经验在全国不少城市得以推广应用，是杭州献给世界的一份礼物，有力地推动了智慧城市的建设和发展。

V Hangzhou City Brain

Hangzhou City Brain, headquartered in the Cloud Town, is a "city operating system" and a digital interface for city management and daily life, and a great experiment and revolution in the construction of a smart city. It helps to modernize city management via big data, cloud computing, artificial intelligence and other means. The City Brain project started in April 2016, taking the solution to traffic congestion via big data as the breakthrough point. Now it has extended from traffic congestion addressing to overall city governance. Its application is increasingly diversified, with 11 systems of policing, traffic, cultural tourism, health, etc., and 48 scenarios. The City Brain is based on the top-level structure of "Five-in-One", which covers the five fields of economy, politics, culture, society and ecology, being the core engine of urban digitalization. And the five fields are subdivided into smaller branches supported by the information system. At the same time, government departments take the best of their informatization achievements and fusion calculation, aiming to create an integrative city brain system. With the help of the City Brain, the citizens can "feel" the city and enjoy its services, and the city administrators can scientifically allocate resources, make sound decisions and improve administration efficiency. In the second half of 2020, the average daily collaborative data reached over 200 million pieces.

In the City Brain, a "531" logical architecture is applied. "5" means: "one network" that ensures the barrier-free flow of data and caters to the data needs of the "brain" via unified standards; "one cloud" of logic that connects all kinds of cloud resources; "one database" at the municipal level which is well managed, updated and accessible; "one hub" that is the core of data and interconnection of all systems, and realizes system access, data fusion and effective feedback; "one brain" that unifies the structure and implementation in the whole city, eradicating the traditional uncoordinated administration style, realizing the coordination and linkage between the sectors of municipal and district level, as well as preventing repetitive constructions. "3" refers to "3 interconnections": interconnection among the municipality, districts and departments, interconnection among the hub, systems, platforms and scenarios, and interconnection between government and market. "1" means "one new urban infrastructure". The City Brain aims to build for the city a digital infrastructure that can think and evolve iteratively by comprehensively accessing all kinds of data, connecting various business systems and implementing fusion calculation. In the future, the City Brain will provide services for Hangzhou citizens and tourists at any time as part of utility and an essential component of the city infrastructure.

Hangzhou City Brain has brought substantial experience and great convenience to its citizens and tourists. The "One Payment" service reduces the original multiple payments at the doctor's room and the self-service machine to one payment for each visit.The service of "Convenient Parking, Departure First Bill Later" allows the drivers to pull out of the parking lot with no payment on the spot, saving time for the drivers. What's more, the parking lots distributed at every corner of the city integrate into one "super parking lot" via the Convenient Parking System, which brings a great convenience. The "One-button Escort" service enables ambulances to pass through every intersection safely, quickly and smoothly without running red lights or affecting social vehicles, which creates an automatic green lane for emergencies. The "Hangzhou Health Code" was invented and launched on February 11, 2020 in Hangzhou, then spread nationwide, providing a substantial guarantee for the epidemic prevention and control of COVID-19, and helping the resumption of normal life and work. "Qin-qing Online", a new digital platform for the interaction between the government and the commerce, has realized the "instant online responds to enterprises' appeals to the government", "online implementation of the government policies", "online addressing of business affairs", "online evaluation of administrative service", "online approval and licensing", and so on.

Hangzhou City Brain has received many groups of leaders and city managers from home and abroad, and won lots of praise and admiration. The idea and mechanism of the City Brain have spread to many other cities across the country, which is a gift from Hangzhou and a powerful driving force for the construction and development of smart cities.

第八章　温暖之城

　　杭州不仅风景秀美，还有许许多多的故事，温暖着每一个人。斑马线前司机的一脚刹车、一个手势、一个微笑，公交地铁上照顾老弱病残的爱心座位，城市随处可见的公共自行车，医院、车站等公共场所的志愿者身影，早已成为城市一道亮丽的风景线。

Chapter Eight
City of Warmth

Hangzhou not only has beautiful scenery, but also has many stories, which warm everyone. The driver presses the brake, makes a gesture or gives a smile to the pedestrians while they are in front of the zebra crossing; priority seats are designed for the elderly or the sick on buses and metros; public bicycles can be seen everywhere in the city; volunteers serve in many parts of the city such as hospitals, stations and public places. What mentioned above is just part of the story, and they have long been a part of the city's landscape.

第一节 公共自行车

当大多数人习惯开车或乘坐公共交通出行的时候，骑行文化却在杭州兴起，随处可见的公共自行车是杭州街头流动的风景。杭州公共自行车服务始于 2008 年，旨在缓解城市的交通拥堵。如今，它已发展为全世界最大的公共自行车系统，同时也是世界最佳之一。杭州公共自行车外形小巧、颜色鲜艳，被人们亲切地称为"小红车"。由于其便捷、经济、安全、共享的特征，以及"自助操作、智能管理、通租通还、押金保证、超时收费、实时结算"的运作方式，公共自行车已经成为来杭中外游客和杭州市民出行必不可少的城市交通工具，为大众提供了许多便利。

杭州有着完善的公共自行车租赁系统。城市里分布几千个公共自行车服务点，许多靠近公交、地铁及旅游景点。租用自行车一小时内归还不收取费用，游客可以免费骑公共自行车游览城市。自 2017 年 3 月起，杭州公共自行车实现 24 小时服务。通过交通卡、市民卡等，充值 200 元人民币后即可租车，也可用智能手机扫码进行租车还车。市民和游客可在城市任何一个服务点还车。基于"随时可以享受共享单车"的理念，政府鼓励市民和游客利用新的交通组合方式，提高公共交通效率。在杭州市中心的街道旁，每隔几百米就有一个租车点，有许多移动设备应用程序告诉用户最近的租车点在哪里，一小时免费期之外的租车费用为每小时 1 元。杭州公共自行车服务深受欢迎，每天有近 20—30 万人次使用租赁自行车服务。

目前，杭州已形成了公交、地铁、公共自行车、共享单车无缝转换的绿色出行网络，被英国广播公司（BBC）旅游频道评为"全球 8 个提供最棒的公共自行车服务的城市之一"。

Ⅰ Hangzhou Public Bicycle Service

While most people are used to driving or taking public transportation, cycling culture is thriving in Hangzhou, and public bicycles seen everywhere in Hangzhou is a beautiful view. Hangzhou Public Bicycle Service (Bicycle Sharing System) was launched in 2008. In an effort to ease traffic congestion in the city, Hangzhou developed China's first bike-sharing system. It has since grown into the world's largest—and one of the world's best—public bicycle renting systems. As they are small in size and bright in red color, public bicycles in Hangzhou are called "small red bicycles". Because of its convenient, safe, economic and sharing characteristics, as well as "self-help operation, intelligent management, rent and return at any service stations, the deposit guarantee, overtime charge, real-time settlement" operation, public bicycle has become an indispensable means not only for citizens of Hangzhou, but also for visitors at home and abroad.

Since 2008, Hangzhou has a well-developed bicycle renting system. There are thousands of service stations around the city, many of which are in close proximity to bus and metro stations, as well as popular attractions. You can borrow a public bicycle free of charge if you return it in one hour. Visitors can rent a bicycle and tour around the city freely. Since March 2017, Hangzhou has provided 24-hour public bicycle service. For renting a bicycle, one needs a transportation card or citizen card, and stores at least RMB 200 yuan in the new card. People can ride public bicycles simply by scanning QR code with a smart phone. Bicycles are available at any public bicycle spot, and return it at any other service station in the city. Based on the development concept of "bicycles for public use at any time", visitors and citizens are encouraged to adapt the newly public transportation system of combining transportation with bicycles, which could improve the efficiency of public transportation. With a rental stand every few hundred meters in downtown areas, mobile apps that tell users where to find the closest available bicycle, and fees of RMB 1 yuan an hour. The schemc is already very popular: As many as 200,000－300,000 people use it every day.

Buses, metro, public bicycles and sharing bicycles, Hangzhou's public transport network has made it possible for green commuting. Travel Channel of BBC regarded Hangzhou as one of the "Top Eight Cities Providing the Best Public Bicycle Service in the World".

第二节　斑马线前礼让行人

在杭州，斑马线前礼让行人是一道风景。骑自行车，杭州有专门的骑行道路；在十字路口等待通过时，头顶上有遮阳遮雨棚；杭州的机动车，在人行道前一律让行……类似这样的细节，在杭州比比皆是，它反映了这座城市对每个个体的尊重与关爱。

斑马线前礼让行人已经是浙 A 牌照车辆的一种习惯和涵养。这一现象最早从公交车开始。2007 年，杭州市公交集团制定了《公交营运司机五条规范》，其中明确规定"行经人行横道时减速礼让"，从制度上保障"礼让"的实施。2009 年，杭州市内出租车也加入了"礼让斑马线"行动中。其后，"斑马线前礼让行人"首次被写入地方性法规，该条例于 2016 年 3 月 1 日起正式施行。在今天的杭州，斑马线前遇行人过马路，公交车、出租车、私家车都能主动停下，耐心地礼让，这已成为杭城街头日常的风景线，让市民和游客"感动和温暖"。司机在斑马线前礼让，让行人安全通行；行人则竖起大拇指给予回报，甚至鞠躬致谢……这样温暖的场景在杭州街头随处可见。斑马线前礼让行人逐渐成为司机们的共识和基本素质。即使是在拥挤的早晚高峰，无论是私家车还是公交车，大多数司机都能踩下刹车，做到车让行人，这使得整座城市更温暖了，也让人们越发喜欢杭州了。

Ⅱ Give Way to Pedestrians at a Zebra Crossing

Giving way to pedestrians at a zebra crossing is a beautiful view in Hangzhou. When riding bicycles, there are specially-designed bicycle lanes; when waiting at the intersections, there are sunshade over you to protect the sunshine in summer and rain; when crossing the zebra line, vehicles come to a stop waiting for your pass ... These practices are very common in Hangzhou, which reflects the respect and caring for the people.

Cars of Zhejiang A license give way to pedestrians at a zebra crossing is now a common practice and self-restraint. In 2007, Hangzhou Public Transport Group constituted a guideline for bus drivers, totally there are five rules. When driving in front of a zebra crossing, they are required to slow down and give way to pedestrians. In 2009, taxi drivers were involved in this action and it was first written into the local regulation, which took into effect on March 1, 2016.

Today, it has become a common scene for bus drivers, taxi drivers and private car drivers to give way at zebra crossings; this practice made citizens and tourists moved and feel warm. They usually thumb up or even bow to the drivers to show their gratitude. Drivers whether they are in Hangzhou or from other cities will slow down and wait pedestrians very patiently at zebra crossings; it's common practice and basic quality for drivers. Whether it's rush hour in the morning or late in the afternoon, whether they are bus drivers or private car drivers, they step on brakes and give way to passers-by. Residents and visitors in Hangzhou feel warm and like the city better.

第三节　志愿者活动

1993 年，"保护西湖绿色行动"拉开了杭州志愿服务工作的序幕；1995 年，杭州志愿者协会成立，迄今为止，全市注册志愿者超过 200 万人。杭州的机场、火车站、汽车站、医院、办事中心、景区、十字路口，到处都有志愿者的身影，他们身着红色马甲，给一个个需要帮助的市民和游客以温暖。杭州的志愿者也成为城市文明形象的闪亮名片。

志愿者曾服务 2007 年女足世界杯、2011 年全国残疾人运动会、2016 年全国大学生运动会、2017 年全国学生运动会、2018 年世界游泳锦标赛和世界水上运动大会。但最引人注目的是 G20 峰会期间的会场志愿者"小青荷"。G20 峰会前，当招募志愿者的通道开启时，10 多万志愿者报名参加高层次的国际论坛服务，有近 26000 名志愿者是大学教师和他们的学生。经过严格的挑选和培训，最后招募了 3000 人。峰会现场志愿者需要较高的语言能力和峰会工作经验。城市志愿者则协助公共安全、环境和文化宣传。他们的服务成为 G20 峰会一道亮丽的风景，得到了中外嘉宾的一致好评。

杭州志愿者参与服务工作意愿很高，积累了多年的服务经验，为志愿服务奠定了基础。志愿者活跃在各个领域，无私奉献，用微笑和热情感动和温暖着杭州，传播丰富多彩的志愿文化，书写志愿名城的新篇章。

Ⅲ Volunteer Activities

In 1993, the "Protect the West Lake Green Action" kicked off the volunteer service work in Hangzhou. In 1995, Association of Hangzhou Volunteers was founded. Up to now, more than two million people have registered volunteers. Whether you are at airports, railway stations, coach stations and bus stops, or you are in the hospitals, service centers, scenic spots and intersections, you'll surely not miss these volunteers. Dressed in red vests, they offer help to citizens, visitors and tourists, which warms those who are in need of help. Today, volunteers in Hangzhou have become a shining card of the civilized image of the city.

Volunteers in Hangzhou did excellent jobs in the service of the FIFA Women's World Cup in 2007, the National Games of Disabled Persons in 2011, the National University Games in 2016, National Student Sports Games in 2017, the FINA World Swimming Championship (25 m) and the FINA World Aquatics Convention in 2018. But the most impressive one were the volunteers at the venue during the G20 summit "Xiao Qing He". In the drive to recruit volunteers ahead of the G20 Summit, when the recruitment channel opened, more than 100,000 volunteers signed up to participate in high-level international forum services, and nearly 26,000 of them were university teachers and their students. After strict selection and training, 3,000 people were recruited. Summit site volunteers need high language skills and summit work experience. City volunteers assist with public safety, environmental and cultural advocacy. The service of "Xiao Qing He" has become a beautiful scenery during the G20 Summit and won unanimous praise from guests at home and abroad.

Hangzhou volunteers have a high willingness to participate in service work, and they have accumulated years of experience, which has laid a foundation for service work. Volunteers are active in all fields. With their selfless dedication, they touch and warm Hangzhou with their smiles and enthusiasm, spreading a rich and colorful volunteer culture and composing a new chapter in the famous volunteer city.

第四节　公羊队

浙江省公羊会公益救援促进会，始创于 2003 年，是具有独立社团法人资格的民间公益社团组织，截止到 2022 年 6 月，已拥有浙江、北京、上海、陕西等 7 个国内公羊会分会，美国（加利福尼亚州、得克萨斯州）、意大利、奥地利、埃塞俄比亚、厄瓜多尔、法国 7 个海外公羊会。开展的公益活动涉及全国和海外多个国家，累计达 3000 多次，参与过 50 余起抗震、抗台风救援行动，深入一线救助救治了 10000 多名受灾群众，赈灾捐款捐物 800 多万元。公羊会受到社会各界的广泛关注，注册的专业志愿者从初期的 15 人增加到如今的 24500 多人。[1]2008 年 5 月，公羊会设立了一支专门执行应急救援任务的志愿者队伍——公羊队，专门开展自然灾害应急救援、突发性城市应急救援、国家次生灾害抢险救援，以及城市走失和失智老人搜寻救助等公益救援行动。公羊队以"救危助难，为社会出力；扶弱帮困，为政府分忧"为宗旨。

公羊队目前拥有百余名经过严格挑选、培训、考核并具有扎实救援知识及实战经验的志愿者，在浙江、四川、陕西、新疆拥有 4 支救援力量，并建立了 3 个战备装备库，配备有应急救援车辆、冲锋艇、充气船、无人机、卫星通信设备、专业医疗帐篷以及众多山地和水上救援器材等专业救援装备。先后在国内执行山林走失驴友救援任务 30 余次，执行 24 小时公益急

---

[1] 张志强. 全球华人公益组织：公羊会［EB/OL］.（2022-06-24）［2023-04-06］. http://edu.cnr.cn/nxjy/tgy/20220624/t20220624_525880937.shtml.

寻任务 100 多次，^①参加了汶川、玉树、雅安、鲁甸、景谷、康定、九寨沟等地震救援。在浙江省内，公羊队曾多次参加台风等极端天气灾害救援以及山体滑坡等地质灾害救援。2016 年，台湾发生地震，公羊队第一时间派出救援先遣队，成为首支大陆赴台民间救援队，救援行动促进了两岸关系，加强了两岸民众的深度交流。公羊队还走出国门，代表中国民间救援力量参加了尼泊尔、巴基斯坦、厄瓜多尔、意大利、印度尼西亚等海外地震救援。

公羊会除了执行应急救援行动以外，每年向社区居民及户外活动爱好者、学生进行百余次应急救援安全知识培训及常见意外伤害急救处理实际操作培训。2014 年 9 月，公羊会"公益大学"成立，这是全国首家面向残疾人的公益性"大学"，是政府购买公益服务的典型范例。公羊会"公益大学"为学员们免费开设了陶艺、美术、手工串珠、景泰蓝、手工编织等 5 大系统课程。除负责教学外，还提供日间照料、心理咨询、康复娱乐、手工劳动、社会适应性能力训练等综合性服务。公羊会被授予"杭州红十字救援队""杭州市城市管理社会应急救援队""西湖区志愿者大队"等称号。2020 年 10 月，荣获"抗击新冠肺炎疫情青年志愿服务先进集体"称号。

Ⅳ Rescue Team of Ramunion

Founded in 2003, Zhejiang Public Relif Promotion Association of Ramunion is a non-governmental public welfare organization with the qualification of an independent legal person. Until the June of 2022, there are 7 branches in Zhejiang, Beijing, Shanghai and Shaanxi Province, etc., in China, and 7 overseas branches in America (California and Texas), Italy, Austria, Ethiopia, Ecuador and France. The Ramunion has carried out more than 3,000

① 李静.首届全国应急管理系统先进集体——浙江省公羊会公益救援促进会事迹介绍［EB/OL］.（2021-12-21）［2023-04-06］. https://www.mem.gov.cn/shjyfw/dwfc/202112/t20211221_405362.shtml.

public welfare activities nationally and internationally, participated in more than 50 earthquake and typhoon relief operations, rescued more than 10,000 people, and donated goods and materials valued at more than RMB 8 million yuan. It has attracted wide attention from all walks of life, and the registered professional volunteers has numbered from 15 to over 24,500.

In May 2008, the Ramunion set up a voluntary team, the Rescue Team of Ramunion, which is specialized in rescues of natural disasters, emergency in urban areas, national secondary disasters, as well as in searching for and rescuing the lost and disoriented elderly in urban areas. The aim of the Rescue Team of Ramunion is "to rescue those in disaster and help those in difficulty to contribute to the society; to relieve the weak and help the poor to shoulder social responsibility".

At present, the rescue team has more than 100 volunteers who have been strictly selected, trained and assessed, and have solid rescue knowledge and practical experience. The team has four rescue forces in Zhejiang, Sichuan, Shaanxi and Xinjiang, and has established three rescue equipment depots storing emergency rescue vehicles, assault boats, inflatable boats, unmanned aerial vehicles, satellite communication equipment, professional medical tents and a large amount of mountain and water rescue equipment and other professional rescue equipment. In China, the team has rescued lost travelers in mountains and forests for more than 30 times, carried out all-day emergency searches for more than 100 times. It conducted rescues in earthquakes in Wenchuan, Yushu, Ya'an, Ludian, Jinggu, Kangding, Jiuzhaigou and many other places. In Zhejiang Province, the team has participated for many times in the rescue of extreme weather disasters like typhoons and geological disasters such as landslides. In 2016, when Taiwan was hit by an earthquake, the team immediately sent a group of experienced rescuers, as the first non-governmental rescue team from the Mainland to Taiwan. This rescue promoted cross-straits relations and strengthened the in-depth exchanges between the Chinese of both sides. The rescue team has also gone abroad on behalf of China's non-governmental rescue forces to participate in earthquake relief in Nepal, Pakistan, Ecuador, Italy, Indonesia and some other countries.

In addition to emergency rescues conducted by the rescue team, on a yearly basis the Ramunion carries out for residents, outdoor activity enthusiasts and students more than 100 training activities on emergency rescue and practical operation of emergency treatment to common accidental injuries. In September 2014, the "Ramunion Charity College" was established, which is the first charitable education organization for the disabled in China, and a representative example that the government purchases public welfare services for the disadvantaged groups. The "Ramunion Charity College" offers five free handcraft programs, including pottery, fine arts, beading, cloisonne and knitting. In addition to teaching, it also provides day care, psychological counseling, rehabilitation and entertainment, handwork, social adaptability training and other comprehensive services. The Ramunion was entitled "Hangzhou Red Cross Rescue Team", "Hangzhou City Management and Social Emergency Rescue Team" and "Xihu District Volunteer Brigade". In October 2020, it won the title of "Advanced Collective for Youth Volunteering Services Against COVID-19".

第五节　春风行动

2000 年，杭州市总工会首创了以"社会各界送温暖、困难群众沐春风"为主题的"春风行动"。多年来，在社会各界的支持下，该慈善爱心行动实现了由"一阵春风"向"春风常驻"的跨越，帮扶救助对象不断扩大，帮扶救助内容不断丰富，逐步发展为着力保障和改善困难群众生活，帮扶救助困难群众的杭州模式。"春风行动"表现出社会各界齐参与、帮扶对象广覆盖、帮扶内容全方位、工作机制长效化、城乡统筹两延伸等特点。

"春风行动"年年如约而至，不负芳信，截止到 2020 年，已累计募集社会资金 27.71 亿元，各级财政补充资金 7.04 亿元，有 6.95 万余家单位、335.63 万人（次）向"春风行动"捐款献爱心，为"春风行动"深入开展奠定了坚实的物质基础；20 年来，"春风行动"共向 338.12 万户（次）困难家庭发放助困、助医、助学、反哺、应急等各类救助金 36.03 亿元，成为政府保障和改善困难群众生活的有力补充。[①] 目前，"春风行动"已建立起了党委领导、政府组织、工会牵头、部门配合、全社会参与的综合帮扶体系。

V The Spring Breeze Campaign

In 2000, the General Labor Union of Hangzhou initiated the "Spring Breeze Campaign" with the theme of "all sectors of society giving a helping hand, the spirits of the needy lifted as in the spring wind". Over the years, with the support from all walks of the society, this charity action has evolved into a routine, and the number of beneficiaries have grown larger and larger and the aid coverage has increasingly expanded. It gradually develops into a "Hangzhou Model" of charity, which focuses on the basic life security for the people in need, gradual improvement to their lives, and helping enable them to gain employability. The Campaign features extensive participation from people of all walks of life, wide coverage of target subjects, overall supporting, long-term helping mechanism, as well as balanced helping measures covering both the urban and rural areas.

The Campaign is launched year after year and lives up to its noble

---

① 佚名. 春风概览［EB/OL］.［2023-04-19］. http://www.hzcfxd.org/news2.htm.

original intention. Up to 2020, it has raised a total of RMB 2.771 billion yuan from the society, RMB 704 million yuan of financial support from levels of governments; and over 3.3563 million people have donated to the Campaign, laying a solid foundation for its development. Over the past 20 years, it has provided 3.3812 million families (some need continual help) with RMB 3.603 billion yuan for poverty alleviation, medical care, education, nursing and emergency response. It has become a powerful supplement to the government's efforts to aid the disabled, poor, sick, orphans, laid-off workers, etc. At present, the Campaign has established a comprehensive support system, which is led by the Party Committee, organized by the government, hosted by the Workers Union, coordinated by related sectors and participated by the whole society.

第九章　最忆是杭州

要了解一个城市，最快的方式就是成为一名市民。如果是一名游客，可以通过参与活动的方式了解城市的文化，可参与一个或多个活动来体验杭州。《印象西湖》是一台大型山水实景演出，歌舞剧《宋城千古情》再现了1000多年前杭州的历史故事与传说，钱江新城灯光秀、西湖音乐喷泉可以让游客感受现代杭州的韵味，舒缓压力。只有去体验才能了解真实的杭州文化，感受杭州的魅力。

Chapter Nine
Hangzhou—The Most Memorable City

The fastest way to access a city is to become one of the citizens. But as a tourist, there are also some activities you can participate in which helps you understand its culture. You may choose one or more activities to experience Hangzhou. *Impression of the West Lake Show* is a large-scale real landscape performance. *The Romance of the Song Dynasty* is a drama based on the historic stories and legends in the city of Hangzhou a thousand years ago. Watching Qianjiang New Light Show and the Musical Fountain of the West Lake, you may experience the beauty of the modern city, comforting your mood from the pressures. It is true that you never know what the real culture is and the charm of Hangzhou until you have experienced it fully.

第一节　《印象西湖》

　　《印象西湖》是由杭州市委市政府、浙江广播电视集团及浙江凯恩集团共同组建的印象西湖文化发展有限公司打造的一台大型山水实景演出，由张艺谋、王潮歌和樊跃导演。张艺谋曾执导 2008 年北京奥运会开幕式和广西桂林阳朔的《印象刘三姐》。《印象西湖》音乐由日本音乐家喜多郎担纲，张靓颖主唱，于 2007 年 3 月公演。该剧以西湖浓厚的历史人文和秀丽的自然风光为创作源泉，深入挖掘杭州的古老民间传说和神话，在波澜起伏、柔美多变的西湖上表演，生动自然。西湖的神话传说将观众引入一个甜美的千年之梦。

　　《印象西湖》分为"相遇""相恋""再见""回忆"和"印象"等 5 场，根据流传在中国数千年的白娘子和许仙、梁山伯和祝英台的爱情故事创作而成。这台演出以西湖为舞台，以天空为幕，以周围的风景为景，在五彩缤纷的灯光和音乐的衬托下，十分引人入胜。中国年轻歌手张靓颖演唱的主题曲《印象西湖——雨》成为她的代表作之一。《印象西湖》的舞台建在湖面上，所以演员看起来像在水面上跳舞和行走。特殊的隐藏式看台提供了开阔的鸟瞰视野。每个座位都是不看表演也能欣赏西湖全景的好地方。开创性的个性化音响系统，结合以声音为导向的系统，提供了令人惊叹的音乐享受。

　　《印象西湖》让西湖人文历史的代表性元素得以重现，同时借助高科技手法再造"西湖雨"，从一个侧面反映雨中西湖和西湖之雨的自然神韵。整场山水实景演出，通过动态演绎、实景再现，将杭州城市内涵和自然山水浓缩成一场高水准的艺术盛宴，向世人推出。

Ⅰ *The Impression of the West Lake Show*

The Impression of the West Lake Show is a large-scale real landscape performance created by the Impression West Lake Cultural Development Co., Ltd. which is jointly established by Hangzhou Municipal Party Committee and Government, Zhejiang Broadcast Television Group and Zhejiang Kane Group. First performed in public in March, 2007, *The Impression of the West Lake Show* is a large-scale live performance directed by Zhang Yimou, Wang Chaoge and Fan Yue. Among them, Zhang Yimou directed Olympics Opening Ceremony in 2008 and *The Impression Liusanjie Night Show* in Yangshuo, Guilin, Guangxi Province. Music of the show is by Japanese musician Kitaro and the lead singer is Jane Zhang (Zhang Liangyin). The show presents the history of the West Lake and beautiful natural scenery as the creative source, with excavation of the Hangzhou ancient folklore and mythology in-depth. Staged on the wavy, mellow and changing the West Lake, the performance appears vivid and natural. Contented with the myths and legends of the West Lake, the show leads spectators to a sweet thousand-year dream.

The Impression of the West Lake Show is divided into five acts, respectively "Meeting", "Love", "Farewell", "Reminiscence" and "Impression", which are created based on the love stories between the White Snake and Xu Xian, Liang Shanbo and Zhu Yingtai (Butterfly Lovers), which spread in China for thousands of years. This show is performed on the West Lake as the stage, the sky as the curtain, the surrounding landscape as the scenery, with the colorful lights and music, which is quite attractive. The young singer in China Jane Zhang sings the theme song *Impression West Lake—Rain*, which becomes one of her masterpieces. The stage is built on the lake, hence performers are seen like floating, dancing and walking on water. The special concealable auditorium provides a wide and bird's-eye view. Each seat is a wonderful place to enjoy the panoramic view of the West Lake even without watching the show. The pioneering individualized sound system, combined with the sound-oriented system, is surely to offer a surprising musical enjoyment.

The representative cultural and historical elements of the West Lake can be reproduced, and the "West Lake Rain" can be recreated with the help of high-tech techniques to reflect the natural charm of the West Lake in the rain and the rain of the West Lake from one side. The whole landscape performance, through dynamic interpretation and real scene reproduction, the connotation of Hangzhou city and natural landscape are condensed into a high level of art feast and presented to the world.

第二节　《宋城千古情》

《宋城千古情》是一部由宋城全力制作的大型立体音乐剧，1997 年开始在宋城景区上演。该剧以杭州的历史故事和传说为基础，将世界音乐与杂技艺术融为一体，运用高科技创造出梦幻般的诗意意象，成为杭州宋城景区的灵魂。《宋城千古情》与拉斯维加斯的《O》秀、巴黎的《红磨坊》并称"世界三大名秀"。《宋城千古情》用最先进的声、光、电等科技手段和舞台机械，以出其不意的呈现方式演绎了良渚古人的艰辛、宋皇宫的辉煌、岳家军的惨烈、梁祝和白蛇传的千古绝唱，把丝绸、茶叶和烟雨江南表现得淋漓尽致，极具视觉体验和心灵震撼。《宋城千古情》也成为来杭游客必看的演出之一。

120 平方米的 LED 屏幕、300 平方米的水上舞台、3000 平方米的烟雨场景、100 米的时间隧道，产生强烈的视觉冲击，让观众仿佛生活在 1000

年前。"给我一天，还你千年"，这也是《宋城千古情》的宣传口号。20多年来，《宋城千古情》创造了世界演艺史上的奇迹：年演出1300余场。到目前为止，《宋城千古情》的观众超过千万，并赢得了大量的好评。对于每一位来杭州的游客来说，这是一场不容错过的演出。

Ⅱ *The Romance of the Song Dynasty Show*

The Romance of the Song Dynasty Show (Eternal Love of the Song Dynasty) is a large stereoscopic musical drama which was wholeheartedly made by Song Dynasty City, it began to be performed in Songcheng Scenic Area in 1997. Based on the historic stories and legends in the city of Hangzhou, the drama integrated the world music with acrobatic art, applied the high technology to create a dreamy poetic imagery. The drama has been the most important activities for visitors. The Romance of the Song Dynasty, together with *O* show in Las Vegas, USA, and *Moulin Rouge* in Paris, France, are "World's Top Three Famous Shows". With the most advanced technological means of sound, light and electricity as well as stage machinery, it presents the hardships of the ancient people in Liangzhu, the magnificence of the imperial palace in Song Dynasty, the tragedy of the army led by General Yue Fei, and the epic song of Butterfly Lovers and Xu Xian and the White Snake. It presents the silk, tea and the smoky rain south of the Yangtze River incisively and vividly, which is full of visual experience and spiritual shock. *The Romance of the Song Dynasty Show* is a must for the visitors coming to Hangzhou.

With 120 square meters LED screen, 300 square meters water arena, 3000 square meters scene of misty rain and 100 meters time tunnel, You can have a strong visual impact and the spectators may be impressed as if they live one thousand years back. With the slogan "Give me a day, returning you for a thousand years", for more than twenty consecutive years, *The Romance of the Song Dynasty Show* created a miracle in the history of world performing arts: It performed more than 1,300 times a year. Till now, the drama has received more than ten million audiences and wins a large outpouring of favorable comments. It is a not-to-be-missed performance for tourists to Hangzhou.

第三节　钱江新城灯光秀

　　钱江新城灯光秀是杭州市人民政府为迎接 2016 年 G20 峰会的召开而倾力打造的灯光工程，是 G20 峰会后杭州的一张新名片。灯光秀地点位于杭州市钱江新城，沿着钱塘江，以钱江新城市民中心、杭州国际会议中心和杭州大剧院为中心，由 70 万盏 LED 灯组成，分别安装在钱江新城核心区沿岸的 30 栋高层建筑外立面上，运用声、光、电等现代化的视听效果配以大型音乐喷泉、自然山水、人文、建筑及杭州标志等元素，使得文字、灯光、影像显示在钱塘江沿岸 30 多栋高楼串成的一幅"巨幕"上，呈现一幅幅具有"中国气派、江南韵味"的画卷。现场观众无不感受到灯光的震撼。每周二、周五、周六的 19：30、20：30 各 1 场，每场持续 30 分钟。灯光秀为杭州市民和国内外游客献上一场场视觉和听觉的盛宴。白天游西湖，晚上看灯光秀，成为来杭州旅游的标配。钱江新城灯光秀也成为杭城标志性景观之一，深受市民和游客喜爱。

　　钱江新城是杭州最繁华的地方之一，这里的城市阳台是观看灯光秀的最佳位置，对面就是杭州奥体中心，也是 2022 年杭州亚运会的场馆。灯光秀是杭州对外展示的一个重要窗口，场景里有杭州本土特色文化的展示，也有一些与杭州发展相关的内容及主题等。在"2019 全国双创活动周"主题灯光秀中，通过各种元素的创意演绎，钱塘江沿岸的"巨幕"向世界呈现创新活力之城的开放之美，传递杭州的别样精彩和独特韵味。2020 年，钱江新城首次举办跨年灯光秀活动，杭州市民与游客会聚在杭州钱塘江畔，共同欣赏。疫情期间，灯光秀根据疫情变化进行更新，并通过媒体直播，为广大市民坚定信心，传递温暖。

Ⅲ Qianjiang New CBD Light Show

Qianjiang New CBD Light Show is a light project created by Hangzhou Municipal Government for the convening of G20 Summit in 2016. It is a new name card of Hangzhou after G20 Summit. Located in Qianjiang New City, Hangzhou, along the Qiantang River and centered on Hangzhou Qianjiang New City Civic Center, Hangzhou International Conference Center and Hangzhou Grand Theater, the light show consists of 700,000 LED lights installed on the facades of 30 high-rise buildings along the core area of Qianjiang New CBD. Modern audio-visual effects such as sound, light and electricity are combined with elements such as large musical fountains, natural mountains and rivers, culture, architecture and Hangzhou's logo. The words, lights and images are displayed on the "giant screen" made up of more than 30 tall buildings along the Qiantang River, presenting a picture scroll with "Chinese style and Jiangnan charm". The spectators felt the shock of the lights. Three nights a week, Tuesday, Friday and Saturday at 19:30 and 20:30, each lasting for 30 minutes. The light show presents a visual and auditory feast for Hangzhou residents and visitors from home and abroad. Visiting the West Lake during the day and watching the light show at night has become a standard part of a visit to Hangzhou. Qianjiang New CBD Light Show has also become one of the iconic sights of Hangzhou and is loved by citizens and tourists.

Qianjiang New CBD is one of the most bustling areas in Hangzhou. The City Balcony is the best place to watch the light show; opposite is the Hangzhou Olympic Sports Center, which will be the venue for the 2022 Asian Games in Hangzhou. The light show is an important window for Hangzhou to show to the outside world. The scene includes Hangzhou's local characteristic culture, and there are also some light shows related to Hangzhou's development and themes. In the light show with the theme of "2019 National Mass Entrepreneurship and Innovation Week", the "giant screen" along the Qiantang River presents to the world the open beauty of an innovative and dynamic city and conveys the wonderful and unique charm of Hangzhou through creative interpretation of various elements. In 2020, Qianjiang New CBD held the New Year's Eve Light Show for the first time. Citizens and tourists gathered along the Qiantang River to welcome and enjoy the beautiful light show. During the epidemic period, the light show was updated according to the changes of the epidemic and broadcast live through the media to strengthen the confidence of the public and pass warmth.

第四节 西湖音乐喷泉

西湖音乐喷泉位于湖滨三公园附近的湖面上，2003 年西湖综合保护工程时创建。西湖音乐喷泉长达 126 米，在程序控制喷泉的基础上加入音乐控制系统，计算机通过对音频及 MIDI 信号的识别进行译码和编码，最终将信号输出到控制系统，使喷泉及灯光的变化与音乐保持同步，从而达到喷泉水型、灯光及色彩的变化与音乐完美结合，使喷泉表演更生动，更富有内涵。西湖音乐喷泉近 400 个喷头，其中 224 个能 360 度旋转，实现 600 多种水形变幻，最中间的大喷头，可以将水柱喷到 60 多米高。音乐播放时，电脑里编排好的新曲，经过软件处理后形成不同的脉冲信号，通过变频器控制水泵，射出高低不同、大小不同的水柱，水柱再通过旋转的喷头，或摇曳或奔放，和着配乐，给人的感觉就像喷泉在跳舞。

西湖音乐喷泉通过千变万化的喷泉造型，结合五颜六色的彩光照明来反映音乐的内涵及主题。使用的音乐主要有西湖特色歌曲、中国古典音乐及流行音乐、外国古典音乐及流行音乐等。播放时，藏于湖底的喷泉设备在水压控制下慢慢临近水面，精心设计过的喷泉喷嘴360度旋转，配合音乐喷出多种形状的水柱、水雾、水球，时而波涛汹涌，时而婉约动人，吸引了众多游客。

西湖音乐喷泉是夜晚西湖边的一处胜景。每天晚上还没到喷泉演出时间，附近人流如织，很多游客更是提前两三个小时前来排队，高峰期一晚多达五六万人观看。[①]西湖音乐喷泉最佳的观赏位置是湖边摆出的四五百张喷泉观赏椅所在，这些座椅是免费的，完全遵循"先到先得"原则。每晚2场，每场时长为3首曲目的时间，约15分钟（2020年1月，由于新冠疫情，西湖音乐喷泉关闭，预计2023年下半年正式开放）。

Ⅳ Musical Fountain of the West Lake

Musical Fountain of the West Lake is located on the lake near the third park of the West Lake shore. It was built in 2003 during the comprehensive protection project of the West Lake. The fountain is 126 meters long. On the basis of program control, music control system is added, the computer decodes and encodes the final output signals to the control system based on audio and MIDI signal identification, which makes the fountain water be in pace with the

---

① 佚名.首秀引5万人观看！西湖音乐喷泉被"挤停了"！［EB/OL］.（2016-05-02）［2021-10-28］. https://www.sohu.com/a/72998648_349120.

change of light and music, so as to achieve the fountain water type. With the change of light and color and the perfect combination of music, the fountain show is more vivid and rich in connotation. The Musical Fountain of the West Lake has nearly 400 sprinklers, among which 224 can rotate 360 degrees to realize more than 600 kinds of water shape changes. The largest sprinkler in the middle can spray water column to a height of more than 60 meters. When the music is playing, the new music arranged in the computer will form different pulse signals after being processed by the software. The water pump will be controlled by the frequency converter, and the water column of different height and size will be emitted. Water column through the rotating nozzle to form or swaying or bold and unremittingly different transformation. With the soundtrack, it feels like the fountain is dancing.

Musical Fountain is to reflect both the connotation and the theme of music through the ever-changing fountain shape and the combination of colorful lighting. The music used in the Musical Fountain mainly includes songs with the West Lake characteristics, Chinese classical music and popular music, foreign classical music and popular music, etc. When music starts, the fountain equipment hidden in the bottom of the lake slowly rises to the water surface under the control of water pressure, the carefully designed fountain sprinklers rotate 360 degrees, with the music, and spouts a variety of shapes of water column, water mist, water balloons. Sometimes they are turbulent, sometimes graceful and moving, which attracts many tourists.

Musical Fountain of the West Lake is an attraction especially at night. In the evening, there are full of people before performance time and many tourists queue up two or three hours in advance. During peak time, as many as 50,000 to 60,000 people watched it. The best viewing position is the place where the four or five hundred fountain viewing chairs set up by the lake. The seats are free and are based on a "first come, first served" principle. There are two performances each night, each of which lasts about 15 minutes for three songs (Music Fountain of the West Lake was closed in January 2020 due to the COVID-19 pandemic, it's expected to be officially opened in the second half of 2023).

第五节　杭州韵味

　　杭州以美丽的风景、众多的历史遗迹、辉煌的文物和丰富的土特产而闻名，被称为"人间天堂"。中国有句古话"上有天堂，下有苏杭"，马可·波罗称杭州为世界上最迷人的城市。这不仅因为杭州拥有美丽的湖泊、山脉和许多景点，还因为凭借多年的历史积淀，其独特的江南韵味和大量优秀的文化景观入选了世界遗产名录。西湖是中国唯一一个湖泊类文化遗产，千百年来西湖周围有着许多动人的故事或传说。

　　传说西湖是天上掉下来的一颗宝石，这颗"宝石"是杭州最精彩的地方，所有的景点都被它包围着。杭州西湖风景名胜区融名胜古迹、园林山水为一体，总面积超过48平方千米，周边有无数道路纵横。青山环绕的西湖周边，散落着宝塔、楼阁、寺庙和园林。西湖及其周围的青翠山峦成为中国历史上无数艺术家、诗人与哲学家的灵感源泉。北山路上可见大片荷花与莲叶，似乎一直延伸到天际。清晨或日落时分登上保俶山，最能领略西湖的魅力。沿着白堤漫步，可以感受城市的宁静，更深刻地体会"上有天堂，下有苏杭"的名言。漫步街头或是西湖，你可以在这座迷人的城市中度过休闲时光，感受这座充满诗意的城市的韵味。

　　作为有着8000多年文明的历史文化名城，杭州不仅有世界文化遗产西湖、京杭大运河和良渚文化遗址，还有世界非物质文化遗产龙井绿茶、中华医药、金石篆刻、南宋官窑、古琴艺术、蚕桑丝织等。杭州是一个充满活力的城市，不仅有世界三大潮之一——钱塘江潮（另外两个是南美的亚马孙潮和印度的恒河潮），还是一座懂得将安宁、幸福的感受化为活力和财富的城市，一个能够创造奇迹的地方。杭州是中国最具幸福感和安全感的城市之一，也是一座幸福和谐的东方品质之城，一个能让你放松精神的绝佳之地。杭州也是中国最适宜居住的城市之一。

办好一个会，提升一座城。亚运会将使杭州这座城焕发出新的魅力。欢迎来自五湖四海的朋友，让我们共同见证亚运盛会，一起感受日新月异的杭州。

V Charm of Hangzhou

Reputed for its beautiful scenery, a multitude of historical sites, brilliant cultural relics and a profusion of native products, Hangzhou is known as "Paradise on Earth". An old Chinese saying also goes, "There is heaven above, Suzhou and Hangzhou below." Marco Polo, an Italian tourist, called Hangzhou the most enchanting city in the world. This is not only that Hangzhou boasts beautiful lakes, mountains and many attractions, with its accumulation of years of history, its unique southern charm and a large number of outstanding cultural landscape help itself to be selected into the World Heritage List. The West Lake is the only China's cultural heritage in the class of lakes, and for centuries, there are so many touching stories or legends about the West Lake.

Legend has it that the West Lake was a heavenly jewel fallen to earth, so the West Lake in Hangzhou is the highlight and all the attractions are surrounded of it. Scenic area of the West Lake is the integration of historic site and garden landscape. The entire site covers more than 48 square kilometres and there are numerous paths around the lake. The mountain-fringed West Lake grounds are speckled with pagodas, pavilions, temples and gardens. The surrounding lush hillsides has been a great source of inspiration for artists, poets and philosophers throughout the Chinese history. Walking along Beishan

Road, you can see large patches of lotus blooms and leaves that seemingly stretch to the horizon. To best experience the lake's charms, you can hike up to Baochu Hill in the early morning or at sunset. Taking a stroll along the Bai Causeway by the lake, you'll feel the peaceful ethos of the city and better understand its time-honored fame as "Up above there is heaven, down below there are Suzhou and Hangzhou". Walking on the streets or around the West Lake, you can spend leisure time by losing yourself in this charming city full of poetic factors.

As a famous historical and cultural city with a civilization of 8,000 years of history, Hangzhou has not only the world cultural heritage of the West Lake, Beijing-Hangzhou Grand Canal and Liangzhu Culture Ruins, but also the world intangible cultural heritage of Longjing Green Tea, the Traditional Chinese Medicine, the Art of Chinese Seal Engraving, the Traditional Firing Technology of Longquan Celadon, the Guqin and Its Music, Sericulture and Silk Craftsmanship of China. Hangzhou is a city full of vitality. Not only is it home to Qiangtang River Tidal Bore—one of the world top three tidal bores (the others are the Amazon in South America and the Ganges in India), but also a city that masters the art of turning the sense of calmness and happiness into productivity and fortune. It is a place where miracles can be made. This is a city where citizens have the top sense of happiness and security among China, a wonderful oriental city full of happiness and harmoniousness. Being a place for meditative and spiritual retreat in times of trouble, Hangzhou is one of the most livable cities in China.

Upgrading the city by hosting the Games. The Asian Games will surely make the city of Hangzhou glow with greater charm. Welcome friends from all over the world to witness the Asian Games and experience the ever-changing Hangzhou together.